MW01613873

"This gift from the most hig
the heart which reaches down into our soul and touches us in ways that
not only encourage but teach, cleanse and reveal truths that facilitate the
emotional healing that the Holy Spirit desires for all of us."

Dr. Maureen E. Young
Executive Director of Pastoral Counseling Center

"Carolyn's keen insights into everyday life will inspire and encourage you
as you allow her words to touch and challenge your paradigm of thinking.
Her Daily Cup of encouragement is refreshing and uplifting. I look
forward to it every day."

Rev. Stan Roberts, Pastor
Victory Life Church, Brownwood Texas

"As Carolyn's former manager, I can tell you her passion for life and
healing is evident through her music, her writing and simply the way she
lives. Time spent with this woman of God is like balm for the soul. What
better way to spend time with her than through her inspiring Daily Cup?"

Tami Rowbotham, Incubator Creative Group

"The Daily Cup is such a blessing to me and my family. This is not your
average daily devotional book. It is a much needed source for inner
freedom and healing that combines wisdom with real life experiences.
There is no doubt you will be pointed to Biblical truth that will change
your life. It is sound both psychologically and scripturally. Carolyn has an
authentic and unmistakable love for God and people. She definitely has
a divine call on her life to help others shed pounds from their past. This
book holds that potential. When I attended one of her musical concerts,
I was mesmerized by her performance, her talent and her witness for our
Lord."

Peggy Joyce Ruth, Published Author 91st Psalm, Live
Radio Host, Conference Speaker, Bible Teacher

If we come closer to Jesus, He will come closer to us. Reading this book
daily will help you draw closer to Him. It contains the Word of God as
well as words of encouragement from the author and will help you fill your
"cup" so that you are not running on empty.

Dr. Phyllis J. Arno
Research and Developer of the Arno Profile System
Co-Founder of NCCA & SACC

# DAILY CUP

## FILLING UP WITH GOD'S WORD

### CAROLYN SCHWARTZ

**TATE PUBLISHING**
AND ENTERPRISES, LLC

# FORWARD

This gift from the most high God is a true work of both the spirit and the heart which reaches down into our soul and touches us in ways that not only encourage but teach, cleanse and reveal truths that facilitate the emotional healing that the Holy Spirit desires for all of us.

As all divine instruments Carolyn begins with the word of God followed by a time of worship & praise that exemplifies the revelation her soul experiences as she presses in and touches the hem of his garment with faith and passionate intimacy.

Desperate and dependent we are drawn to the purity, truth and glory that flows daily into our life as we open ourselves up to encountering more of what Jesus has for us.

What is more glorious than knowing, feeling and experiencing the presence of the spirit of God as we are transformed by the renewing of our minds?

The soft, comforting, warm and tender touch of unconditional love we embrace through the "Daily Cup" is an ongoing reminder of who we are, whose we are and what we can do as a result of the miracle of the cross. We need to be reminded or else the challenges of our earthly life will lead us to wither and grow weak under the stress of our own works. Christ has allowed us to trade our shame, rejection and weaknesses in for his unconditional acceptance and love. The heart-felt communication inspired by this devotional fills us up with the fruit of the spirit that flows divinely as we "go out with joy and are led forth with peace".

I have been privileged to recognize the call of God on my life into the ministry of counseling many years ago and have been searching and praying for a nurturing devotional which would feed my spirit and soul as I encourage other believers to make a demand on the measure of faith God has given them to not only be used as an instrument of healing in the redeemers hand but to operate in his righteousness and profound peace.

My Daily Cup reminds me that God's grace is available to me and it is new every morning. Grace allows us to live in his righteousness and our Daily Cup is the instrument that reminds us of whose we are and what we can do through him. There was a time when I thought that I could live on the glorious fruits and gifts received upon Baptism. I now know that this cup of grace is preordained to provide me with all the divine and glorious treasures I will use to remain in his presence as I am accustomed to walking with others from victimized to victorious with freedom in Christ.

How grieved is the Father when we fail to realize that the gift is there, ready to be opened, new every morning but our un-renewed selves fail to receive and glory in the righteousness and favor that is ours because of the work of the cross.

The Daily Cup reminds us of the grace, mercy, love, joy, peace, patience, kindness, goodness, faithfulness, gentleness and self-control available to us every day, not because we deserve it but because we make a conscious choice daily to receive and unwrap it.

This unmerited gift through such an inspirational and acclaimed journal reminds us of the freedom he won for us, the treasures we inherit and the principles we get to live by. Principles that exceed and excel all of man's brilliant theories and are filled with hope, passion and promise to all who partake. What we as mediators of this unique work is that it is just that, unique. Rarely have I seen the word of God so passionately interpreted into daily principles that we earthly creatures get to apply to our own daily challenges and practice these heavenly principles into solutions that allow us to practice these principles in our everyday affairs. The sense of holy yet humble empowerment unleashes more enlightenment on a daily basis that allows us to grow ourselves and encourages those we encounter personally and professionally.

What a joy it has been to see one of my most gifted students say, "Yes, Lord." and begin allowing the Holy Spirit to use her to pour out his wisdom and grace as she waiting obediently with pen in hand and allowed the wisdom of the creator to fill our lives daily with *rhema* from the word applied as solutions to our thirsty, yet soluble souls. Thank you Dr. Carolyn and may all who are gifted with this journal use it to become one step closer to the intimacy, purity and holiness that we crave.

I have observed the seeds of the Daily Cup produce a great and magnificent harvest of love, mercy, grace, and forgiveness that is more bountiful and necessary than I could ever imagine. This prayer journal reminds us that we are greatly blessed, chosen, highly favored and deeply loved.

Dr. Maureen E. Young

*Dr. Maureen E. Young is the Executive Director of the Pastoral Counseling Center located in Bradenton Florida. The Pastoral Counseling Center is the Certified Academic Institution of the National Christian Counselors Association. Dr. Young oversees supervision for students who are pursuing Christian Education in Counseling. Dr. Young has a rich background helping people. She earned her BSW in social work from the University of South Florida and a Masters Degree in Public Health (MPH) specializing in Maternal and Child Health. She holds a PhD from Cornerstone University in Christian Psychology and Counseling. She has been a NBCCT board certified clinical supervisor since 1998, training students to become professional Christian Counselors for the National Christian Counselors Association. Dr. Young is also an active member of the American Association Christian Counselors and certified by the International Board of Christian Counselors.*

# LIFE'S A GIFT...OPEN YOURS!

Isn't life amazing? We live in uniquely designed earth suits made in the image of God and live in a world that wants us to believe it can meet our needs. That dynamic in itself is challenging. We face relational ups and downs, disappointments, unmet expectations, unrealized dreams, unresolved pain from our past, and often carry around emotions of confusion, doubt, fear, shame, guilt, and anger.

Perhaps I've just "read your personal mail". The good news...... first, God knows our condition...second, He's provided us a way out,... and third we are not alone.

We're all on a journey. No matter where we are or where we've been, our destination is the same–Eternal life. How we arrive at God's desired destination is the same – accepting Jesus Christ as our personal Lord and Savior. God has provided us the gift to life and the gift for life. What happens in-between the gift to life and the gift for life is where we have a say. Our source will determine our course.

Perhaps you accepted Jesus as Your Lord and Savior years ago. Even today, in the secret and hidden depths of your heart, you wonder where's the zeal for living, the love for giving, the peace of forgiving, and the joy for thanksgiving? Your secret's safe with me. I lived many years asking myself the same questions and a few more..... like, "What's wrong with me?" "Is joy reachable in this lifetime or a benefit in the next?" "Is peace more than just the absence of conflict?" "Is this all there is?" "What am I missing?" "Is there something else I need to do?"

Maybe like me, you've invested countless hours in doing (trying), verses being (trusting). You've found yourself captive to the belief that if you persistently work hard or give more something different will happen. Einstein spoke to that theory when he said, "Insanity is doing the same thing over and over and expecting a different result." I had accepted that God was my Creator and my Redeemer. I believed Jesus died to give me life. I believed God was loving enough to meet me right where I was and powerful enough to take me from where I'd been. I believed Heaven was my final resting place. So what was I missing between salvation and Heaven? Why wasn't I enjoying the trip?

I was sitting in the worship area of my music studio one morning having just finished reading the story about David and Goliath when I heard deep within, "Do you love Me?" I closed my eyes and allowed my memories to take me on a journey of recall of countless victories God had won over Goliaths in my own life. I realized God wasn't asking me that question because He didn't know the answer, He was calling me to a place of self-reflection. God often uses questions to get us to take a look inside ourselves. I began praying the words of Psalm 139:23-24. "Oh Lord, search me and know my heart; test me and know my anxious thoughts. Point out anything in me that offends you and lead me along the path of everlasting life." (NLT)

Just so you know, God is faithful to His Word. My awareness of shadows of pride and smudges of unforgiveness I'd buried alive began to rise up in my thoughts. As I began to cast my cares on Jesus and ask Him to heal my hurts, awareness welled up within me that life was not about what I could do, but all about what Jesus did for me on the cross. Seeking Him, yielding to Him, and resting in His finished work was my part. God had completed His work so how would I respond to what I've already been given and why did I continue to think I could add something to what God had already given to me through my own works?

Over time, as I continued to ponder the question, "Do you love Me?", and read the Word, the wonder of Jesus living on the inside of me, became more and more intimately and personally real. His aliveness inside of me allows me to stand in wonder before His throne of Grace and say, "Thank You!" I continue to see God's Good News as not a call to do something, but an awesome wondrous announcement of love by a sovereign God that in Christ all is done. The Christian life is not living in our own strength and resources so we can do, it's yielding to, relying on, trusting in, and submitting our will to Christ Jesus so He can do through us. The unveiling of the blessings of love, joy, righteousness, and peace come from being plugged into the power source of Christ Himself, who is our abundant supply. He is The Truth, The Life, and The Way – He's also My Truth, My Life, and My Way.

Now, I no longer read scripture, pray, write praise music, or attend church because it's the right thing to do, I do so because it's the humble response to what He has already done for me. There's something more wonderful than words can describe when revelation of what God did for us through the cross makes its incredible connection to Jesus living on the inside of me. The Creator of the Universe lives on the inside of me! The King of all Kings and the Lord of all Lords lives on the inside of me. When God's revelation becomes illumination, nothing can snuff out His Light. Unexpected blessings, amazing inner freedom, renewed strength, incredible creative expressions, new unexpected relationships, deeper connections in old relationships, closed doors now opening, deep joy and peace unaffected by circumstances begins to unfold in miraculous wonders. It doesn't mean I don't have challenges or face pain – it means I can cast my cares on Christ and live free. It means I can ask Christ the Forgiver to heal my hurts. It means I can know peace because I know the Prince of Peace. It means I am loved and accepted now and forevermore. It means He turns my weaknesses into strengths for my good and His glory.

We all share many commonalities like pain, struggles, questions, emotional challenges, disappointments, circumstances beyond our control, abuse at the hands of others, losses, battles in our health, families, and finances, and the question of where to find our true value, our genuine purpose, and our divine calling on our lives. I found as my hunger and thirst grew to seek Christ I began to manifest more of Him to others even in the midst of my human weaknesses, frailties, and failures. What a joy! I'm the clay and He's the Master Potter!

As I continue to seek Christ, ponder the question, "Do you love Me?" and look at myself through the mirror of God's Word, Christ is transforming me from the inside out.

I continue to realize that Jesus is not only my Savior, past tense, He is the Lord of my life, present tense. Scriptures I'd read many times before, now jump off the pages and stir my heart as if Jesus is right beside me in

# JANUARY 1

God is indeed
powerful enough
to remove
any circumstance
from our life, yet
His depth of love
is revealed
for us, as He walks
with us through
every circumstance.

We don't yet see things clearly. We're squinting in a fog; peering through a mist. But it won't be long before the weather clears and the sun shines bright. We'll see it all as clearly as God sees us.... knowing directly just as He knows us!

I Corinthians 13:12 *(The Message)*

Lord, you are loving enough to meet me right where I am and powerful enough to take me from where I've been. You are a God of personal restoration. I yield myself to your feast of love and Grace. You are my Infinite source. You supply every need I have. In you, I am never alone or forgotten. You hold me with your Righteous Right hand and keep my feet from slipping. You go before me and behind me. You dance all around me with power, provision, love, and safe- keeping. In you, I am convinced that neither death, nor life, nor angels, nor rulers, nor things present, nor things to come, nor powers, nor height, nor depth, nor anything else in all creation, will be able to separate me from your love in Christ Jesus my Lord. I draw near to you and you draw near to me. Your fullness of grace living inside of me in Christ supplies all my needs. You are able to make all grace abound to me so that having all sufficiency in all things at all times, I abound in every good work to glorify you. Thank you.

# JANUARY 2

Faith that is exercised
does not perish.
Hope that is stretched
does not evaporate.
Love that is genuine
produces miracles.

But for right now, until that completeness, we have three things
to do to lead us toward that consummation: Trust steadily in God,
hope unswervingly, love extravagantly. And the best of the three is
love."

I Corinthians 13:13 *(The Message)*

Lord, I release this day to you and your love that lives inside of me to those around me. As I come to the Christ living in me, I am one with you. My spirit and soul are open to you. I receive your blessings of wonders and miracles. You are my source for all good things. My faith is a gift from you. As I look to your Word in faith, you enlarge my territory. I receive the unlimited blessings you have lavished on me with thanksgiving. The light of your Spirit brings illumination to all things. My hope grows in the light of your reflection. My creativity explodes as you fill my mind with prosperous visions and ideas. In you, I live rich and abundant in every way. I receive your overflowing love and pour out your love on those I meet. I live in the hope of your Glory. My ministry of reconciliation is alive and flowing like a gentle flowing uninterrupted stream. I live by faith in Jesus Christ knowing that you will bring every good work in me to completion at the day of Jesus Christ. My being is in you. Thank you.

# JANUARY 5

Freedom is making choices
and love is a fruit
of forgiveness.
The more we own our weaknesses
and yield them to grace,
the more loving we will become.

Don't pick on people, jump on their failures, and criticize their faults—unless, of course, you want the same treatment. That critical spirit has a way of boomeranging. It's easy to see a smudge on your neighbor's face and be oblivious to the ugly sneer on your own. Do you have the nerve to say, 'Let me wash your face for you,' when your own face is distorted by contempt? It's this whole traveling road-show mentality all over again, playing a holier-than-thou part instead of just living your part. Wipe that ugly sneer off your own face, and you might be fit to offer a washcloth to your neighbor.

Matthew 7:1-5 *(The Message)*

Lord, you are divine love. I choose to look through the eyes of your love and see the very best there is to see in others. As I rest in, trust in, and experience your constant, loving presence in my life, I am an open joyful vessel of your love, your Grace, and your life. I pour out Christ within me to those around me. As I yield to him, he supplies love, patience, and forgiveness through me. Through Christ in me, my words and actions are full of compassion and understanding. The mercy you have lavished on me is the same mercy I lavish on those I meet. My words are those that build others up and give grace to those that hear. My actions are filled with love, patience, and compassion as I yield to Christ in me. In you, I have well-founded and everlasting hope that comforts and encourages my heart and strengthens me in every good work. Search my heart O God and see if there is any wicked way in me. As you bring to mind those areas of my life that need remolding by your Grace, I yield to you. You are the Potter and I am the clay.

# JANUARY 6

The demanding
nature of our
pride is the master
architect of walls
that separate us
from the discovery
of authentic truth,
rewarding relationships,
lasting joy, and true
inner freedom
with God,
others,
and ourselves.

Investigate my life, O God, find out everything about me; Cross-examine and test me, get a clear picture of what I'm about; See for yourself whether I've done anything wrong— then guide me on the road to eternal life.

Psalm 139:23-24 *(The Message)*

Lord, you are life. I yield myself to you. Take the clay of my life and shape it into your likeness. Mold me into your Divine masterpiece. As you examine me, make known those areas of my thoughts that do not line up with your Word. Enlarge my understanding. Lead me in the way of the Everlasting. In your light of love, I am whole and free to be all you created me to be. In gratitude, I receive your guidance, correction, and direction. Your Word is life. Your spirit is life- giving freedom. You are my God. I humble myself before you and you lift me up. With Christ living in me, I purpose my words to be those of life and encouragement to others. I live in the life of your spirit alive in me in Christ Jesus. I take the yoke of Christ Jesus upon me and rest in His fullness of Grace. I clothe myself in humility and you lift me up. As your beloved and chosen in Christ, I put on love and mercy. I am your child and you are my God. Thank you.

# JANUARY 11

Life is a constant journey.
Unless each moment
is lived by faith,
our years will pass in fear;
Unless each step
is taken in humility,
our legacy
will lend itself to worry;
Unless each day
is under girded
with God's presence;
our lives will be governed
by unrest.

THE LORD is my Light and my Salvation—whom shall I fear?
The Lord is the Stronghold of my life—of whom shall I be afraid?

Psalm 27:1

Lord, you have placed your gift of life in me. Today I plant seeds of love with the expectation of a bountiful harvest. In faith, I step out to fulfill your Divine calling on my life. Every circumstance and every person who is a part of your calling on my life is lining up and responding to your voice. Your perfect order is in motion as I build on the foundation of Jesus Christ. Every measure of faith I express multiplies. I cast off any thoughts of doubt, fear, confusion, and unrest as I stand on your Word. The thoughts I have and the words I speak reflect the fullness of the God-head living within me. I live joyfully and victoriously. Your perfect love casts out all fear. You supply all my needs according to your riches in Glory in Christ Jesus. In my weakness, your Grace super abounds. I yield to the Prince of Peace living within me and live in his peace. Peace, Grace, and Truth live within me in Jesus. The peace of Christ rules my heart. I live filled with every blood bought blessing of Christ Jesus. Jesus is my stronghold.

# JANUARY 12

Sorrow
looks back;
Worry
looks around;
Faith
looks inward.

And without faith it is impossible to please God, because anyone who comes to him must believe that he exists and that he rewards those who earnestly seek him.

Hebrews 11:6

Be strong! Be courageous! Do not be afraid of them! For the Lord your God will be with you. He will neither fail you nor forsake you.

Deuteronomy 31:6 (TLB)

Lord, you are my source. You are all things and know all things. You are my shield, my glory and the lifter of my head. Joined to the Christ within me, I have abundant life. I overflow with your joy. Your Covenant promises are mine now and forever more. You are my strength to face all things. You are my provision for every need. You are my provider as you make a way when in the natural my way is unclear. Even when I am pressed on every side, I am not crushed, nor shaken, nor broken. In your presence and through your Grace, your divine plan for my life is in motion. Nothing or no one has the power to destroy that which is divinely mine. I take hold by faith of all favor and blessing that you richly lavish on me in Christ Jesus. You are my God. I am your accepted and beloved child. All I am rests in your being. I am the anointed workmanship of your hands. I live gratefully in your Grace which is never-ending. I am your loved and accepted child now and forever. My soul magnifies your wonderful name. Thank you.

# JANUARY 15

The heart
that holds
onto the hurts
of the past
invites the soul
to look through
rose colored
glasses which
distorts the present
and the future.

Do not judge, and you will not be judged. Do not condemn, and you will not be condemned. Forgive, and you will be forgiven. Give, and it will be given to you. A good measure, pressed down, shaken together, and running over, will be poured into your lap. For with the measure you use, it will be measured to you.

Luke 6:37-38 *(The Message)*

Lord, you are my healer, my future and my hope. When the enemy attempts to distort my faith in you by bringing thoughts of insecurity, fear, rejection and condemnation, they clear up in light of your Word. As I look to your Word, Christ sheds his light of Truth through the Holy Spirit. As I look through the lenses of your love, I receive your everlasting healing. I become what I behold. In you, I am a divine instrument of truth, peace and joy. As I join with the Christ within, I am a ballad of symphony, pleasing to you, and singing songs of joy to those I meet. Every measure of the song within me flows in your perfect timing. In your presence, my harmony deepens so I can pour out blessings of love to those around me. I live in your unforced rhythms of Grace. My oneness with you is the song of joy I sing. I am one in spirit with you in Christ Jesus. I lean on, trust in, and rely on Christ who lives in me. It is no longer I that live but Christ who lives me the hope of Glory. My lips sing your praises. You are worthy to be praised. Thank you.

# JANUARY 16

The
greatest
mountains
we will
climb
start in the
deepest
valleys
of our
hearts.

If your heart is broken, you'll find God right there; if you're kicked in the gut, he'll help you catch your breath.

Psalm 34:18 *(The Message)*

Lord, you are perfect wisdom and everlasting power. In my day of trouble, you hide me in the secret place of your Tent. You set me high upon a rock where I can see through the eyes of faith. There is only one plan and it's your plan. Nothing can hinder or come between your divine purpose for my life. Everything you have planned for me is opening and coming forth in your Grace. Your love is unfailing and your comfort all encompassing. You send orders from Heaven to protect me. You are my shield, my salvation, my defender and my fortress. I live, breathe, and move in your divine provision. Blessed God, your comfort delights my soul. You are for me so who can be against me. I rest in your abundant provision. In Christ, I am more than a conqueror. As I renew my mind to your Word and yield myself to Christ within, I rise above because Jesus lifts me up. Not by power, not by might, but by your spirit I shout, "Grace, Grace" to my mountains and they become plains. I confess your Word sending it forth by faith and wait expectantly as you work all things together for my good. I rest in Christ who is my strength.

# JANUARY 17

When God's
forgiveness
makes the
journey
from our
heads
to our hearts,
transformation
begins
to takes place
from the
inside out.

In prayer there is a connection between what God does and what you do. You can't get forgiveness from God, for instance, without also forgiving others. If you refuse to do your part, you cut yourself off from God's part.

Matthew 6:14 (MSG)

Lord, you are Grace restoration. Today I see everyone I meet as your divine creation created in your image and worthy of value. I have the mind of Christ. In Christ, as I am holy, chosen and beloved. I put on a compassionate heart, kindness, humility, meekness and patience, bearing with others through the presence of Christ living in me. I forgive others with the grace of Christ in me and His presence overflows to others. No offense is worth holding onto that interrupts your flow of Grace in me. I put on love which binds everything together in your perfect harmony. I draw near to you knowing in full faith, all my sins are forgiven. I am washed white as snow. I hold steadfast to the hope within me because you are my ever present, faithful Savior and Friend. By the power of your holy blood, I am free once and for all from shame, guilt and condemnation. I sing of your Glory and live in your freedom. In Christ, You have adopted me through your Love and forgiven me completely. By your Grace I am righteous, justified and redeemed. My soul magnifies your name. I live in the fullness of your immeasurable love. Thank you.

# JANUARY 18

Anger is hurt
turned inward
and its
lingering
presence will
produce distance
in all our
relationships.

Post this at all the intersections, dear friends: Lead with your ears, follow up with your tongue, and let anger straggle along in the rear. God's righteousness doesn't grow from human anger. So throw all spoiled virtue and cancerous evil in the garbage. In simple humility, let our gardener, God, landscape you with the Word, making a salvation-garden of your life.

James 1:1-21 *(The Message)*

Lord, you are perfect Love. As you live in me and I yield to you, the love you first loved me with over flows to those I meet. I recognize that anger is a warning signal that something is wrong. I acknowledge its presence within me and ask you to search me in your loving grace. I choose to lay the weight of anger before your throne of Grace and I invite Christ the healer to go to it and through it. My heart desires your will and not my will. In Christ, I am slow to anger, bountiful in grace and alive in mercy. In you, I see beyond the human frailty of behavior and let go of any beliefs, thoughts, or emotions that do not line up with the truth of who I am in you. I look to and rest in your bountiful Grace to supply my needs. I bear the fruits of the spirit because I abide in you. Through your eyes, I see everyone I meet as a beautiful masterpiece. Every moment of this day, I connect more deeply with the Christ in me. I humble myself before you. My desire is to be the mirror that reflects you, the Lord of my life. I live free by the blood of the Lamb. Thank you.

# JANUARY 21

The clay of our lives,
already belongs to God
as it rests on the divine wheel
for the Holy Spirit to mold,
but it needs daily shaping
into the masterpiece
that God wants
for those
who belong to Him.

God, investigate my life; get all the facts firsthand. I'm an open book to you; even from a Distance, you know what I'm thinking. You know when I leave and when I get back. I'm never out of your sight. You know everything I'm going to say before I start the first sentence. I look behind me and you're there, then up ahead and you're there, too—your reassuring presence, coming and going. This is too much, too wonderful—I can't take it all in!

Psalms 139:1-4 *(The Message)*

Lord, you are the Master Potter. I am an open vessel to you. Take the clay of my life and mold it into your purposed masterpiece. Press into me where I need pressing. Shape me where I need shaping. You have placed treasures in every fiber of my being by your divine design. Your eyes watch me, your hands guide me, your spirit holds me, your Grace empowers me, your blood cleanses me, and your Word feeds me. Your spirit is alive in me in Christ Jesus. You are King of Kings and Lord of Lords. You created me in your image to have dominion and authority in Christ Jesus. I surrender to the Holy Spirit alive on the inside of me through Christ to guide, teach, correct, and bring wisdom over every area of my life. I rest in Christ by faith and in His provision I rise above every storm. Your Grace is my full provision. You surround me with songs of victory. Thank you that in Christ I have every spiritual blessing in heavenly places. Thank you for your abounding and never-ending love. Thank you for creating and loving me. Halleluiah.

# JANUARY 22

When we rest
in the finality
of the cross,
we experience
the reality
of the
resurrection;
Christ living
in us and
through us.

Whatever God has promised gets stamped with the Yes of Jesus. In him, this is what we preach and pray, the great Amen, God's Yes and our Yes together, gloriously evident. God affirms us, making us a sure thing in Christ, putting his Yes within us. By his Spirit he has stamped us with his eternal pledge—a sure beginning of what he is destined to complete.

2Corinthians 1:21-22 *(The Message)*

Lord, you have equipped me with every gift. I am signed, sealed and delivered in the Holy Spirit. I am equipped for every good thing through your Grace. I am victorious in my beginning and victorious in my ending. I am stamped with a "Yes" in Christ which can never be altered or removed by any circumstance, any person, any devil or any demon. I am a child of the Light. No darkness lives in me. I am chosen and ordained by Christ to bear much fruit. Every detail of your divine design for my life is coming true. My hands are anointed to fulfill the divine call on my life. Divine power and strength live within me. I can do all things through Christ. I boast in the cross of Christ Jesus who is my resurrection and life. In Christ, the world has been crucified to me, and I to the world. In Christ, I live holy and blameless. I live in the freedom of his joy and the fullness of his Grace. I am seated in Heaven with Christ. My spirit dances to the rhythms of his unending love. My soul magnifies you. My lips sing your praises. Thank you.

# JANUARY 23

Grace
is God's gift
of how we are saved;
it's also
the power source
for living.

For it is by grace you have been saved, through faith—and this is not from yourselves, it is the gift of God.

Ephesians 2:8

Since we've compiled this long and sorry record as sinners (both us and them) and proved that we are utterly incapable of living the glorious lives God wills for us, God did it for us. Out of sheer generosity he put us in right standing with himself. A pure gift. He got us out of the mess we're in and restored us to where he always wanted us to be. And he did it by means of Jesus Christ.

Romans 3:23-24 *(The Message)*

Lord, you are my salvation and redemption. Jesus placed his blood on the mercy seat to pay my sin debt in full. Your work at the cross is finished. Your will, not my will; Your Way, not my way; Your time, not my time; Your works not my works be done. In you, I am perfected with everlasting wholeness. Your finished work on the cross has delivered me from judgment. Through faith, I am a partaker of salvation once and for all. I receive your gift of Grace and joyfully confess, "You are my God, my Lord, my Savior, my Redeemer and my Friend." You see and accept me as complete and whole in Christ. No bondage to sin lives within me. Jesus has broken the power of sin over me. You came to set the captive free and to heal the broken-hearted. You are my divine healer and my divine supply. You came to give life and give it abundantly. I gratefully and humbly receive your gift of life. I am forever free to live in the fullness of your divine design – forgiven and redeemed. My lips sing your praises. Thank you.

# JANUARY 24

Self-blame
over the past
leads to
depression
in the present
and
hopelessness
for our future.

Who will bring any charge against those whom God has chosen? It
is God who justifies. Who then is the one who condemns? No one.
Christ Jesus who died—more than that, who was raised to life—is
at the right hand of God and is also interceding for us.

Romans 8:33-34

Lord, You are Grace and Forgiveness. Your Grace and Forgiveness
cover me. I readily admit my mistakes and receive restoration, for in my
weaknesses you are strength. In and through Jesus, I'm empowered to live
in his newness of life. I humbly come to your banquet table and feast on
your goodness, your truth, your mercy and your amazing Grace. I drink
of your living water. You quench my longing thirst. Your Word nourishes
me. Your living Presence brings purpose, passion, energy and life to my
mind, body, soul, and spirit. I gratefully receive your blessing of life and
all your Covenant promises. I live in divine aliveness to complete all that
you have called me to and created me for. My spirit is alive to God in
Christ Jesus. I am called to great things in the Kingdom and it is Christ
in me who supplies all that I need to complete His work through me. I
live in the blood bought blessings of Christ Jesus. My cup overflows in the
joy of Christ living in me. I live in praise every day for you are worthy to
be praised.

# JANUARY 27

Blessing those
who have
hurt us
is an
opportunity
to master
what is already
ours in Christ.

Make a clean break with all cutting, backbiting, and profane talk. Be gentle with one another, sensitive. Forgive one another as quickly and thoroughly as God in Christ forgave you.

Ephesians 4:31-32 *(The Message)*

Lord, you are living and lasting Grace. Christ Jesus living within me is my supply. Your Grace is sufficient for my every need. I offer blessings of favor on those I meet because I am filled with blessings from you. I pour out what you have poured in. I trust in, rely in and lean on your presence. You are ever faithful and dependable. When I fail or those around me fail, I forgive through Christ the Forgiver who lives in me. I exercise my power of choice and engage my right of responsibility to release any offenses alive in my heart. I cherish an uninhibited flow of relationship with you. I lay down offense by your strength so that nothing comes between or interferes with my fellowship with you. My thoughts, my emotions, my words and my actions are renewed and purified as I look to your Word. I rest in you and receive your healing restoration. I cast my cares on you and live free. As I rest in Christ, I put on the truth of your words that direct my way in his love and guide my way into his peace. Thank you.

# JANUARY 28

Integrity means
refusing to cheat
yourself
with lies or half truths
regardless of the cost.
The fertile ground for seeds
of truth to spring forth in a
harvest of blessings
is the place where
honesty and love meet.

Summing up: Be agreeable, be sympathetic, be loving, be compassionate, be humble. That goes for all of you, no exceptions. No retaliation. No sharp-tongued sarcasm. Instead, bless—that's your job, to bless. You'll be a blessing and also get a blessing. Whoever wants to embrace life and see the day fill up with good, Here's what you do: Say nothing evil or hurtful; Snub evil and cultivate good; run after peace for all you're worth. God looks on all this with approval, listening and responding well to what he's asked; But he turns his back on those who do evil things.

I Peter 3:8-12 *(The Message)*

Lord, you are Grace and Truth. Your divine supply in Christ Jesus is my grace and truth as I yield to Him. I bear much fruit because I live connected to the vine of Christ Jesus. As I live with and embrace the Christ in me, my nature mirrors your nature. You are transforming me from the inside out. You have stored up sound wisdom for the upright. You are a shield to me as I walk in integrity. You guard the paths of justice and watch over the ways of your saints. I draw near to you and you draw near to me. Your steadfast love is alive within and I walk in your bounty. As I plant seeds of integrity, harvest comes for your glory and my good. I overflow in the love of Christ and share his love with everyone I meet. I see others as created in your image with immeasurable value and great worth. I greet others with the love of Christ in me. My words honor and encourage those I meet. As you treasure me, I treasure others. Thank you.

# JANUARY 29

Beliefs fuel thoughts,
thoughts feed perceptions,
perceptions feed attitudes,
attitudes feed emotions,
emotions feed words and
words fuel our actions.

Trust in the LORD with all your heart and lean not on your own understanding; in all your ways submit to him, and he will make your paths straight.

Proverbs 3:5-6

Lord, you are Infinite Wisdom in my life. My spirit is alive in Christ Jesus. I make the choice to yield to you, listen to you, follow you, and submit to the gift of the living Holy Spirit within me. In and of myself there is no good thing within me. You are my goodness, my restoration, and my life. I set my mind on you, for you are Living Water. I feast on your Word for you are Truth and Life. Submitting to Christ within me, I overflow in his love, his peace, his grace, his joy, his mercy and his forgiveness to myself and others. In Christ, I am a new creation predestined with hope and an expected outcome. I renew my thoughts with the truth and life of your Word. I take my thoughts captive to the obedience of Christ. As I look into the mirror of your Word and confess it from my mouth, I become a mirror that reflects Christ Jesus. By faith, I partake of his divine nature. I am being transformed from glory to glory as I keep my eyes on Jesus. Every blood bought blessing of Jesus is mine by faith. My flesh has been crucified with Christ and it is Christ in me that transforms me from the inside out. I yield all that I am to you. Thank you.

# JANUARY 30

Often times what
or who we
perceive as our
greatest enemy,
offers the best
opportunity of friendship
and the greatest invitation
for our own inner growth.

Celebrate God all day, every day. I mean, revel in him! Make it as clear as you can to all you meet that you're on their side, working with them and not against them. Help them see that the Master is about to arrive. He could show up any minute! Don't fret or worry. Instead of worrying, pray. Let petitions and praises shape your worries into prayers, letting God know your concerns. Before you know it, a sense of God's wholeness, everything coming together for good, will come and settle you down. It's wonderful what happens when Christ displaces worry at the center of your life.

Philippians 4:4-7 *(The Message)*

Lord, you are my Promised Land. I see every obstacle as a stepping stone towards my Promised Land. You go before me and your Loving Grace is all around me. You uphold and uplift me with your Righteous Right Hand. Nothing compares to your Goodness. You are faithful to your Word as I confess it over my life. Every blood bought promise of Christ Jesus is mine by faith. You enlarge my territory as I humble myself to Christ who lives within me. Your works are to wonderful for words. You hold me in your Loving Arms. Your hedge of protection is all around me. In you, I have complete and Divine victory. No weapon formed against me shall prosper. You work all things together for my good in Christ Jesus. You will never abandon me or leave me orphaned. I live in the fullness of your love and love others as you love me. My cup overflows in the joy of your presence. My soul magnifies you. My lips sing your praises. Goodness and mercy follow me all the days of my life. Thank you.

# JANUARY 31

Our lives
are constantly
sending forth
messages
as if we were
wearing signs
for others
to read.
What are you saying?

I call heaven and earth to witness this day against you that I have set before you life and death, the blessings and the curses; therefore choose life that you and your descendants may live.

Deuteronomy 30:19

Lord, you are the full measure of blessing. You are the Rock on which I stand. You are my fortress, my strong tower, my refuge, my shield, my strength and my supply. Your Grace supplies my every need in Christ Jesus. By the Word of my Testimony and the Blood of the Lamb, I am more than a conqueror. You are watching over your Word to perform it. I open my mouth and speak your Word over my life. Thank you for being faithful to your Word. Faith in your living Word brings forth your supernatural manifestations into my natural circumstances. As I wait on and rest in Christ, He brings forth His life and abundance to me and through me. I am an open vessel to receive your blessing of Life and unlimited favor. The Grace of Christ Jesus flows uninterrupted as I walk in his love. I am prosperous in all I do bearing the fruit of Christ. My mind is a garden of perpetual seeds ripe with harvest which bursts forth for Kingdom glory. My hands are creative and fruitful by faith. I am what I am by the grace of Christ Jesus. Thank you.

# FEBRUARY 1

When our
vertical
alignment
is right,
we will
reap
the fruits
of the Spirit.

But what happens when we live God's way? He brings gifts into our lives, much the same way that fruit appears in an orchard—things like affection for others, exuberance about life, serenity. We develop willingness to stick with things, a sense of compassion in the heart, and a conviction that a basic holiness permeates things and people. We find ourselves involved in loyal commitments, not needing to force our way in life, able to marshal and direct our energies wisely.

Galatians 5:22-23 *(The Message)*

Lord, you are my harvest. You have given me dominion to plant seeds. Your Living Water and your presence within produces and multiples my harvest beyond anything my eyes can see or my mind can imagine. I water my thoughts with your Word. You are the Light of my harvest. My faith is fertile soil. I gratefully receive every portion of the harvest that is mine in Christ Jesus. I prosper in your favor. By faith, my storehouses are filled through the blood bought blessings of Christ Jesus who is my life. You have anointed me with the oil of gladness. My cup runs over. Goodness and mercy follow me all the days of my life. Life and creativity flows into me through the abundance of Christ Jesus. The branches of my life bear an overflowing abundance of love, joy, peace, patience, kindness, goodness and faithfulness because I abide in the vine of Christ Jesus. Search me Lord and prune those areas of my life that need pruning. I yield to your wisdom. I submit to your will. Thank you for your immeasurable love and abundant life.

# FEBRUARY 2

When we increase
in God,
we increase in love;
for where there is love,
mercy finds a way.

Be completely humble and gentle; be patient, bearing with one another in love. Make every effort to keep the unity of the Spirit through the bond of peace.

Ephesians 4:2-3

What marvelous love the Father has extended to us! Just look at it—we're called children of God! That's who we really are. But that's also why the world doesn't recognize us or take us seriously, because it has no idea who he is or what he's up to. But friends, that's exactly who we are: children of God. And that's only the beginning. Who knows how we'll end up! What we know is that when Christ is openly revealed, we'll see him—and in seeing him, become like him. All of us who look forward to his Coming stay ready, with the glistening purity of Jesus' life as a model for our own.

1 John 3:1-3 *(The Message)*

Lord, you are my Portion. Everyday is a gift of opportunity and privilege to increase in you. I live by faith in your Covenant promises. Your Word is life. You are able to do exceeding abundantly above all that I can ask, think or image according to the power that is at work in me. I receive my inheritance through Christ by faith. I live in unlimited freedom and share perfect harmony with those I meet because Christ lives in me. I yield my heart and mind to your living presence within me and connect to your endless supply of grace and unconditional love. Through you, I pour out your love, mercy and compassion to everyone I meet. As I pour out, my Divine supply increases. In me there is no good thing. Apart from Christ Jesus, I can do nothing. I live, I love and I forgive through Christ who lives within. I love those I meet because you first loved me. I glory in your goodness. My spirit is one with Christ. My soul magnifies you. My lips sing your unending praises. I am what I am by Your Grace. I am your child and you are my God.

# FEBRUARY 3

God is not just
delivering us
from something;
He is drawing
us to someone.

My sheep listen to my voice; I know them, and they follow me. I give them eternal life, and they shall never perish; no one will snatch them out of my hand. John 10:27-28

> So, friends, we can now—without hesitation—walk right up to God, into "the Holy Place." Jesus has cleared the way by the blood of his sacrifice, acting as our priest before God. The "curtain" into God's presence is his body. So let's do it—full of belief, confident that we're presentable inside and out. Let's keep a firm grip on the promises that keep us going. He always keeps his word. Let's see how inventive we can be in encouraging love and helping out, not avoiding worshiping together as some do but spurring each other on, especially as we see the big Day approaching.
>
> Hebrews 10:19-25 *(The Message)*

Lord, you are limitless possibilities and abounding supply. I come boldly to your throne of Grace by the blood of Christ Jesus. I am seated in heavenly places in Christ Jesus. I am a joint-heir with Christ. I am redeemed by the blood of the Lamb. I live with no condemnation. I am one spirit with Christ. As I behold Jesus, I become like him. I am God's workmanship, created in Christ Jesus to do good works, which God prepared in advance for me to do. You are drawing me to every predestined open door as I hear your voice in my spirit. My spirit is alive and one in Christ. I can do all things through Christ who gives me strength. I receive the fulfillment of my heart's desire in all you designed me to be. By faith, I confess every blood bought blessing is mine. As I draw near to you, you draw near to me. You hear my prayers and meet my needs according to your riches in glory in Jesus. As I live in your presence, I follow your voice within me. You are my God. I am your forever loved and accepted child. Thank you.

# FEBRUARY 4

Where we seek
nourishment,
reveals the true
condition
of our
hearts.

Look to the LORD and his strength; seek his face always.

Psalm 105:4

Search me, God, and know my heart; test me and know my anxious thoughts. See if there is any offensive way in me, and lead me in the way everlasting.

Psalm 139:23-24

Lord, you quench my hunger and thirst. You fill my very being as you live in me. I am living in your kingdom of fulfillment in Christ Jesus. You preserve me and give me life. You are my righteousness, my portion and my deliverer. Your Righteous Right Hand holds me and keeps me safe. Your Light fills my life with grace and truth. As I join with the Christ in me, I receive divine instruction, wisdom, strength, and resurrection power through the Holy Spirit. I am signed, sealed and delivered by the Holy spirit. Your Word is life to my spirit and health to my soul. I love your Word. Living in and through you is as natural as breathing. As I plan my way, you direct my steps. In Christ, every place my foot touches is sure ground. You are my Rock, standing strong and ever faithful. My greatest standing comes on bended knees. Humility and reverence of you brings wealth, honor and life. You are my God. I am your child. I live in the provision and confidence of Christ Jesus. Highest praises. Glory halleluiah. Thank you.

# FEBRUARY 5

A revelation
without
manifestation
is a
missed
opportunity.

This is how God showed his love among us: He sent his one and only Son into the world that we might live through him. This is love: not that we loved God, but that he loved us and sent his Son as an atoning sacrifice for our sins. Dear friends, since God so loved us, we also ought to love one another. No one has ever seen God; but if we love one another, God lives in us and his love is made complete in us.

I John 4:9-12

Lord, you are the eyes of my heart. My vision in you is beyond anything possible in the natural. Your plans for my life are coming to pass in every moment of my life. All that I need to know comes to me in your perfect timing and in your perfect way. I respond to your pleadings inside of me and follow your voice to guide me into all your favor and blessings. Even when I am uncertain, you are steady and sure. I cast my anxieties on you and live free and full of confidence to go where you lead. I declare your praises as I wait for abundant harvest in your timing. No road block and no detour can come against your Word which covers my life. Every revelation from you is anointed and connected to your divine design of my life. I gratefully celebrate your rich, abundant blessings. Thank you for watching over your Word to perform it. As I confess your Word in faith, I release the faithfulness of Christ into my natural circumstances and wait expectantly for him to bring it to pass. I live in the abundant provision of Christ Jesus. My lips sing your praises. My soul magnifies your name. Thank you for creating and loving me.

# FEBRUARY 6

Our hard places
often hold the
undiscovered
treasures
of our high
places.

Though the fig tree does not bud and there are no grapes on the vines, though the olive crop fails and the fields produce no food, though there are no sheep in the pen and no cattle in the stalls, yet I will rejoice in the LORD, I will be joyful in God my Savior. The Sovereign LORD is my strength; he makes my feet like the feet of a deer, he enables me to tread on the heights.

Habakkuk 3:17-19

Lord, you are my Strength. You supply all my needs according to your riches in Glory in Christ Jesus. As I delight myself in you, you give me the desires of my heart. I live by faith calling forth that which is not seen as though it were. Faith comes by hearing and hearing by the Word of God. I feast on your Word which nourishes my spirit. You take me to new heights and open my eyes to see Your Goodness. No man and no powers of darkness can spoil your divine plans for my life. Perfect wisdom, perfect order and perfect power are gifts you lavish upon me in Christ. It is Christ in me who brings forth all your divine goodness. Every morning I thank you for your new mercies. At noonday, my lips shout your praises. As evening falls, I rejoice in your faithfulness. As I lay my head down to sleep, I rejoice in the fullness of your Grace. I have my being in you through faith. In Christ, all things are possible. My mind is set on the prize you have ordained and created for me. I am an open channel of your love, your grace, your strength and your provision. You are life to my soul and health to my body. Thank you.

# FEBRUARY 7

Before we will
take a
step towards
coming home,
we have to
admit
we've been
away from home.

Do you want to stand out? Then step down. Be a servant. If you puff yourself up, you'll get the wind knocked out of you. But if you're content to simply be yourself, your life will count for plenty.

Matthew 23:11-12 *(The Message)*

Lord, you are my Infinite immediate supply of all good. You are my unfailing Guide. Where you lead, I will follow. Your Word guides me as a lamp unto my feet and lights my path. You are my lasting and faithful provision. Angels surround and keep me safe under your tender mercies. You guard me when I leave and return. You never leave or forsake me. All evil that comes against me cannot prevail in your name. You are my strength, my comfort, my protector, my defender, my light, my fortress and my peace. I live in the incomparable riches of Christ Jesus. I humble myself before you and yield myself to Christ living within. I share in the promise of Christ Jesus. By faith, I have the full measure of the God-head living in me – Father, Son, and Holy Spirit. Every gift you lavish on me is living within me in Christ Jesus. It is Christ who brings forth every blessing of abundant grace. By faith, I receive and release every blood bought blessing of covenant in Christ. My lips sing your praises. I step out to claim all that you desire to give me.

# FEBRUARY 8

We overcome what we choose to embrace.

First pride, then the crash— the bigger the ego, the harder the fall.

Proverbs:16:18 *(The Message)*

Lord, you are my Supply. I lay myself before your throne of Grace in Christ Jesus. Your Divine Wisdom and planned Goodness for my life pours into me as I humble myself in Christ. Apart from Christ, there is no good thing in me. I acknowledge your holy presence and give thanks for the full and complete provision of your love, grace, mercy and forgiveness. By faith, I receive every portion of your Goodness and Divine presence in my life. Every breath I breathe is Divinely ordained. You are revealing your will in all my affairs. Your Divine plan for my life is in motion, in your way and in your timing. Nothing or no one can interfere with or hinder your Divine call. I gratefully and openly receive the blessings you shower upon me. I sit amazed at your wonder. I glory in your splendor. I rest in your majesty knowing that your love is unfailing and unwavering. I am your child and you are my God. Christ Jesus is the author and finisher of my faith. All good things dwell and come forth in me through Christ. As I yield to Christ, I exhibit his goodness, his righteousness and his truth. I bear the fruit of his nature. Thank you.

# FEBRUARY 9

At some point in our
relationships,
the inner baggage
we work so hard
to carry around,
will become the
very hindrance
we trip over.

Work at getting along with each other and with God. Otherwise you'll never get so much as a glimpse of God. Make sure no one gets left out of God's generosity. Keep a sharp eye out for weeds of bitter discontent. A thistle or two gone to seed can ruin a whole garden in no time. Watch out for the Esau syndrome: trading away God's lifelong gift in order to satisfy a short-term appetite. You well know how Esau later regretted that impulsive act and wanted God's blessing—but by then it was too late, tears or no tears.

Hebrews 12:14-17 *(The Message)*

Lord, you are Perfect Order. You know my beginning and my end. I am created for your pleasure and your glory. Though my flesh may fail, you are the strength of my Spirit. I stand steadfast as no one or nothing can come against your Grace for me. Grace is the person of Christ Jesus who lives in me and His supply through me. I am an heir to every blood bought promise. In you, I am unmoved by appearances, therefore appearances move. I am a new creation alive unto God by the spirit of Christ. As I feast on your Word, I am renewing my mind to the truth of who I am in Christ. My mind is the fertile ground open to receive all the fullness of your goodness and truth. I am growing in oneness with you as I yield to you. My flesh was crucified in Christ Jesus and I now live the life of Christ by his spirit living in me. The strength of Christ is made perfect in my weakness. I offer my life to you as clay and thank you that you are molding me into your divine masterpiece. Praise is an unending song I sing throughout the day. Thank you. Halleluiah.

# FEBRUARY 10

The longer
we reject the
light and
choose
to live in the
darkness,
the more we will
believe our darkness
is the light.

Jesus summed it all up when he cried out, "Whoever believes in me, believes not just in me but in the One who sent me. Whoever looks at me is looking, in fact, at the One who sent me. I am Light that has come into the world so that all who believe in me won't have to stay any longer in the dark.

John 12:44-46 *(The Message)*

Lord, you are the Light that lives inside of me and guides me into the knowledge of your truth. I live in the Light as you are in the Light. Your light which you spoke forth on the first day of creation was your glory. In Christ, I am clothed in your Glory. I live as a righteous child because Christ imparted his righteousness to me. I no longer lived condemned or in bondage to sin. I live by grace through faith in Christ. Your living Word nurtures my spirit with life and truth. As I renew my mind to the truth of your Word, Christ is changing my beliefs, my thoughts, my perceptions and my attitudes. My emotions reflect the peace of Christ in me as I yield to the Prince of Peace in my spirit. Joy radiates from me as I count my blessings. I hold fast to you Lord and receive your favor. I trust in you and lean not on my own understanding. I look to you to light my way and to make my path straight. Wisdom enters my heart and knowledge is pleasant to my soul. As I listen for your voice, I live in safety and security. I seek your kingdom and your righteousness and you add these things to me. Thank you. You are amazing.

# FEBRUARY 11

Every issue of
unrest
relates to
cover up....
our own
or
someone else's.

God means what he says. What he says goes. His powerful Word is sharp as a surgeon's scalpel, cutting through everything, whether doubt or defense, laying us open to listen and obey. Nothing and no one is impervious to God's Word. We can't get away from it—no matter what.

Hebrews 4:12-13

Lord, you are Sovereign God, all seeing and all knowing. You have saved me and called me to a holy life not because of my works but through the finished works of Christ Jesus which you purposed ahead of time. I am crucified with Christ living in the fullness of his Grace by faith. I died with Christ and was resurrected with Christ to live by his spirit alive in me. My spirit is one with Christ. I am holy and blameless because you see me through the perfect and holy sacrifice of Christ Jesus. I no longer live under the weight of shame and guilt. I have no need to hide or cover up my weaknesses. I bring them to the light of your Grace where Christ Jesus in me turns them into his strengths. I can't do enough or quit enough in my own effort to obtain any greater favor with you. You created me in love and saved me by Grace. Christ has already purchased my favor through his blood in accordance with your love. Your Word supplies my spirit with life and truth. I live complete in the fullness of your love and the wonder of your amazing Grace. Thank you for creating me, saving me and supplying my every need in Christ Jesus. Halleluiah.

# FEBRUARY 12

God's answers
come in ways
only
spiritually
focused eyes
can see.

Take a good look, friends, at who you were when you got called into this life. I don't see many of "the brightest and the best" among you, not many influential, not many from high-society families. Isn't it obvious that God deliberately chose men and women that the culture overlooks, exploits, and abuses; chose these "nobodies" to expose the hollow pretensions of the "somebodies"? That makes it quite clear that none of you can get by with blowing your own horn before God. Everything that we have—right thinking and right living, a clean slate and a fresh start—comes from God by way of Jesus Christ. That's why we have the saying, "If you're going to blow a horn, blow a trumpet for God.

I Corinthians 1:26-31 *(The Message)*

But I tell you that everyone will have to give account on the Day of Judgment for every empty word they have spoken. For by your words you will be acquitted, and by your words you will be condemned.

Matthew 12:36-37

Lord, you are my fortress, my rock, and my provider. Songs of joy pour from my heart because you are my God. My ways are in your full view. You examine my paths. You set me straight and crown me with a crown of Righteousness in Christ. I follow your voice of wisdom. My spirit is open to your revelation and I hear you call my name. Through the finished work of Christ, I have the mind of Christ and reflect His nature as I abide in him by faith. In Christ, I have every spiritual blessing in Heavenly places. By your Grace and through your love for me, you have revealed the hidden mystery of your kingdom which is Christ in me the hope of glory. My lips sing your praises. My soul exalts you. The songs that pour from my heart are for your glory. My every boast is for the awe of your unending love and life in Christ who lives in me. Thank you.

# FEBRUARY 13

Excuses provide
fertile ground
for
murmuring,
complaining,
and
complacency.

May my prayer be set before you like incense; may the lifting up of
my hands be like the evening sacrifice. Set a guard over my mouth,
LORD; keep watch over the door of my lips.

Psalm 141:2-3

Lord, you are Perfect Excellance. In Christ, I'm created for mighty and
powerful kingdom works. I yield every part of my being to Christ who
lives in me. My mouth is a fountain of life flowing to all those I meet. As
I yield to Christ, I partake of his Divine nature. Your will not my will be
done. I see others as your divine creation worthy of honor and respect. I
love others with Heaven's love that builds up and encourages those I meet.
You are alive in all things and living in all circumstances. My life aligns
with your perfect will. I glorify you and you pour out your blessings in me.
I open my heart to receive every portion of blessing that you pour in me
and cause to overflow from me. In Christ Jesus, I am grateful with hope.
In Christ Jesus, I am alive with purpose. My heart sings with joy and
praise for your everlasting goodness. From the fruit of your labor, I enjoy
the abundance of Christ Jesus. You are the vine and I am the branches.
As I abide in Christ, I bear much fruit. In Christ, I have supply, favor and
everlasting life. You are beautiful. Receive my praise oh magnificent God
as a fragrant offering of thanksgiving.

# FEBRUARY 14

Sacrifice
and
blessing
go hand
and hand.
Sacrifice
always
comes
before the
blessing.

Love GOD, all you saints; GOD takes care of all who stay close to him, but he pays back in full those arrogant enough to go it alone. Be brave. Be strong. Don't give up. Expect God to get here soon.

Psalm 31:23-25 *(The Message)*

Lord, you are Grace. I find no words to describe the wonder of your Grace offered to me through the sacrifice of your son, Christ Jesus. The blood of Jesus paid my sin debt in full. It is no longer I that lives in the flesh, but Christ who lives in me. Your grace saved and redeemed me. As I yield to Christ by faith, your favor is working through unexpected places, unexpected people and in unexpected ways to perform your wonders for my life. I commit all that I do to you, and my plans succeed according to your Divine Design for my life. My cheerful heart is forever filled as I feast on your goodness. I draw living water from your continuous spring of Life. I live every day as a new creation in Christ. I take my thoughts captive to the obedience of Christ. I renew my mind with your Word. The rebirth of my spirit in you brings growth in every area of my life. Thank you for placing the fullness of your nature in me at the time of my salvation. Thank you for unveiling your wonder, your goodness and your love as I yield to and abide in Christ. New wonders, and new revelations unfold all around me by your Grace. I rest in Christ Jesus.

# FEBRUARY 15

Walking in the Spirit
is a faith
mindset
that
determines
our life-step.

For you were once darkness, but now you are light in the Lord. Live as children of light (for the fruit of the light consists in all goodness, righteousness and truth) and find out what pleases the Lord. Have nothing to do with the fruitless deeds of darkness, but rather expose them. It is shameful even to mention what the disobedient do in secret. But everything exposed by the light becomes visible—and everything that is illuminated becomes a light. This is why it is said: "Wake up, sleeper, rise from the dead, and Christ will shine on you." Be very careful, then, how you live—not as unwise but as wise.

Ephesians 5:8-16

Lord, you are life and light living on the inside of me. I am alive in Christ and nothing today will distract me from who I am in you or what you've called me to do. No power can come against your plan for my life. No person can place a stumbling block in my way. My obstacles are springboards to the next level of victory Christ Jesus brings to me, for me, and through me. The kingdom gates of blessing swing open to me by faith as I walk though them led by the Grace of Christ Jesus. I worship you oh God in Spirit and in Truth. Your Word nurtures and fills my spirit. As I live redeemed by the power of Jesus's blood, I come before your throne of Grace boldly and humbly in reverent awe of you. You are Worthy of honor and praise. You are my God and I am your child. I live in Covenant blessings. I live in the light of your living Word. I cherish spending time in your presence. Your Word illuminates the glory of Christ Jesus living within me. In Christ, I live abundantly. Praise your name for the Light of your grace that supplies me.

# FEBRUARY 16

It's Grace
that keeps us
walking in the
Light,
and fear
that keeps us
stumbling in the
dark.

For God, who said, "Let light shine out of darkness," made his light shine in our hearts to give us the light of the knowledge of God's glory displayed in the face of Christ.

2 Corinthians 4:6

Whoever believes in him is not condemned, but whoever does not believe stands condemned already because they have not believed in the name of God's one and only Son. This is the verdict: Light has come into the world, but people loved darkness instead of light because their deeds were evil. Everyone who does evil hates the light, and will not come into the light for fear that their deeds will be exposed.

John 3:18-20

Lord, you are the light of glory. I live in the light of your imparted righteousness. My old sinful nature of darkness is dead once and for all. You paid my sin debt in full at the cross. The life I live now is the life of Christ. In Christ, I am a new creation. My spirit is alive in Christ. Christ living in me is the hope of all glory. I yield myself to Christ within asking the spirit of God to search me as I renew my mind to the truth of your Word. I yield my mind and will to you so the flow of your spirit in me comes through me. As I confess your Word over my life, you are watching over it to perform it. As I live led by the spirit, I do not commit the deeds of the flesh. As I yield myself to your molding and shaping, I openly and honestly confess what needs confessing, grieve what needs grieving and forgive what needs forgiving. The shame and guilt of my sin nature has been broken by the blood of Christ Jesus. I live free from condemnation in Christ Jesus. The fullness of your Glory within me is the light that shines to everyone I meet. My lips sing your praises. My soul magnifies you. I live in the fullness of your wonder. Thank you.

# FEBRUARY 17

The roots
of joy grow
the deepest
where seeds
of love
are planted
in the
fertile soil
of service.

You, my brothers and sisters, were called to be free. But do not use your freedom to indulge the flesh; rather, serve one another humbly in love.

Galatians 5:13

Lord, you are everlasting Love and perfect Joy living in me. Everyday in honor to you and through service to others, I plant seeds of love. I see others as a gift of your creation. As you healed my brokenness, I pour out words of encouragement to others. Through my humble act of serving and your supernatural presence, the Kingdom harvest you create in me is flowing freely from me. I am free to love what you love by your grace. I am free to grow under your love. You water the soil of my heart with your Living Water. Reveal to me others who need the touch of your love. Pour me out as your living vessel of life, hope and encouragement to those you divinely place in my path. Christ Jesus is my everlasting source and supply. The sacrifices I make to serve others pale in comparison to the sacrifice you made for me at the cross. Your blood which you poured out for me is the ultimate demonstration of your love for me. My source of loving and serving others is supplied by Christ Jesus who lives in me. Thank you.

# FEBRUARY 18

The most
precious treasure
discovered cannot
be purchased,
it must be opened
with our hearts.

The King will reply, "Truly I tell you, whatever you did for one of the least of these brothers and sisters of mine, you did for me."

Matthew 25:40

Lord, you are perfect, unconditional and everlasting love. Give me eyes to see who I can reach out to in your love and an open heart to connect to others in the same love you have for me. My eyes are open and my spirit quickened to the Christ within me. I am a vessel through which your supply flows. I am ready, willing and able to bring your encouragement to someone who is downtrodden. My words are those of encouragement as your presence nourishes my spirit. Your love quenches my deepest thirst. Your Goodness is all around me. You are my Dwelling Place. You feed my spirit. Your presence within me is peace to my soul. In you, I am high and lifted up and I go forth to lift others up. Your love is never-ending and all sustaining. Reflect your presence through me so others can taste and see your Goodness. I taste and see that you are good. Your love lives in me through the Holy Spirit. In Christ, I am chosen, blessed and highly favored. My lips sing your praises. My soul magnifies you. Thank you Jesus for being my source.

# FEBRUARY 19

Our inner light often
shines as a beacon
over another's path
in ways
only God knows.

Be especially careful when you are trying to be good so that you don't make a performance out of it. It might be good theater, but the God who made you won't be applauding. "When you do something for someone else, don't call attention to yourself. You've seen them in action, I'm sure—'play actors' I call them— treating prayer meeting and street corner alike as a stage, acting compassionate as long as someone is watching, playing to the crowds. They get applause, true, but that's all they get. When you help someone out, don't think about how it looks. Just do it—quietly and unobtrusively. That is the way your God, who conceived you in love, working behind the scenes, helps you out. And when you come before God, don't turn that into a theatrical production either. All these people making a regular show out of their prayers, hoping for stardom! Do you think God sits in a box seat? Here's what I want you to do: Find a quiet, secluded place so you won't be tempted to role-play before God. Just be there as simply and honestly as you can manage. The focus will shift from you to God, and you will begin to sense his grace.

Matthew 6:1-6 *(The Message)*

Lord, you are Excellence and Perfection. I live in your Light and in your Grace by faith in Christ Jesus. Any goodness in me is a reflection of the goodness of Christ living in me. You have created me in your image. My spirit is alive unto you in Christ Jesus. Your Word is a lamp to my feet and light for my path. The light of Christ illuminates my very being and his light shines to those around me. In the quietness of my soul, I hear your voice. Being in your presence, I receive spiritual nurture and guiding insight throughout my day. My cup overflows with joy. Lord, you supply my every need according to your Riches in Glory in Christ Jesus. The Divine plan of my life is in motion under the faithful leadership of Christ within. I am completely loved and totally accepted. I am one spirit with Christ. I surrendered myself to you when I accepted you as my Lord and

Savior. It is no longer I that live, but Christ that lives in me. As I call out to you in prayer, you answer me showing me great and mighty things that stir my faith and leave me in awe of your wonder. I am your yielded vessel filled with your goodness to pour out on others.

# FEBRUARY 20

It's our choice whether
we pencil our hurts
in the sand,
where the winds of
forgiveness
can erase them,
or carve them in our
hearts as stone,
where the winds
of pride
may never blow.

But I tell you, love your enemies and pray for those who persecute you, that you may be children of your Father in heaven. He causes his sun to rise on the evil and the good, and sends rain on the righteous and the unrighteous. If you love those who love you, what reward will you get? Are not even the tax collectors doing that? And if you greet only your own people, what are you doing more than others? Do not even pagans do that? Be perfect, therefore, as your heavenly Father is perfect.

Matthew 5:44-49

Lord, you are Restoration and Wholeness. I let go of all that is in my flesh that needs releasing. I sing to you a new song because I am forgiven and free. I offer all offenses to Christ the forgiver who lives within asking Christ to go to my brokenness and change it to his peace. I sow in peace because Christ is my peace. No offense is worth holding onto and giving the devil a foothold in my life. My relationship with Christ is more valuable than any act of revenge. Holy Spirit search me and bring to mind any area of unresolved pain still alive on the inside of me. I yield myself to Christ Jesus and cast my burdens on him. I receive his healing and transformation. I am open to hear his voice as the sheep hears their Shepherd. I willingly confess what needs confessing, grieve what needs grieving and forgive what needs forgiving. By your Blood that covers me and your Grace that forgives me, I can forgive others who have hurt me. I am gracious and merciful to others because Christ is my source. As I yield to Christ, his life in me flows from me.

# FEBRUARY 21

Who we
turn to in our
deepest hour
of need will
determine
our source.
Our source
will determine
our course.

I am the gate; whoever enters through me will be saved. They will come in and go out, and find pasture. The thief comes only to steal and kill and destroy; I have come that they may have life, and have it to the full.

John 10:8-10

Lord, you are my Source. There are no lost opportunities in the Kingdom. As one door shuts another opens. In your Grace, I go where you lead. Nothing can come against all you have for me. No weapon formed against me shall prosper. Even though I live in the flesh, I am not carrying on warfare according to the flesh or using mere human weapons. The weapons of God's Word and the blood of Christ are mighty before God for the overthrowing and pulling down of strongholds. In Christ, I resist the devil and he has to flee. I overcome by the blood of the lamb and the word of my testimony. I am established in righteousness and oppression is far from me. I yield my will to the Christ within. Christ is my open gate to blessings and favor. Christ is my open gate to Eternal life. Doors once closed are now open in the presence of your loving Grace. Walls come tumbling down under the power of your love. Change is taking place in me from the inside out. Your loving kindness covers me like a blanket. In Christ, I can do all things.

# FEBRUARY 22

We can
search
for answers
looking
over here
and over
yonder,
but the one
true answer is
Jesus Himself.

Jesus answered, "I am the way and the truth and the life. No one comes to the Father except through me. If you really know me, you will know my Father as well. From now on, you do know him and have seen him."

John 14:6-8

Lord, You are the way, the truth, and the life. You have called me according to your purpose and I have nothing to fear as I go forth in your wisdom and strength. You are my lasting love. You are my unmovable rock. You are my everlasting shelter. You are my faithful friend. You are my living Lord. You are my protective shield. You are my constant comfort. You are my unyielding strength. You are my indestructible fortress. You are everlasting. You are the same yesterday, today and forever. I receive the favor of your awesome and wondrous presence of Christ living in me. Faithful is he that has called me in Christ, and he will bring it to pass. I rest in the abundant provision of Christ Jesus. Thank you God that you arm me with the strength of Christ and he makes my way perfect. I bear the fruits of the spirit of Christ as I abide in Him. No works of my flesh can produce fruit. I am a branch resting in Christ Jesus the vine and the fruit I bear is the fruit He creates and produces. Christ is life seed. Thank you for the life seed of Christ living in me and springing up in me to bring about an abundant harvest for your glory. Halleluiah.

# FEBRUARY 23

We can exercise
our bodies,
lose a
few pounds
and affect
ourselves;
we can exercise
our hearts,
gain much joy,
and affect
countless others.

You make known to me the path of life; you will fill me with joy in your presence, with eternal pleasures at your right hand.

Psalm 16:11

Lord, your Joy is my strength and my guide. My body, mind and soul are molded according to your Divine design within. You strengthen my heart as I exercise my faith. You are my Portion. You hold me with Your Righteous Right hand and guide me into all truth by the counsel of the Holy Spirit. I delight myself in you and you give me the desires of my heart. I commit my ways to you and you bring them to pass. All that I am you have created. Apart from Christ, I can do nothing. Christ is my wisdom and my grace supply. All that I plant in your love and Grace brings a bountiful harvest. The works of my hands and the manifestations of my heart are anointed in your presence to serve others and glorify you. I walk the path you have predetermined for me in victory, joy, peace and strength as I yield to Christ living within me. Lord by your favor you have made my mountain to stand strong. Thank you for circumcising my heart with your spirit.

# FEBRUARY 24

Our background
and circumstances
may contribute to
what we think,
but we can
choose whose
we are.

This mystery has been kept in the dark for a long time, but now it's out in the open. God wanted everyone, not just Jews, to know this rich and glorious secret inside and out, regardless of their background, regardless of their religious standing. The mystery in a nutshell is just this: Christ is in you, so therefore you can look forward to sharing in God's glory. It's that simple. That is the substance of our Message. We preach Christ, warning people not to add to the Message. We teach in a spirit of profound common sense so that we can bring each person to maturity. To be mature is to be basic. Christ! No more, no less. That's what I'm working so hard at day after day, year after year; doing my best with the energy God so generously gives me.

Colossians 1:26-30 *(The Message)*

Lord, you are Life and Provision. You live inside of me in Christ Jesus and constantly equip me to do all you've predestined me to do. You have anointed all the details of my life to line up in your perfect will. Christ is my unending unlimited source. In Christ, I am fully and totally equipped to do all you have purposed me to do. The glorious mystery of the Gospel lives in me through Jesus. In Jesus, I am high and lifted up, reborn, restored, redeemed and saved. I renew my mind with the truth of your Word and live free, empowered, reconciled and healed. I am your child and you are my God. I rest in your unending provision. Lord, you are my sun and shield. I live in the glory and grace of Christ Jesus. In the righteousness of Christ, there is no good thing you will withhold from me as I walk in his righteousness. As I renew my mind with your Word, I see myself and others through the eyes of Christ. My lips sing your praises as Christ transforms me into His image. I rest in Christ. I glory in you. I am your child. You are my God. Thank you.

# FEBRUARY 25

Outer
credentials
do not
define
our inner
identity.

For by the grace given me I say to every one of you: Do not
think of yourself more highly than you ought, but rather think of
yourself with sober judgment, in accordance with the faith God has
distributed to each of you.

Romans 12:3

Lord, you are my Truth and lasting Identity. I live accepted by the Father
by the blood of Christ. I live chosen, blessed and highly favored. I am your
workmanship created in Christ to do good work which you predestined
for me to do. Your grace establishes and gives me access to every spiritual
blessing in heaven. Even when circumstances are rocky and relationships
pain-filled, you can work all things out for my good as I abide in Christ
Jesus. Lord, you are my overflowing source of love, grace, mercy and
forgiveness. Your continuous embracing presence permeates me with
peace. I am an instrument of blessing and service to others as I yield to
Christ in me. Your holy presence living in my spirit serves as a magnet to
draw others unto you. My mouth is a mouthpiece of encouragement, love,
peace, hope and joy to others as my words honor your presence alive in
me. I live high and lifted up not because of my works, but because of your
Grace that flows in me and through me in Christ Jesus. Thank you for
creating and loving me.

# FEBRUARY 26

Each of us
has untapped
potential
that God
has placed
within us;
our faith
holds the key
to unlock all the
possibilities God already knows.

Through him all things were made; without him nothing was made that has been made. In him was life, and that life was the light of all mankind. The light shines in the darkness, and the darkness has not overcome it.

John 1:3-5

And without faith it is impossible to please God, because anyone who comes to him must believe that he exists and that he rewards those who earnestly seek him.

Hebrews 11:6

Lord, you are the Master of all Creation. I write love and faithfulness on the tablet of my heart. As I live in harmony with the Christ within and seek you with all that I am, you unleash miracles and wonders beyond measure. My faith brings forth your Divine Design for my life. I have my being in you. You are my God and I am your child. I receive your mercy, kindness and divine plans through the life of Christ within me. Covenant promises from your Word are taking root in my life and producing abundant Kingdom fruit. In Christ, I have a future and a hope. My hands bring forth great works as I yield to your will in Christ Jesus. I rest in Christ Jesus who brings all the fullness of your abundance in me and through me. You are my God and I am fully loved and totally accepted in Christ. My lips sing your praises for your gift of eternal life and daily supply in Christ. Thank you for the measure of faith you placed within me. I gratefully receive.

# FEBRUARY 27

It takes courage
to look in the mirror
of self-reflection,
acknowledge the walls
we've built around ourselves,
lay down our crutches
and stop playing
the self-destructive
games of
denial and blame.

Post this at all the intersections, dear friends: Lead with your ears, follow up with your tongue, and let anger straggle along in the rear. God's righteousness doesn't grow from human anger. So throw all spoiled virtue and cancerous evil in the garbage. In simple humility, let our gardener, God, landscape you with the Word, making a salvation-garden of your life. Don't fool yourself into thinking that you are a listener when you are anything but, letting the Word go in one ear and out the other. Act on what you hear! Those who hear and don't act are like those who glance in the mirror, walk away, and two minutes later have no idea who they are, what they look like.

James 1:20-22 *(The Message)*

Lord, you have ransomed and redeemed me. In Christ, I am blessed with all spiritual blessings in heavenly places. I live by your spirit and not by my flesh. Love, compassion, understanding, patience, joy, hope, mercy and forgiveness are bursting forth like flowers touched by a shower of rain. I am rooted in your fertile soil of your tender mercies. Your Word is my Light that shines forth your goodness towards me and all those I meet. Your Word is a mirror that reflects the fullness of your nature. My mouth shouts your praises. My spirit is alive and filled with the abundance of Christ Jesus alive within me. I yield myself to Christ and live in His abundance and freedom. I joy in opening myself to you to search me. Thank you for molding me into Christ likeness. My eyes are fixed on you and I am becoming what I behold. Thank you.

## FEBRUARY 28

Every offense provides the
opportunity to plant a seed
of forgiveness, and the
opportunity to bring
forth a harvest of peace in
our own souls.

Therefore, my friends, I want you to know that through Jesus the
forgiveness of sins is proclaimed to you.

Acts 13:38

Lord, You are my Fountain of Grace. In you, I overflow with forgiveness towards others. I release all thoughts and mindsets of unforgiveness, impatience, irritation, agitation and selfishness. I put off self-serving pride and put on humility. I communicate my needs to others openly and without demand. I allow others to be who you created them to be. I live in your Spirit of reconciliation. I am open to hear and consider others opinions. I value others as created in your image. I live for God's approval and not man's approval. I live free in the gift of forgiveness that Christ gives me. I speak unity over all things and to all those I meet. Envy and strife have no place in my heart. I refuse to give the devil or any power of darkness a license to bring confusion, fear or any evil work in my life. I yield to and abide in your love in Christ Jesus. I am a Kingdom child. I live in freedom. I pursue God's peace. I am filled with the Divine nature of Christ and escape the corruption that is around me. I am the Righteousness of God in Christ Jesus. I increase with the increase of Christ and abound in his love. Thank you.

# FEBRUARY 29

Our
greatest
standing
always
comes
on
bended
knees.

And being found in appearance as a man, he humbled himself by becoming obedient to death— even death on a cross! Therefore God exalted him to the highest place and gave him the name that is above every name, that at the name of Jesus every knee should bow, in heaven and on earth and under the earth, and every tongue acknowledge that Jesus Christ is Lord, to the glory of God the Father.

Philippians 2-11

Lord, I bow before your throne of Grace because you are worthy. As you live in me, I live in you. You are Lord of Lords and King of Kings. You are Creator and Master of all. You are my beginning and my end. You called me according to your purpose before the foundations of the world. The hairs on my head are numbered. You knitted me together in my Mother's womb. You created me in your image and breathed life into me. You supply my every need in Christ Jesus. Your Grace has saved me and your love has redeemed me. In you, I am destined to do great things for the Kingdom in Christ Jesus. My boast is not in my own works or in my filthy rags of righteousness, but in the finished works of the cross and the righteousness Christ imparted to me. In Christ, I am the head and not the tail. I am above and not beneath. I am chosen, blessed and highly favored. My name is written in the Lamb's book. In Christ, I am empowered to live by faith in His never-ending supply of grace. In Christ, I can do all things. Apart from him, I can do nothing. I humble myself before you. I joyfully confess, "You are my God." Thank you.

# MARCH 1

The seeds
we plant
are the
mirror image
of our faith.

Now faith is confidence in what we hope for and assurance about what we do not see.

Hebrews 11:1

By entering through faith into what God has always wanted to do for us—set us right with him, make us fit for him—we have it all together with God because of our Master Jesus. And that's not all: We throw open our doors to God and discover at the same moment that he has already thrown open his door to us. We find ourselves standing where we always hoped we might stand—out in the wide open spaces of God's grace and glory, standing tall and shouting our praise. There's more to come: We continue to shout our praise even when we're hemmed in with troubles, because we know how troubles can develop passionate patience in us, and how that patience in turn forges the tempered steel of virtue, keeping us alert for whatever God will do next. In alert expectancy such as this, we're never left feeling shortchanged. Quite the contrary—we can't round up enough containers to hold everything God generously pours into our lives through the Holy Spirit!

Romans 5:1-5 *(The Message)*

Lord, You provided my destiny in Christ who lives in me. In faith, I plant faith seeds of your Word in my mind and Christ brings forth his harvest. Faith is the substance of things hoped for the evidence of things not yet seen. Christ is my substance and my supply. Every seed bears after its own kind. I plant seeds of faith in the truth of God's Word. No devil, no demon, no person nor any circumstance can hinder or stop the Divine call on my life in the provision of Christ. Greater is Christ Jesus living in me than he that lives in the world. I reap in Divine Favor because I yield to the source of all blessings. I abide in Christ Jesus and he abides in me.

The Blessings of Abraham are upon me. I am a righteous saint equipped to do every good work. In Christ, I live, I move and have my being. My lips sing your praises. My thoughts rest on you. My cup overflows. My soul magnifies you. You are my God. I am your child loved and accepted in the abundance of Christ. I joy in the wonder of living in the abundance of Christ Jesus. Thank you.

# MARCH 2

Spiritual and emotional growth
can only be separated
in theory, not in reality.
All growth is spiritual if it
involves the biblical
processes of love,
responsibility
and forgiveness.

For I know the plans I have for you," declares the LORD, "plans to prosper you and not to harm you, plans to give you hope and a future. Then you will call on me and come and pray to me, and I will listen to you. You will seek me and find me when you seek me with all your heart.

Jeremiah 29:11-13

Lord, You are the source of life. In Christ, I am alive in my spirit. As I walk in the spirit of Christ, my soul aligns to him and I partake of his divine nature. The issues of life are in my heart. You search me as I yield to Christ within to bring to my mind those areas of my life that need to be touched and healed by your love. Offered to Christ, I see my past as a springboard to my future. Christ is my healer. Christ is my rock. Christ is my fortress. Christ is my refuge. Christ is my strong tower. Christ is my strength. Christ is my comfort. Christ is my provider. Christ is my defender. Christ is my salvation. Christ is my restoration. Christ is my shield. Christ is my redemption. Christ is my light. Christ is my life. Christ is my portion. Christ is my righteousness. Christ is my guide. Christ is my wisdom. Christ is my teacher. Christ is my friend. I receive your Divine favor and unending blessings as you live in my Spirit, dance over my life, and unleash your Grace in my life. I live engrafted and rooted in Christ Jesus. Let your light break forth in my life as the morning sunshine. You supply Grace upon Grace. I am what I am by your Grace.

## MARCH 3

God's Word
holds
mountain moving
power, because
He's the one
that moves them
when we ask in faith.

Jesus replied, "I tell you the truth, if you have faith and do not doubt, not only can you do what was done to the fig tree, but also you can say to this mountain, 'Go, throw yourself into the sea,' and it will be done."

Matthew 21:21 (NIV)

Lord, you are my Rock, my Fortress, my Wisdom and my Provider. Thank you for placing the measure of faith in me at salvation. As I rest in and rely on Christ living within me, he supplies resurrection power to triumph and overcome. I trust in your Word and speak your promises over my life. I live in faith. I speak your truth. I claim your promises as living and purposed for my life. You supply all my needs according to your riches in Glory in Christ Jesus. Nothing can disrupt the Divine purpose you have called me to. Thank you Lord, that in Christ I can see each circumstance through your promises and not just as a problem. Thank you for working all things together for my good and your glory. In Christ, I have complete and total victory. I overcome by the blood of the Lamb and the word of my testimony. Your Word is your living provision which you are faithful to perform. I shout your praises. I shout, "Grace, Grace" over my mountains and I joy in you as I wait expectantly knowing you will turn my mountains into plains. Thank you.

# MARCH 4

Focusing
on our problems,
increases their
magnitude.
Focusing
on Christ
increases our
altitude.

And that about wraps it up. God is strong, and he wants you strong. So take everything the Master has set out for you, well-made weapons of the best materials. And put them to use so you will be able to stand up to everything the Devil throws your way. This is no afternoon athletic contest that we'll walk away from and forget about in a couple of hours. This is for keeps, a life-or-death fight to the finish against the Devil and all his angels. Be prepared. You're up against far more than you can handle on your own. Take all the help you can get, every weapon God has issued, so that when it's all over but the shouting you'll still be on your feet. Truth, righteousness, peace, faith, and salvation are more than words. Learn how to apply them. You'll need them throughout your life. God's Word is an indispensable weapon. In the same way, prayer is essential in this ongoing warfare. Pray hard and long. Pray for your brothers and sisters. Keep your eyes open. Keep each other's spirits up so that no one falls behind or drops out.

Ephesians 6:10-17 *(The Message)*

Lord, You are abounding and everlasting supply. I cast my cares on Christ and breathe in His life. I walk in freedom knowing that I can do all things in Christ who lives in me. I have within me undiscovered territory and I go forth in faith to claim it. No mountain is too tall and no ocean too deep that I cannot rise above, walk over or tunnel through in your Grace. You are my source and my portion. Trials and tribulations will come, but I am of good cheer for Christ has overcome the world. Nothing or no one can hinder your work in my life. I keep my eyes on the prize which is you, Christ Jesus. I am called according to your purpose and empowered to bring forth all you have predestined for me to do. As I draw near to you, you draw near to me. I live in the wonder of your love and rejoice over your resurrection power that lives in me in Christ Jesus. Thank you.

# MARCH 5

Wrong beliefs
based on half truths
steal our joy,
kill our peace
and rob us of
God's Divine
purpose
for our lives.

So here's what I want you to do, God helping you: Take your everyday, ordinary life—your sleeping, eating, going-to-work, and walking-around life—and place it before God as an offering. Embracing what God does for you is the best thing you can do for him. Don't become so well-adjusted to your culture that you fit into it without even thinking. Instead, fix your attention on God. You'll be changed from the inside out. Readily recognize what he wants from you, and quickly respond to it. Unlike the culture around you, always dragging you down to its level of immaturity, God brings the best out of you, develops well-formed maturity in you.

Romans:12:1-2

Lord, you are Truth alive and manifested in Christ Jesus. As I rest in Christ, I am in harmony with your perfect wisdom for my life. I lay before you every detail of this day and receive every ounce of power, strength and wisdom, to keep moving forward to what you have called me to. I trust all that I am and all that I have to you. I persevere in faith looking to Christ as the author and finisher of my faith. Every creative seed you have placed in me is producing a Divine Harvest. I bear much fruit because I abide in Christ. My eyes are on you. My spirit is one with you in Christ Jesus. My mind is filled with your peace as I look to Christ. I am high and lifted up in you. I rest in your provision and rejoice at your unending supply. The angel of the Lord encamps around me and protects me. The name of Jesus and the blood of Jesus is my victory. I confess your Word over my life and joy in your faithfulness. Thank you. Halleluiah praises.

# MARCH 6

As we
acknowledge the
weaknesses
we desire to
overcome,
we've already
won half the battle.

For the LORD your God is the one who goes with you to fight for you against your enemies to give you victory.

Deuteronomy 20:4

Who shall separate us from the love of Christ? Shall trouble or hardship or persecution or famine or nakedness or danger or sword? As it is written: "For your sake we face death all day long; we are considered as sheep to be slaughtered." No, in all these things we are more than conquerors through him who loved us.

Romans 8:35-37

Lord, you are my victory. To you, O God, belongs the greatness and the might, the glory, the victory, the majesty and the splendor. Everything in heaven and everything on earth is yours. Your have given me resurrection power to overcome by faith in the blood of Christ Jesus. I embrace the power of the living Christ within me proclaiming victory in His name. His redeeming blood has marked me as saved and redeemed. I am signed, sealed and delivered by the Holy Spirit. Nothing or no one can separate me from your love. Every power of darkness coming against me fails in the name of Christ Jesus who has won the victory for me. In you, I am a victorious warrior. You are my shield and my protection. Your Righteous Right Hand upholds me. My mind is in perfect peace as I abide in Christ. You rescue me from every evil attack and bring me safely into your Heavenly Kingdom. You are near to the brokenhearted and save the crushed in spirit. The living truth of your Word is my defense and my shield. I rest in you. I confess your Word over my circumstances and rest in Christ by faith to perform it.

# MARCH 7

Consider what might happen
if we spent as much time
getting our inner man
ready as we
do our outer.

Trust God from the bottom of your heart; don't try to figure out everything on your own. Listen for God's voice in everything you do, everywhere you go; he's the one who will keep you on track. Don't assume that you know it all. Run to God! Run from evil! Your body will glow with health, your very bones will vibrate with life! Honor God with everything you own; give him the first and the best. Your barns will burst, your wine vats will brim over. But don't, dear friend, resent God's discipline; don't sulk under his loving correction. It's the child he loves that GOD corrects; a father's delight is behind all this.

Proverbs: 3:5-12 *(The Message)*

Lord, you are abundant supply. In Christ, I have life and have it abundantly. I put on the Lord Jesus Christ, and take no forethought for the flesh to fulfill its lusts. I put off the old man which has been crucified and buried. As I feast on your Word, I reflect the spirit of Christ to those around me. All of life flows in perfect harmony and rhythm in the spirit of Christ. I rely on, trust in, and lean on Christ Jesus. He supplies all my needs according to his riches in glory. I rest in Christ and his peace empowers me. God is at work in me to make me willing and able to obey his purposes. The infilling of your Spirit imparted to me in Christ Jesus overflows into my soul. You have not given me a spirit of fear and timidity, but of power, love and self-discipline. Your eyes are watching over me. You are watching over your Word to perform it. My soul magnifies you. My spirit is alive unto Christ. My lips sing your praises. I dance to the unforced rhythms of your Grace. Thank you for creating me, saving me and providing my every need in Christ Jesus.

# MARCH 8

There is
power in
humility
and
surrender
is
victory.

When pride comes, then comes disgrace, but with humility comes wisdom. The integrity of the upright guides them, but the unfaithful are destroyed by their duplicity.

Proverbs 11:2-3

Humility is the fear of the LORD; its wages are riches and honor and life.

Proverbs 22:4

Lord, you are life giving Grace. I let go of everything that is not divinely designed for me and the perfect plan for my life through Christ unfolds minute by minute, and hour by hour. As I spend time with you, the Holy Spirit brings to mind that which needs confessing, grieving and forgiving. I respond by faith and in obedience to your voice. I open myself to your loving kindness and receive your outpouring of Grace, love, restoration and transformation. As I offer myself to you, you change the scars of my life into your bright shining stars for my good and your glory. Thank you Jesus that in you I can do all things through your strength that is at work in me. Thank you that your Grace is sufficient to meet all my needs. My lips praise you. My heart joys in your presence. I yield myself to Christ at work within me to bring forth the masterpiece you have created in me. I abide by faith in Christ Jesus and he supplies. I cast my cares on Christ and live in peace and freedom. The love of Christ in me overflows to those around me. I joy in submitting to you and reaping the riches of Christ Jesus. Halleluiah.

# MARCH 9

To become a true
Masterpiece
of the Spirit
of God,
we must
yield to the hand of
the Master Potter
and submit
to the fiery furnace.

Yet you, LORD, are our Father. We are the clay, you are the potter;
we are all the work of your hand.

Isaiah 64:8

Lord, you are the Potter and I am the clay. I am moldable in your nail
scarred hands. Shape and mold me into your likeness. Move what needs
moving, change what needs changing and fire what need firing. I yield
in surrender and humility so that I am becoming all that you have called
me to be in your Masterful Hands. Transformation from the inside out is
bursting forth as I yield to Christ living inside of me. I am Your creation
fearfully and wonderfully made. You have anointed the works of my hand
to serve others and glorify you. You are my God. I am your chosen, loved
and accepted child. Thank you that Christ in me is bringing forth the
masterpiece you created me to be. His work abounds as I rest in Him. My
life is a vessel of his Grace filled with his love. Christ brings increase and
brings forth your fruit which you predestined for me in him. Thank you for
the measure of faith that is mine in Christ Jesus. As I feast on your Word
and confess it out my mouth, you bring it to pass. I live as your treasured
vessel. Thank you.

# MARCH 10

Our obedience toward God,
molds our character.
Our reliance on God,
shapes our heart.
Our faith in God,
determines our destiny.

It's in Christ that we find out who we are and what we are living for. Long before we first heard of Christ and got our hopes up, he had his eye on us, had designs on us for glorious living, part of the overall purpose he is working out in everything and everyone. It's in Christ that you, once you heard the truth and believed it (this Message of your salvation), found yourselves home free—signed, sealed, and delivered by the Holy Spirit. This signet from God is the first installment on what's coming, a reminder that we'll get everything God has planned for us, a praising and glorious life.

Ephesians 1:11-14 *(The Message)*

Lord, you are my destiny. I am signed, sealed and delivered by the Holy Spirit. Every step of my destiny is ordered by your divine presence. In Christ, I have abundant life. I hear your voice in the quietness of my spirit. I joy in spending time with you. You sustain me daily with Living Water and nourish me with a feast of your Grace. I honor and revere you. I worship you in Spirit and in truth. As I rest on, trust in and rely on Christ, there is no lack of any good thing in my life. I live in your peace and joy. You fill my borders with peace and bless my storehouses with abundance. You are the prince of peace reigning and ruling in my life. I live in peace as I fix my mind on you. I glory in your wonder. I live amazed by your Grace. I joy in your presence. I shout your praises. The presence of Christ Jesus in me and the work of His righteousness is my peace and assurance forever. Nothing and no one compares to you. Thank you. Halleluiah praises.

# MARCH 11

When we
sow in anger,
there is strife.
When we
sow in pride,
there is destruction.
When we
sow in forgiveness,
there is peace.
When we
sow in love,
there is life.

Don't be misled: No one makes a fool of God. What a person plants, he will harvest. The person who plants selfishness, ignoring the needs of others—ignoring God!—harvests a crop of weeds. All he'll have to show for his life is weeds! But the one who plants in response to God, letting God's Spirit do the growth work in him, harvests a crop of real life, eternal life.

Galatians 6:7-8 *(The Message)*

Lord, you are pure and unconditional Love. Your seed of love is alive in me in Christ Jesus. As I choose to plant seeds of love, Christ in me abundantly manifests his harvest through me. Your love for me is the love I share with others. I live under the favor and blessing of God. My storehouses are full by the grace of Christ Jesus. You are the Master Gardener. All that I am is because of you. You provide and weave the gardening principles of sowing in faith, fertilizing in prayer, watering in hope and living in your light into my life. I am bearing everlasting and divine kingdom fruit. You fill my storehouses by anointing my hands and the works of my heart. Your loving, unlimited, abundance prospers and blesses every area of my life. I receive my divine harvest with thanksgiving and praise. I joy in your Word which is living seed. Thank you.

# MARCH 12

Prayer heightens
our inner
awareness of God;
it's a direct connection to
our spirit and it's
a Divine manifestation on
our world.

Don't fret or worry. Instead of worrying, pray. Let petitions and praises shape your worries into prayers, letting God know your concerns. Before you know it, a sense of God's wholeness, everything coming together for good, will come and settle you down. It's wonderful what happens when Christ displaces worry at the center of your life.

Philippians 4:6-7 *(The Message)*

Lord, you are Sovereign over all things. All you have for me reaches me in your perfect way under Grace. As I spend time with you, I hear your voice that leads my every step. I am a joint heir with Christ Jesus. In Christ, I live in confidence knowing that when I ask anything according to your will, you hear me. Thank you that you supply all my needs according to your riches in glory in Christ Jesus.

I am anxious for nothing, but in everything by prayer and supplication with thanksgiving I make my requests known to you and the peace of God which surpasses all comprehension guards my heart and mind in Christ Jesus. I rejoice in all things for this is your will in Christ Jesus. I am not rejoicing for all things but in all things. I know that you are working all things together for my good. I come boldly before your throne of grace that I may obtain mercy and find grace to help in my time of need. Thank you Father that your eyes are watching over me. My lips sing your praises. My soul shouts for joy. My spirit is one with you in Christ Jesus. Thank you.

# MARCH 13

When
thanksgiving
is a part of our
living,
our living becomes
thanks-living.

Be cheerful no matter what; pray all the time; thank God no matter what happens. This is the way God wants you who belong to Christ Jesus to live.

1 Thessalonians 5:16-18 *(The Message)*

Rejoice always, pray continually, give thanks in all circumstances; for this is God's will for you in Christ Jesus. Do not quench the Spirit. Do not treat prophecies with contempt but test them all; hold on to what is good, reject every kind of evil. May God himself, the God of peace, sanctify you through and through. May your whole spirit, soul and body be kept blameless at the coming of our Lord Jesus Christ. The one who calls you is faithful, and he will do it.

1 Thessalonians 5:16-24

Lord, you are Provision and Life. I live in the righteousness and provision of Christ Jesus. In Christ, I live with an inexhaustible supply. I thank God no matter what my circumstances for this is the will of God in Christ Jesus who is the revealer and mediator of God's will. My words praise you for your completed work of the cross which saved and redeemed me now and forevermore. The roots of my being are firmly and deeply planted in Christ, fixed and founded in him, continually built up in him and becoming increasingly more confirmed and established in faith and overflowing with thanksgiving. You have fashioned me in your image and anointed me to do the work which you have called me to do. In Christ, I am whole and blameless. You are my God and I am your blessed and loved child. I rejoice in the endless abundance of Christ who lives in me. My lips sing Your praises. My words shout thanks to you. My soul magnifies you.

# MARCH 14

God in His
mercy usually
does not
allow us to
see the
real depth
of our pain
until our
healing
is already
well under way.

But he said to me, "My grace is sufficient for you, for my power is made perfect in weakness." Therefore I will boast all the more gladly about my weaknesses, so that Christ's power may rest on me. That is why, for Christ's sake, I delight in weaknesses, in insults, in hardships, in persecutions, in difficulties. For when I am weak, then I am strong.

2 Corinthians 12:9-10

Lord, you are Grace fulfillment and Grace supply. Thank you that your power is made perfect in my weakness. Thank you for your resurrection power that lives in me in Christ Jesus. In Christ, I can do all things. Personal weaknesses, hardships, persecutions and offenses are stepping stones in your Grace offering me the privilege of yielding to Christ who supplies all Grace. All that others have meant for harm, you turn into good. Your love and your faithful presence living in me through Christ Jesus strengthens and carries me through every adversity. I am blessed in my going out and my coming in. I am blessed in the city and the field. The works of my hands are anointed by the Christ within. The labor of my mind, hand and body bring forth favor, blessing, and a plentiful harvest. I abide in Christ by faith and you supply. In Christ, I am empowered, healed and restored. Halleluiahs and praise now and forevermore. You are life. Thank you.

# MARCH 15

Forgiveness begins with a
conscious choice,
but emotions
linger until
the hurt has been
touched by Christ the Healer.

Blessed is the one who perseveres under trial because, having stood the test, that person will receive the crown of life that the Lord has promised to those who love him.

James 1:12

Lord, you are Healer. I rest in you for my victory and healing. I yield myself to Christ living within me. I cast my cares on Christ and live in His freedom. The time I spend with you is like a refreshing rain. Your peace rules my mind as I consider you. I breathe in life because you are life in me. Because you were pierced for my transgressions, crushed for my iniquities, took on the punishment that brought me peace and healed me by your wounds, I live free in the grace of Christ Jesus. I truthfully confess every offense, every wound and every buried hurt that has come upon me as I ask Christ the Forgiver to go to and through my pain. I lay my thoughts and emotions before you bringing my need to your light. In my weakness, Christ is my strength. I let go of offense because it hinders your flow of grace in my life. I acknowledge my emotions as gifts as part of your divine design in creating me. I love, nurture, and forgive myself and others as you forgave me at the cross. I live in the fullness of the Spirit of Christ Jesus alive in me.

# MARCH 16

What we call the past
makes no difference
to the power of
God's love because,
no pain is too deep,
no hurt so wide, or
no memory so
longstanding that the
love of God cannot
reach it, heal it and
transform us
in the process.

I'm not saying that I have this all together, that I have it made. But I am well on my way, reaching out for Christ, who has so wondrously reached out for me. Friends, don't get me wrong: By no means do I count myself an expert in all of this, but I've got my eye on the goal, where God is beckoning us onward—to Jesus. I'm off and running, and I'm not turning back. So let's keep focused on that goal, those of us who want everything God has for us. If any of you have something else in mind, something less than total commitment, God will clear your blurred vision—you'll see it yet! Now that we're on the right track, let's stay on it.

Philippians 3:12-16 *(The Message)*

Lord, you are Divine perfection, perfecting all that is in me, my past, my present and my future. My heart is full of joy and peace as I live in Christ. My soul joys in the salvation work Christ completed at the cross that is mine by faith. My spirit is alive unto you. Your Word brings life and supply to me as I renew my mind to your truth. Thank you for sifting, molding and shaping me through your living Word. Christ in me empowers me with his grace to live your truth and honor the gift of life you have given. I am an open vessel to you Lord. I receive all the good you have for me. I praise your wonderful name. I live filled with your love and rejoicing in your abundant supply of grace that lives in me and through me in Christ Jesus. My soul magnifies your name. Your inner transformation is a blessing and a wonder. Halleluiah.

# MARCH 17

Life has
many choices,
eternity only has
two.

Very truly I tell you, whoever hears my word and believes him who sent me has eternal life and will not be judged but has crossed over from death to life.

John 5:24

Jesus said, "You don't have to wait for the End. I am, right now, Resurrection and Life. The one who believes in me, even though he or she dies, will live. And everyone who lives believing in me does not ultimately die at all." Do you believe this?

John 11:25-26 *(The Message)*

Lord, You are the source of life. My spirit man is alive in Christ Jesus by faith. I am one with Christ in undivided love and life. Christ Jesus is my Lord and Savior. In Christ, I reap everlasting life by your Spirit. You lead me to living fountains of water. I am running my race empowered by your Grace. Power, anointing and blessing are mine in Christ Jesus. Eternal life is my finish line. My trophy is the crown of your Glory which I humbly wear in praise and adoration. I am blameless because God sees me through Christ. I no longer live under condemnation, guilt and shame. I am the righteousness of God in Christ Jesus. I am one Spirit with Christ. I am filled with the divine nature of Christ. The fullness of the God-head lives within me in Christ. In Christ, I have every spiritual blessing in heavenly places. I am chosen, favored and blessed in Christ. Thank you for your blood which has restored the blessings of God in me and over me. I live by faith in your blood bought blessings. My lips sing your praises. Thank you.

# MARCH 18

As we seek growth
from the inside out,
we grant our
unspoken wounds
permission to take hold of
God's outstretched arms of love.

He brought me out into a spacious place; he rescued me because he delighted in me.

Psalm 18:19

He heals the brokenhearted and binds up their wounds.

Psalm 147:3

Lord, You are everlasting healing. You know every space in my heart that needs your touch of healing restoration. Your arms are wrapped around me in love and grace. As I join with the living Christ within, light streams through every area of my body. I give thanks for radiant energy and endless joy. I offer praise for the divinely planned journey I am on. Christ Jesus within me is turning my tests into his testimony of thanksgiving and praise by his Grace. In Christ, my steps are ordered and anointed with divine supply. Thank you for bringing others into my life as your chosen vessels of healing. I confess your living Word of healing over my life and receive the bounty of Christ's finished work of the cross. As I yield to you and ask you to search me, every area of darkness once occupied by hurt and anger are now filled with the light of your healing and love. I wait on you Lord and trust your process of transforming Grace. I am rooted and established in your love and love others as you have loved me. Thank you.

# MARCH 19

God is light
and where
His healing light
meets our wounded souls
through the invitation
of our own openness,
change begins
to take place.

I don't think the way you think. The way you work isn't the way I work. God's Decree. For as the sky soars high above earth, so the way I work surpasses the way you work, and the way I think is beyond the way you think. Just as rain and snow descend from the skies and don't go back until they've watered the earth, doing their work of making things grow and blossom, producing seed for farmers and food for the hungry, so will the words that come out of my mouth not come back empty-handed. They'll do the work I sent them to do, they'll complete the assignment I gave them.

Isaiah 55:8-11 *(The Message)*

Lord, you are Healing Supply. All that you have for me is unfolding by faith in Christ Jesus through your grace. I embrace the Christ within me and the truth of your Word to stand strong, steady and empowered. I live as one in spirit with Christ Jesus abiding in him, resting in him and confident by faith in him. Your provision and your supply never runs dry. In Christ, I am free to be and free to give all you have created me to be and do. Your wisdom guides the creativity you placed within me and you anoint my hands to bring it to pass. Christ brings forth a bountiful harvest of his love, Grace and truth as I plant the seeds of your Word in spirit. Thank you for your Covenant promises and for bringing forth their manifestation in every area of my life. Thank you for opening divine doors and inviting me to walk through them by faith. Thank you for closing every door that is not in keeping with your will for my life. I rest in Christ. I trust in the wisdom, instruction and teaching of the Holy Spirit. As my spirit is alive in Christ Jesus, I submit my will to your will. I joy in you as you complete every divine assignment you have predestined for me.

# MARCH 20

Jesus
becomes
Lord
of our
lives
when we
confess,
"Lord, I can't, You can".

If you don't go all the way with me, through thick and thin, you don't deserve me. If your first concern is to look after yourself, you'll never find yourself. But if you forget about yourself and look to me, you'll find both yourself and me.

Matthew 10:38-39 *(The Message)*

Cast your cares on the LORD and he will sustain you; he will never let the righteous be shaken.

Psalm 55:22

Lord, you are Divine Wisdom. I yield to Christ living within me and say, "Not my will, but yours be done." I gratefully receive the divine revelation of the Holy Spirit as I feed my spirit with your living Word. I am open to your wisdom and loving guidance. I gratefully receive your chastening. As I release myself to you, you change me from the inside out. Every door, every miracle and every person who is a part of my healing process is lining up with your divine design. I listen for and follow your voice seeking the promise land you have divinely set before me. Your Righteous Right Hand upholds me as I take the steps orchestrated in the grace of Christ Jesus. I am a recipient of every spiritual blessing in the Heavenly places in Christ. As I rest in Christ, he brings forth his life in and through me. Christ Jesus enlarges my territory. His divine power has granted to me all things that pertain to life and godliness, through the knowledge of Christ who called me to his own glory and excellence. My gift to you is praise and thanksgiving.

# MARCH 21

Whatever in us
that has not been
brought out
into the light,
still has a
life of its own
in our past,
and its presence
will affect all
our relationships.

A good man brings good things out of the good stored up in his heart, and an evil man brings evil things out of the evil stored up in his heart. For the mouth speaks what the heart is full of.

Luke 6:45

Lord, you are Healing Grace. You are able to make all grace abound to me in Christ Jesus. Your Grace nourishes my spirit and waters my soul with life. In Christ, I am a child of the light. In Christ, you have chosen me before the creation of the world to be holy and blameless in your sight. When your eyes look upon me you see me through the righteousness of Christ. As Christ, the source of love lives in me, his love flows to others from me. As I continue to grow into the likeness of Christ, you bring to mind those areas of my life that need to be confessed, grieved and released to you for your healing. I recognize offense in my heart blocks the flow of your grace by love. Offense and love are like oil and water. They cannot mix. As I look in the mirror of my heart, I release to the strength of Christ all smudges and shadows that are rooted in my thoughts and acted upon by my words and actions. I choose to forgive myself and others. I am a victor and not a victim. I release all vengeance to you Lord. I speak blessings over my offenders and call them by name before your throne of Grace. Thank you that Christ in me empowers me to walk as a child of the light and relate to others in his abounding love. I live in gratitude.

# MARCH 22

We choose
to tear down the walls
we've built around
our hearts,
and Jesus
does
the healing.

Our firm decision is to work from this focused center: One man died for everyone. That puts everyone in the same boat. He included everyone in his death so that everyone could also be included in his life, a resurrection life, a far better life than people ever lived on their own. Because of this decision we don't evaluate people by what they have or how they look. We looked at the Messiah that way once and got it all wrong, as you know. We certainly don't look at him that way anymore. Now we look inside, and what we see is that anyone united with the Messiah gets a fresh start, is created new. The old life is gone; a new life burgeons! Look at it! All this comes from the God who settled the relationship between us and him, and then called us to settle our relationships with each other. God put the world square with himself through the Messiah, giving the world a fresh start by offering forgiveness of sins. God has given us the task of telling everyone what he is doing. We're Christ's representatives. God uses us to persuade men and women to drop their differences and enter into God's work of making things right between them. We're speaking for Christ himself now: Become friends with God; he's already a friend with you.

2 Corinthians 5:14-20 *(The Message)*

Lord, you are Complete Restoration. My soul is healed in the light of your love. I nurture my relationships with others in your love and through the Grace of Christ Jesus. I forgive others through Christ the Forgiver who lives in me. In, by and through Christ, I love others as you have loved me. I live in freedom and peace as I cast my cares on Christ. I use my words to build up and encourage others as I take responsibility for my words and actions in light of your Word. I take my thoughts captive to the obedience of Christ. Thank you for giving me living hope through the resurrection of Jesus Christ to an inheritance in him that is imperishable, undefiled and unfading. Thank you for empowering me to live in the grace of Jesus. Halleluiah praises.

# MARCH 23

The more space
we rent in our
thoughts to injury
the bigger the injury gets,
and the more space
we rent to our injury,
the deeper the pain becomes.

Do not conform to the pattern of this world, but be transformed by the renewing of your mind. Then you will be able to test and approve what God's will is—his good, pleasing and perfect will.

Romans 12:2

I keep my eyes always on the Lord. With him at my right hand, I will not be shaken.

Psalm 16:8

Lord, you are my Stronghold. I live in the strength of Christ and his power restores and transforms me. I look in the mirror of my heart and hold my beliefs up to the light of your Word. Through the revelation of the Holy spirit bearing witness with my spirit, my mind is renewed with the truth of your Word. I listen to my thoughts and take my thoughts captive to the obedience of Christ. My inner change is not by power and not by might, but by your Spirit, which is alive in and at work within me. I am a new creation. I fix my thoughts on you. I cast my cares on you and live free. I hold fast to Christ Jesus who is my rock. I rejoice in the privilege and honor of yielding to your reign and rule in my life. My spirit is one with you in Christ Jesus. No hurt I have ever experienced is worth building a wall around that will create distance in my relationship. I guard our divine relationship. I honor others with respect and love as you have respected and loved me in Christ. By the grace of God, I confess what needs confessing, grieve what needs grieving and forgive what needs forgiving. I keep my eyes on you. Thank you.

# MARCH 24

By focusing
outside ourselves,
we misplace the key
to self discovery,
inner growth
and genuine purpose.

In all your ways submit to him, and he will make your paths straight.

Proverbs 3:6

The name of the LORD is a fortified tower; the righteous run to it and are safe.

Proverbs:18:10

Lord, you are Sovereign Provision. You hold the perfect plan for my life. Every detail is coming to pass, as I rest in Christ. The grace of Christ is changing me daily from the inside out. Your love is life to my spirit and the key to my soul. Your Grace unlocks and supplies my very being. I am open to receive your divine feast. I taste and see that you are Good. I put on the garment of praise and speak words of thanksgiving. Your divine power has granted to me all things that pertain to life and godliness, through the knowledge of Christ Jesus who has called me to his own glory and excellence. I trust in you Lord with all my heart and lean not on my own understanding. I acknowledge your ways and you make my paths straight. Holy Spirit you are welcome to search me and mold me with God's Living Word. I welcome your truth and desire to live in its fullness and freedom. As I yield to Christ within, I desire truth in my inmost heart. I joy in the privilege of humbling myself before you. I joyfully submit to you. Thank you.

# MARCH 25

Until we get
ourselves out
of the way,
we won't
see our
true selves,
or
discover God's best.

Summing it all up, friends, I'd say you'll do best by filling your minds and meditating on things true, noble, reputable, authentic, compelling, gracious—the best, not the worst; the beautiful, not the ugly; things to praise, not things to curse. Put into practice what you learned from me, what you heard and saw and realized. Do that, and God, who makes everything work together, will work you into his most excellent harmonies.

Philippians 4:8-9 *(The Message)*

Lord, you are the Potter. I choose to lay myself aside and allow the divine Grace of Christ Jesus to mold and shape me. As I consider your Word, your thoughts become my thoughts. My spirit is filled with joy and stirred by your presence. Your love for me, your blood that covers me and your Grace that supplies me are all unearned gifts from your immeasurable nature of love. I live in awe of you. I love others because you are the creator of unconditional, unmatched love living in me. My trials and tribulations pale in comparison to the price you paid at the cross on my behalf. In Christ, I am a divine and unique masterpiece created to glorify you. My spirit sings a continuous melodious song as I joy in your wonder. The universe declares your majesty. As you knit me together in my mother's womb, your eyes were continuously on me. You have numbered the hairs of my head. Apart from you marvelous grace, I cannot take one breath. I glory in you with every beat of my heart. You are my God. I am your child. My lips sing your praises.

# MARCH 26

Jesus is ready,
willing, and able
to help us
face our hurts,
disappointments,
resentments
and
self-protective
motives, and
emerge as one
changed into his likeness

But those who hope in the LORD will renew their strength. They will soar on wings like eagles; they will run and not grow weary, they will walk and not be faint.

Isaiah 40:31

Lord, you are Faithful and Everlasting Strength. In Christ, I am more than a conqueror. I live rooted and built up in Christ, strengthened in the measure of faith that God placed within me at the moment of my salvation. I overflow in thankfulness for the wonder of God placing the fullness of himself in Christ Jesus on the inside of me. I yield those soul wounds I have carried openly and honestly to his Grace. I face my hurts and disappointments with renewed strength, truth, and courage as I lean on, trust in and rely on Christ. As I make the choice to empty out, the grace of Christ Jesus in me overflows through me. I joy as I rest in you because my hope comes from Christ Jesus. He is my rock and my salvation. He is my fortress. I will not be shaken. I burst forth in song every morning because your mercies are new every morning. I am joyful in hope, patient in affliction and faithful in prayer. I draw near to you and you draw near to me. Every moment in the day the full provision of Christ living within me rises up to meet my needs. The Word alive within me brings life to every fiber of my being. In Christ, I am chosen, blessed and highly favored. My heart's desire is to bring you glory in everything I do and say.

# MARCH 27

Authentic
love flows
from a heart
that has been
genuinely broken
and divinely healed
by God's Grace.

Therefore, as God's chosen people, holy and dearly loved, clothe yourselves with compassion, kindness, humility, gentleness and patience.

Colossians 3:12

Lord, you are Divine Supply. I live in your wondrous presence claiming all that is mine through faith in Christ Jesus. My disappointments, failures and weaknesses are healed as I yield all that I am to your amazing Grace. My obstacles are springboards to my next level of victory in Christ Jesus. Your Grace makes a way where there seems to be no way. As I confess your Word, you are watching over it to perform it. Thank you for your faithfulness. My thoughts reflect your truth as I renew my mind to your living Word. By the Grace of Christ Jesus living in me, my choices propel me to actions that encourage and build up others. I move in the harmony of your Love. I clothe myself with compassion, kindness, humility, gentleness and patience because Christ Jesus empowers me with his grace. By the blood of the Lamb, I am empowered to be all you have created me to be. The works of my hands and the meditations of my heart are acceptable in your sight. Thank you that in Christ I am blessed and highly favored. My being glories in you.

# MARCH 28

Life is an ever evolving,
constantly changing process
that invites us to explore,
to choose, to trust,
to ponder, to imagine,
to reflect, to believe,
to reject and to
continuously
dance with the
changes we are
openly willing
to embrace.

May the God of hope fill you with all joy and peace as you trust in him, so that you may overflow with hope by the power of the Holy Spirit.

Romans 15:13

Lord, you are Everlasting Hope. I know you are working all things for my good and your glory. As your child, I am empowered by the resurrection power of Christ Jesus. I rest in Christ and live in his unending and all supplying hope. I joy in the wonder of being the created living in union with my creator. I celebrate the love of the Father given to me graciously in Christ Jesus. I am a joint heir with Christ Jesus. I joyfully and humbly receive all the promises of God in Christ Jesus as yes and amen. I look at my life in the mirror of your Word and offer myself to you as a living sacrifice. I renew my thoughts to the truth of your Word. Holy Spirit I invite you to teach me your ways and bring revelation to my soul. I gratefully receive the counsel, wisdom and correction of the Holy Spirit. I declare your praises and offer unending gratitude for calling me out of the darkness into your marvelous light. My heart writes a continuous symphony of praise that my lips joy in singing day and night. Thank you for loving me. I overflow with hope.

# MARCH 29

God requires us to look
in the mirror
of His Word
so He can reflect
back the
self-interests in our souls.

You did not choose me, but I chose you and appointed you so that you might go and bear fruit—fruit that will last—and so that whatever you ask in my name the Father will give you.

John 15:16

Lord, you are Divine Reflection. Your Word nurtures my spirit and reflects your nature to my soul. Search me and bring to mind those areas of my life that I have yet to surrender to your Lordship. As I walk in the spirit, I do not fulfill the lusts of the flesh. Thank you for breaking the power of sin. Now I live yielded to Christ within who brings His nature to me and through me. I live in the Grace supply of Christ Jesus who turns my weaknesses into his strengths. Apart from Christ Jesus, there is no good thing in me. Living in Christ and Christ in me, I am redeemed, restored and a new creation. I am one spirit with you in Christ Jesus. You fill me with life, hope and purpose. My soul glories in thanksgiving that you are my source, my provider, my strength, my wisdom, my destiny and my Lord. I cherish the time I spend with you and thank you for bringing revelation to your Word by the Holy Spirit. In Christ, I bear everlasting fruit. I desire to be the mirror that reflects you the Lord of my life. Thank you for supernatural transformation.

# MARCH 30

Coming to Christ is much more
than pulling the rotten fruit
of our behaviors
off the tree; it's taking
all we are and offering
our abandoned selves
back to our Creator.

My response is to get down on my knees before the Father, this magnificent Father who parcels out all heaven and earth. I ask him to strengthen you by his Spirit—not a brute strength but a glorious inner strength—that Christ will live in you as you open the door and invite him in. And I ask him that with both feet planted firmly on love, you'll be able to take in with all followers of Jesus the extravagant dimensions of Christ's love. Reach out and experience the breadth! Test its length! Plumb the depths! Rise to the heights! Live full lives, full in the fullness of God.

Ephesians 3:14-19 *(The Message)*

Lord, You know all that I am and all you created me to be. The fullness of Christ and his purpose are manifesting in my life. My spirit was reborn the moment I accepted Christ as my Savior. Thank you for calling me and equipping me with freedom in Christ. He is the divine seed in my spirit that brings forth his fruit of love, peace, joy, truth, and righteousness. As I abide in Christ relying on him as my source, he brings forth the fruits of affection for others, exuberance about life and peace that passes all human reasoning. Joy floods my soul as I spend time with him, draw life from him, and rest in his provision. Where the spirit is there is freedom. My spirit is one with Christ. His righteousness, his wisdom, his goodness lives in the spirit of my being filling me with his abundance, his peace, and his joy. Thank you for allowing me to come to your throne of Grace day in and day out where you receive me with love and joy. Thank you for paying my sin debt in full and supplying me with unending Grace. I sing your praises.

## MARCH 31

Honestly looking in the mirror
of our hearts where we connect
with the inner thirst of our soul
allows us to embrace our hurts,
face our confusion,
confront our fears,
feel our disappointments
and prayerfully release our needs
to a God who quenches our thirst,
heals our hurts, turns darkness into light,
fills us with hope, loves us
unconditionally, and meets our every need.

And so we know and rely on the love God has for us. God is love. Whoever lives in love lives in God, and God in them.

1John 4:16

So I say to you: Ask and it will be given to you; seek and you will find; knock and the door will be opened to you. For everyone who asks receives; the one who seeks finds; and to the one who knocks, the door will be opened.

Luke 11:9-10

Lord, You are Divine Source and Everlasting Provision. Thank you for Christ Jesus who is the door for entering into your abounding grace. Thank you that in Christ as I throw open the doors of my heart by faith, he allows me to discover at the same moment that he has already thrown open his door to me. Thank you for your immeasurable goodness. Thank you for lavishing your gift of love on me through the cross of Christ Jesus. You are bringing all things together for my good. As I lay my hurts before your throne of Grace and choose to open myself to the people you bring into my life, you are healing my hurts and restoring all my broken Humpty Dumpty pieces. You quench my thirst, feed my soul and nourish life in my spirit. You are Light to my spirit and Hope in all things. I am accepted, blessed and highly favored in your everlasting Grace. You are my God and I am your child. I live in the freedom of your spirit that lives in me in Jesus.

# APRIL 1

Often we turn
to Christ
in consistent prayer,
renewed commitment
and zealous service
insistent on finding our
own relief, rather than
genuinely determining
to deepen our
relationship with Him.

I love those who love me, and those who seek me find me. With me are riches and honor, enduring wealth and prosperity. My fruit is better than fine gold; what I yield surpasses choice silver.

Proverbs 8:17-19

Lord, you are Grace Provision. I draw near to you and you draw near to me. You are my unlimited, ever present source. You cause me to triumph in every circumstance. I trust in you. Throughout every day, I sing and shout my praises to you through Jesus, the Messiah. You shower me with the abundance and grace provision of Christ. In Christ, I can do all things. His Grace super abounds over my weaknesses as I rest in him and abide by faith. Nothing brings greater joy than spending time with you. Your Word is a lamp to my feet and a light of your will for me. You are able to do exceedingly abundantly above all that I ask or think, according to your power working in me. Your Divine power gives me things that pertain to life and godliness. I live with conquering power as I yield to the Christ within me. Nothing can hinder your Divine plan for my life. No weapon formed against me shall prosper. Thank you for Eternal Riches and heavenly blessings here on earth. I live for the praise of your glory. Halleluiah.

# APRIL 2

In our
pursuit of
acceptance,
our hidden
agenda
is often
more revealing
than the
one open
for public view.

But when he, the Spirit of truth, comes, he will guide you into all the truth. He will not speak on his own; he will speak only what he hears, and he will tell you what is yet to come.

John 16:13

Lord, you are Spirit and Truth. As I submit to you, you are guiding me into the knowledge of all truth. As I call on you, you show me great and mighty things. I am a God pleaser not a people pleaser. I am appointed and chosen to bear much everlasting fruit as I abide in Christ who is the true vine. As I speak your Word from my mouth, it is unleashing greatness in your Kingdom accomplishing your will in my life. Every seed of faith I plant in your Word, brings abundant life. Thank you for teaching me as I humble myself to you. Thank you for molding me into your vessel that reflects your glory and holds your grace that pours out your love onto those I meet. Thank you for life in Christ Jesus and his grace that is in me which accomplishes his work through me. My spirit is perfected in Christ and I am one with him. No weapon formed against me shall prosper. Christ delivers and draws me to himself from every assault of evil. He preserves and brings me safely into his heavenly kingdom. I overcome by the words of my testimony and the blood of the Lamb. Thank you that your love is unending. Halleluiah praises.

# APRIL 3

The interminable quest for acceptance,
however well defined or obscured
is often indicative of the unresolved pain
arising out of the lingering rejection
alive in our hearts that's
searching for a voice.

What actually took place is this: I tried keeping rules and working my head off to please God, and it didn't work. So I quit being a "law man" so that I could be God's man. Christ's life showed me how, and enabled me to do it. I identified myself completely with him. Indeed, I have been crucified with Christ. My ego is no longer central. It is no longer important that I appear righteous before you or have your good opinion, and I am no longer driven to impress God. Christ lives in me. The life you see me living is not "mine," but it is lived by faith in the Son of God, who loved me and gave himself for me. I am not going to go back on that. Is it not clear to you that to go back to that old rule-keeping, peer-pleasing religion would be an abandonment of everything personal and free in my relationship with God? I refuse to do that, to repudiate God's grace. If a living relationship with God could come by rule-keeping, then Christ died unnecessarily.

Galatians 2:1-20 *(The Message)*

Lord, you are Pure Love and Complete Acceptance. My worth is sealed once and for all in Christ Jesus. I live my life in faith now and forever. Christ is my righteousness. Christ is my identity. Christ is my acceptance and value. There is no work that is complete enough, good enough or acceptable of my own efforts that can present me as holy and blameless before you. I am holy and blameless in and through my Savior, Christ Jesus. I am fully and completely loved and redeemed by your Grace in Christ. I am your child and I live joyfully and freely in your Grace. Christ is my everlasting source. I put on and clothe myself in Christ. I dress in the wardrobe you picked out for me in Christ. The God attire I wear is compassion, love, humility, quiet strength and obedience. I wear the crown of life in Christ Jesus. I live in his abundance, love through his presence in me, and forgive by his grace. I love others because you first loved me. Apart from abiding in Christ, I can do nothing. I live by faith in Christ Jesus. Thank you.

# APRIL 4

As long as we
cling to unmet
expectations, we will
behaviorally
and relationally
expect someone
else to meet
our needs,
which relinquishes
our power and our freedom.

In him and through faith in him we may approach God with freedom and confidence.

Ephesians 3:12

Lord, you are never ending Supply. I come boldly to your throne of Grace by faith in the blood of Jesus. I receive every portion of his goodness and righteousness as I abide in him. I live with joy and thanksgiving as I live chosen, blessed and highly favored in Christ. In Christ, I am free from condemnation. His blood has washed me white as snow. I am your child and you are my God. I am loved with the same love that you have for Jesus. I am blessed with every spiritual blessing in Christ. I am seated in Heaven with Christ. I stir up my faith by confessing the truth of your Word that lives in me and watches over me. Your Word is life to my spirit and health to my soul. I live in the power and freedom of Christ. I reflect his glory as I abide in him. I take no confidence in my flesh where no good thing dwells. I fix my eyes not on what is seen, but on what is unseen. For what is seen is temporary, but what is unseen is eternal. I live in Christ now and for evermore. I rest in your unending supply. I live in the fullness of Christ Jesus.

# APRIL 5

Every issue
in our flesh
is connected
to our
sense of value
or lack thereof
and determines
how we relate
to God, others
and ourselves.

Stand fast therefore in the liberty wherewith Christ hath made us free, and be not entangled again with the yoke of bondage.

Galatians 5:1 (KJV)

Lord, you are Freedom. In Christ, I live in the Spirit where there is freedom and liberty. You know my strengths and my weakness. Your light penetrates my human spirit, exposing my every hidden motive. Nothing is hidden from your eyes. By my faith in Christ, you have removed the yoke of bondage to sin. Christ replaced my darkness with his light that lives in me and shines forth from me. I am a child of the light living in the light as he is in the light. My need and hunger for love is satisfied in Christ. The love of Christ living in me is the love I share with those I meet. I am ransomed by the blood of the Lamb. In your wholeness, I am a non-resistant instrument for your grace. In Christ, my life is unfolding with wonder, power and amazement. Every day is one of joy as I expect your manifestations of goodness. I am set apart in Christ for greatness on earth and Eternal life in Heaven. All my works bring goodness to me and glory to you. Apart from Christ, I can do nothing. Thank you for your longing to be gracious to me. Thank you for lavishing your love upon me. I am worthy in the Lamb. My lips sing your praises.

# APRIL 6

Lasting
faith never
grows in a
comfortable
mind
or a heart
void of struggle.

Now faith is confidence in what we hope for and assurance about what we do not see.

Hebrews 11:1

So do not fear, for I am with you; do not be dismayed, for I am your God. I will strengthen you and help you; I will uphold you with my righteous right hand.

Isaiah 41:10

Lord, you are Divine Wisdom. You are my power source, leading me to all that is rightfully mine in your Kingdom by faith in Christ Jesus. The perfect love of Christ lives in me, fills me and covers me. Thank you for your perfect love that casts out all fear. Thank you that your eyes are always upon me. Thank you for your amazing gift of Christ Jesus who is my high priest that sympathizes with my weaknesses and turns my weaknesses into his strengths as I cast my cares on him. I draw near to your throne of grace with confidence knowing that in Christ I receive mercy and find grace to help in my time of need. I am not afraid or discouraged because the life of Christ and his strength lives in me. I have victory over principalities, powers, rulers of darkness and spiritual wickedness in high places because of the blood of Christ and the Word of my testimony. What I bind in earth is bound in Heaven. What I loose on earth is loosed in Heaven. You assure me that trials and the proving of my faith bring endurance, patience and steadfastness. Mold me according to your divine purposes. I rest in Christ Jesus. Thank you.

# APRIL 7

Every
aspect of our
lives, involves
a season of
relational connections.

Dear friends, let us love one another, for love comes from God. Everyone who loves has been born of God and knows God. Whoever does not love does not know God, because God is love. This is how God showed his love among us: He sent his one and only Son into the world that we might live through him. This is love: not that we loved God, but that he loved us and sent his Son as an atoning sacrifice for our sins.

1 John 4:7-10

Lord, you are Life. You have created me in your image and called me according to your purpose. The fullness of all you have created and called me to is complete in Christ Jesus. Thank you for your gift of goodness as you bring people into my life through your wisdom to join with me in the work you have called me to do. I yield to the Lordship of Christ abiding in him, trusting in him and following his voice. I am a chosen one, established, anointed and sealed by the Holy Spirit. I am confident that every good work in me through Christ is completed by him as I abide in him. I live by faith, knowing I have been given power, love and a sound mind. I am a branch of Jesus Christ, the true Vine and a channel of his life. I have been chosen and anointed. The fruit I bear in Christ Jesus is bountiful and everlasting. I receive what I ask of the Father because I have access to his Holy of Holies through Jesus Christ. I live high and lifted up in Jesus.

# APRIL 8

The burden
of bridge
building
often falls
on the
strong and
innocent,
not on
the weak
and guilty.

Be completely humble and gentle; be patient, bearing with one another in love. Make every effort to keep the unity of the Spirit through the bond of peace. There is one body and one Spirit, just as you were called to one hope when you were called; one Lord, one faith, one baptism; one God and Father of all, who is over all and through all and in all.

Ephesians 4:2-6

Lord, you are Righteousness, Joy, and Peace. In Christ Jesus, I have the Prince for Peace living within me. I submit myself to Christ, cast my cares on him and ask him to bring forth his strength through me to love others like he loves me. Through the eyes of Christ, I see others as your masterpiece formed in your image and divinely designed with value. Christ has woven the chords of his harmony into my spirit and his goodness flows from my very soul. The love I pour out on others is the finale to the symphony of love that flows through me. I love others because you first loved me. You are the source and the essence of love that brings harmony into every area of my life. You are my God and I am your child. I rest in you. Christ, the Forgiver in me, supplies the grace to forgive others. The fullness of Christ in me brings an alert expectancy and trust that I will never be left feeling shortchanged in him. As I abide in Christ by faith and he abides in me, he is faithful to mold me into his vessel that reflects his love. Halleluiah praises.

# APRIL 9

When
we are
not concerned
with who
gets the
credit,
there is no
limit to
how far
we can go.

He has showed you, O man, what is good. And what does the LORD require of you? To act justly and to love mercy and to walk humbly with your God.

Micah 6:8 (NIV)

Lord, you are Immutable. You have seated me with Christ in the Heavens. You created me in your image. My spirit is alive unto you in Christ Jesus. You have given me dominion over all the earth. In submission to Christ, I have the authority to rule and reign over the power of sin, devils, demonic powers, sickness and poverty. You have given me the honor and privilege of living in relationship with you and others. The presence of Christ in me and the love of Christ through me allows me to honor and encourage others as purposed and divinely created. As I live in the spirit of Christ, I walk in his spirit. In Christ, I live a divinely directed life and not a self-driven or self-centered life. I live trusting in your abundance through Christ and not trying to achieve my own works. My life is your agenda, yielded humbly before you, and created to bring you glory. I receive and live in the wondrous riches of grace in Christ Jesus. My lips offer continual praise to you. I set my affections above and not on earth. In Christ, he opens the hidden treasures of your glory for me as I fellowship with You. Thank you for creating me for the praise of your glory.

# APRIL 10

Our relationships
will thrive
when the
innocent
are merciful,
not because
the guilty are judged.

Finally, all of you, be like-minded, be sympathetic, love one another, be compassionate and humble. Do not repay evil with evil or insult with insult. On the contrary, repay evil with blessing, because to this you were called so that you may inherit a blessing. For, whoever would love life and see good days must keep their tongue from evil and their lips from deceitful speech. They must turn from evil and do good; they must seek peace and pursue it. For the eyes of the Lord are on the righteous and his ears are attentive to their prayer, but the face of the Lord is against those who do evil.

1 Peter 3:8-12

Lord, you are Holy and a Righteous Judge. In Christ, I am holy and righteous. The presence of Christ in me and his love flows through me like a gentle flowing stream. In my flesh there is no good thing. Apart from Christ, I cannot love, extend mercy, show compassion, share patience or forgive my offenders. I live in the spirit where God's nature in Christ rules and reigns in me. As I yield to Christ in me and cast my cares on him, he brings forth his nature to me and through me. I rest in Christ and the fullness of his love which grace supplies and with my cup full of Christ, he overflows to those I meet. I am free to live in love and forgiveness because Christ is my unending source. I realize that hurting people hurt people. In Christ, I have the eyes to see beyond offense. The measure I use to relate to others is the same measure of mercy, love, grace, hope and forgiveness you have given to me. I see others as your unique and precious creation. I value and treasure others with the abundance of value and treasure as you sacrificed your life for me. I live in praise and thanksgiving. I live in thanksgiving and praise of your awesome wonder.

# APRIL 11

There is
a process
and a purpose
to work through,
to go through,
and to run to,
in every
breakthrough.

Then he told them what they could expect for themselves: "Anyone who intends to come with me has to let me lead. You're not in the driver's seat—I am. Don't run from suffering; embrace it. Follow me and I'll show you how. Self-help is no help at all. Self-sacrifice is the way, my way, to finding yourself, your true self. What good would it do to get everything you want and lose you, the real you? If any of you is embarrassed with me and the way I'm leading you, know that the Son of Man will be far more embarrassed with you when he arrives in all his splendor in company with the Father and the holy angels. This isn't, you realize, pie in the sky by and by. Some who have taken their stand right here are going to see it happen, see with their own eyes the kingdom of God.

Luke 9:23-27 *(The Message)*

Lord, you are Healer. Thank you that the sufficiency of Christ in me supplies healing grace to every trial and tribulation that comes my way. I rest in Christ and trust him to make a way where there seems no way. I abide in Christ as I speak peace to the storms of my life and he ceases the waves. My lips sing your praises because I know you are working all things out for my good. Your goodness and mercy follow me all the days of my life. I draw near to you and you draw near to me. The grace of Christ turns my weaknesses into his strengths as I abide in him. You are my healer, my defender, my provision, my shield, my rock, my fortress, my dwelling place and my shelter. As I abide in Christ, he is transforming me from the inside out. I find comfort and strength in knowing Christ is my source. My sufficiency is Christ sufficiency. Inhale my worship. Exhale your Glory. My lips shout your praises. Lead me in the way everlasting.

## APRIL 12

Facing our
insufficiency
and brokenness
by surrendering it to God,
allows Him to ready us
for the cross experience
and reveal the
exchanged life
He's waiting
to give us.

God can pour on the blessings in astonishing ways so that you're ready for anything and everything, more than just ready to do what needs to be done. As one psalmist puts it, He throws caution to the winds, giving to the needy in reckless abandon. His right-living, right-giving ways never run out, never wear out. This most generous God who gives seed to the farmer that becomes bread for your meals is more than extravagant with you. He gives you something you can then give away, which grows into full-formed lives, robust in God, wealthy in every way, so that you can be generous in every way, producing with us great praise to God.

2 Corinthians 9:8-11 *(The Message)*

Lord you are All Sufficient. You are extravagant and wondrous. You are mighty and powerful. You are glorious and worthy. You are Sovereign and King. In you, I am fearfully and wonderfully made. I humbly receive every portion of supply in Christ Jesus. I receive the fullness of every blessing you lovingly shower on me through the exchange of Jesus' precious blood. I draw near to you and you draw near to me. Your Word is seed that I plant in my spirit. I water it with faith. I confess it out my mouth and marvel at your faithfulness to perform it. I joy in the wonder of renewing my mind to the obedience of Christ. I praise you for the measure of faith you placed in me at the time of my salvation. All your promises to me in Christ are yes and amen. I rejoice in my trials knowing that you are working all things out for my good. The resurrection life I received by faith in Christ is adventurous, expectant and abundant as he provides and I abide. I live free from the power of sin and death in Christ Jesus. Thank you.

# APRIL 13

God's
conviction
through true guilt
brings us to
repentance,
while false guilt
brings us under
condemnation.

Therefore, there is now no condemnation for those who are in Christ Jesus, because through Christ Jesus the law of the Spirit who gives life has set you free from the law of sin and death.

Romans 8:1-2

Lord, you are Mercy. Living by faith in your gift of grace, I am not condemned. In Jesus Christ, I approach your throne with confidence. My confidence is resting in the finished work of Jesus. Your drops of blood that fell at the cross had my name written in them. I am a new creation in Christ and all old things have passed away. I am an heir with the Father and a joint heir with Christ. I am reconciled to God and I'm an ambassador of reconciliation for Him. I am God's workmanship created for good works. I joyfully receive your words of correction, because I know yielding to Christ within me allows the Holy Spirit to take me to a deeper relationship with him. I am high and lifted up in Christ. I live in the Heavenly realm. I am just passing through on earth. I am chosen of God, holy, and accepted in the beloved. I partake of my Heavenly calling. I receive by faith every great and precious promise that is mine in Christ Jesus. I live whole, complete and free. A mantle of power rests upon my life. I am clothed in humility. I wear the garment of praise. I yield to and rest in you. Thank you for creating and loving me.

# APRIL 14

One of the greatest and most lasting gifts
we can give ourselves is to reflect on any sadness
hidden in our hearts and let the sadness
drive us to healing tears, because as we
touch our own self-centeredness,
our stubborn self-sufficiency,
and our reality of how often we
refuse to trust God, we realize
God Himself is our
wholeness.

May the God of hope fill you with all joy and peace as you trust in him, so that you may overflow with hope by the power of the Holy Spirit.

Romans 15:13

Lord, you are my Unfailing Supply. I am one with you in Christ Jesus. I am called and ordained with your anointing to do great things for your Kingdom as I abide by faith in Christ. Every door for my good is opened by your divine favor. Your finished work of the Cross set me free from the chains of bondage to sin and condemnation once and for all. I receive forgiveness, healing, prosperity and protection through the blood of Jesus. I am not conformed to this world, but I am transformed by the renewal of my mind, that by testing I may discern what is the will of God, what is good and acceptable and perfect. I humble myself before you and you exalt me. I take the yoke of Christ upon me and learn from him for he is gentle and lowly in heart. In Christ, I find rest for my soul and life to my spirit. I am one with the spirit of Christ Jesus. I readily yield myself to Christ and invite his spirit to search me, test my thoughts and see if there is any hurtful way in me. Lead me in the way everlasting. Thank you for bringing forth your masterpiece.

# APRIL 15

When we willingly
address our
own pain,
we can willingly
share
someone else's.

All praise to the God and Father of our Master, Jesus the Messiah!
Father of all mercy! God of all healing counsel! He comes alongside
us when we go through hard times, and before you know it, he brings
us alongside someone else who is going through hard times so that
we can be there for that person just as God was there for us. We
have plenty of hard times that come from following the Messiah,
but no more so than the good times of his healing comfort—we get
a full measure of that, too.

2 Corinthians 1:3-4 *(The Message)*

Lord, you are Healing, Comfort and Restoration. I live in the resurrection
power of Christ Jesus, my Lord and my Savior. At the cross, you took my
infirmities and bore my sickness. You are the Lord that heals and restores.
I receive your Light that breaks forth like morning and speedily springs
forth healing. My heart is a fertile ground for your love. I share your love
with those I meet. Your grace is my daily companion. I put on the inner
garment of forgiveness and wear it throughout the day. I easily discern
other's pain and share a word of encouragement through your Grace that
flows interruptedly through me in Christ Jesus. I am your ambassador of
loving kindness and transforming love. In the presence of love, miracles
happen. I give thanks for the miracles and wonders that are unfolding in
my life and the lives of others around me. I am a vessel of love and hope
in Christ. I pour out your love, your goodness and your mercy because you
have filled me to overflowing with grace. My life reflects your nature which
is alive in me by faith in Christ Jesus. My soul magnifies you. Inhale my
worship. Exhale your glory.

# APRIL 16

If you have a
Spiritual hernia,
you've picked up something
Jesus never intended for
you to carry.

In him and through faith in him we may approach God with freedom and confidence.

Ephesians 3:12

Christ has set us free to live a free life. So take your stand! Never again let anyone put a harness of slavery on you.

Galatians 5:1 *(The Message)*

Lord, you are Everlasting Freedom. I cast my burdens on Christ Jesus and wait expectantly as his grace supernaturally changes my circumstances for my good and his glory. I live in peace persevering in the strength of Christ Jesus towards the Promised Land you have called me to and empowered me to claim. Every detail of your divine design for my life is unfolding, bit by bit, and moment by moment. You are opening every door that needs to be open and closing every door that needs to be closed for my good. You are bringing into alignment every person and every circumstance that helps, uplifts and imparts favor over me. My ministry of reconciliation moves forth with divine power and divine wisdom. I am strong in Christ and the power of his might. I bear the fruit of the spirit as Christ produces the fruit. Love, peace, joy, gentleness, goodness, faithfulness, meekness and temperance are growing in and pouring out of my heart to everyone around me. I shout lungful praises throughout the day. Thank you awesome God.

# APRIL 17

Revelation becomes transformation
when we understand the
difference between
passionately petitioning
God according to His Word, and
consistently pleading and demanding
His will and our will are one in the same.

For my thoughts are not your thoughts, neither are your ways my ways," declares the LORD. "As the heavens are higher than the earth, so are my ways higher than your ways and my thoughts than your thoughts. As the rain and the snow come down from heaven, and do not return to it without watering the earth and making it bud and flourish, so that it yields seed for the sower and bread for the eater, so is my word that goes out from my mouth: It will not return to me empty, but will accomplish what I desire and achieve the purpose for which I sent it

Isaiah 55:8-11

Lord, You are Sovereign, I live, move and have my being in complete submission to you. You are Creator of all things. I live with power and purpose through the living Christ inside of me. I reign in Heavenly places with Christ. I live in resurrection power. By faith, and in your Grace, I am strong to run my race and fulfill my victorious destiny in Christ. You open the eyes of my heart to know you more. Your Word is life to my soul and health to my bones. You are life. You are able to do immeasurably more than I can think, dream or imagine according to the power that is at work in me. I yield the pieces of my life to the altar of your grace and wait expectantly in faith as you knit them together in your will and by your way. You have rescued me from the pit of pride and the lust of my eyes and flesh and broken the power of sin off my life. I gratefully renew my mind to the truth of your Word. I live in freedom and victory abiding, relying, adhering to and leaning on Jesus who supplies all my needs according to his riches in glory.

## APRIL 18

All behavior has meaning
and its purpose
is to move us
toward something
or someone
or away
from something
or someone.

Show me your ways, O LORD, teach me your paths; guide me in your truth and teach me, for you are God my Savior, and my hope is in you all day long. Remember, O LORD, your great mercy and love, for they are from of old. Remember not the sins of my youth and my rebellious ways; according to your love remember me, for you are good, O LORD.

Psalm 25:4-7

Lord, you are Infinite. I see Christ in me as the open way for every provision in life. I surrendered myself to Christ as he reveals the way and brings me into all truth. Christ is the Way, the Truth, and the Life. I choose to rest in Christ, to cast my cares on him, and to draw my strength from him. I am one with the spirit of Christ. I am anointed with the anointing of Christ. Divine anointing removes every burden and destroys every yoke in my life as my lips praise you and confess your Word. As your Word is seed, so are my words. I use my words to plant seeds of truth and grace. As I renew my mind to your Word, I partake of your divine nature. I cling to Christ Jesus in faith and he is changing me from the inside out. My thoughts and my behaviors reflect the Lord of my life. I am an expression of the life of Christ. I am a child of the Light. Thank you for molding, shaping and illuminating my way. Christ in me is the hope of glory. Thank you for loving me, saving me, forgiving me and supplying me. Halleluiah praises.

# APRIL 19

When a hurt remains alive within and unforgiven,
our self-efforts drive us toward
finding our own relief.
With our focus on ourselves, we tend to
bypass our trust in God, gather facts that prove
our perceived case of injustice, and become
demanding toward God, others and ourselves.

Beloved, never avenge yourselves, but leave it to the wrath of God, for it is written, "Vengeance is mine, I will repay, says the Lord.

Romans 12:19

It is obvious what kind of life develops out of trying to get your own way all the time: repetitive, loveless, cheap sex; a stinking accumulation of mental and emotional garbage; frenzied and joyless grabs for happiness; trinket gods; magic-show religion; paranoid loneliness; cutthroat competition; all-consuming-yet-never-satisfied wants; a brutal temper; an impotence to love or be loved; divided homes and divided lives; small-minded and lopsided pursuits; the vicious habit of depersonalizing everyone into a rival; uncontrolled and uncontrollable addictions; ugly parodies of community. I could go on. This isn't the first time I have warned you, you know. If you use your freedom this way, you will not inherit God's kingdom. But what happens when we live God's way? He brings gifts into our lives, much the same way that fruit appears in an orchard—things like affection for others, exuberance about life, serenity. We develop willingness to stick with things, a sense of compassion in the heart, and a conviction that a basic holiness permeates things and people. We find ourselves involved in loyal commitments, not needing to force our way in life, able to marshal and direct our energies wisely.

Galatians 5:19-23 *(The Message)*.

Lord, you are Forgiveness. I yield to the Christ within me. In Jesus name, I break every yoke of bondage, burden, lack and sickness from my life. I live free, forgiven, redeemed and accepted in the blood of Jesus. As Christ Jesus forgave me, I can forgive others with the grace of forgiveness that I know as he lives his life through me. I am an open channel of your flowing grace. I am a vessel filled with your love and pouring out in service to those around me. I see others as your divine masterpiece worthy of honoring with your love. As I look to and rest in Christ, nothing is impossible. Thank you for rewriting the text of my life when I opened the book of my heart by faith. I am the clay and you are the Master Potter. Thank you for abundant life in Christ Jesus.

# APRIL 20

Until we accept our position
in God's hierarchical
order, we will live
frustrated and remain
hungry for the
deep joy, lasting peace
and unspeakable
fulfillment that God
alone gives as we look to,
rely upon and rest in Him.

Hear, O LORD, and be merciful to me; O LORD, be my help. You turned my wailing into dancing; you removed my sackcloth and clothed me with joy, that my heart may sing to you and not be silent. O LORD my God, I will give you thanks forever.

Psalm 30:10-12

Lord, You are Sovereign. You created me in your image and gave me a free will to choose you or reject you. I have worked to find joy and have come up short. I have looked for peace and have despaired in its escape. Even in my self-efforts and clothed in my pride, you have loved me and poured out your mercy upon me. Your grace has guided me to the truth that apart from you I can do nothing. Thank you for the life imparting revelation that my joy and my peace are in Christ Jesus. I repent of my pride-filled beliefs, thoughts, attitudes, perceptions, emotions, words and ways. The spirit of Christ living me revealing his truth to me has brought me to my knees. Your Grace has made it clear once and for all that in my flesh there is no good thing. I have settled in you that the pride of life is the way of destruction. I have settled in you that I can forgive others in and through your strength and grace. I humble myself before your throne of grace and you lift me up. You have delivered me from the pit of self-destruction. I give you thanks forever.

# APRIL 21

God opposes
the proud
who demand their way,
but He
gives grace
to the
humble
who
openly
yield to His way.

Before a downfall the heart is haughty, but humility comes before honor.

Proverbs:18-12

Lord, You are Divine Creator. Thank you for my eternal destiny complete in my Lord and Savior Christ Jesus. There is no where I can go where your eyes are not watching over me. With the gift of my free will, I choose life in Christ Jesus. Nothing I can do or nothing I can quit makes me holy, blameless and righteous before you. I live by faith in the righteousness of Christ Jesus. Thank you for the saving knowledge that life is about you and not about me. I turn to you in humble gratitude resting in Christ who is my portion. Thank you for the abundance of Christ's Grace which gives me access, identity, authority and power to be all you created me to be. Your blessings and favor are all around me. My spirit joys in your presence and my soul is awed by your unlimited goodness. As I pour out in love towards others and glory in Christ I overflow with his divine presence. I am a radiant being filled with light and love. I express the love of Christ to all those I meet. I accept others as your divine creation. I see life through the eyes of Christ. I see potential and goodness all around me. Your love empowers me to share grace, hope, love, encouragement and forgiveness with others. My lips sing your praises. I stand on bended knees.

## APRIL 22

The longer we suppress
our hurts within us,
the more unremitting
our struggles become,
and the more
blurred our lines of
moral distinction
are crossed.

Then you will know the truth, and the truth will set you free.

John 8:32

For if you forgive other people when they sin against you, your heavenly Father will also forgive you. But if you do not forgive others their sins, your Father will not forgive your sins.

Matthew 6:14

Lord, you are Truth. As I feast on your Word, your living truth lights my way and draws me closer to you. I am open to the spirit of Christ living in me yielding myself to him to bring his abundance of truth from the inside out. I am one by the spirit in Christ Jesus. Where the spirit is there is freedom. In the strength of Christ and by his grace provision, I open myself to be searched, molded and shaped. As I spend time with you and nurture my spirit with your Word, I renew my mind to the truth of who I am in Christ. I live in the kingdom of light as you are in the light. In Christ, I am chosen, blessed and highly favored. I choose to apply the truth of your Word to my beliefs, my thoughts, my perceptions, my attitudes, my emotions, my words and my actions. I release past anger and hurts to Christ inviting his love in me and through me to touch them and heal them. Thank you Jesus for removing my shame, guilt and condemnation and replacing my lack with your complete provision. I am free. Thank you. Halleluiah praises.

# APRIL 23

Fading hope
and unrelenting pain
are fertile ground
for the cultivation
of a demanding spirit
to take root in our lives.

For the flesh desires what is contrary to the Spirit, and the Spirit
what is contrary to the flesh. They are in conflict with each other, so
that you are not to do whatever you want.

Galatians 5:17

Lord, you are Everlasting Life. Christ is the seed from the womb of heaven
that brings forth a bountiful harvest. Christ' seeds of love and grace are
alive in my spirit. My faith is the fertile ground that holds those seeds
of expectation. I water those seeds with the truth of your Word as you
reveal the truth of who I am in you. Christ is the vinedresser and I am the
branch. As I abide in Christ, I bear much fruit. I guard the harvest you
are bringing forth by confessing your Word over it. Thank you that you
are the Master Gardener watching over your Word to perform it. You are
the fertile ground of Life. I am grounded in your Grace through the living
Christ within. I live empowered to stand strong in any circumstance in the
strength of Christ. I am a new creation in Christ Jesus. My past is dead
and buried in the finished work of the cross. It has no power over me. I
renew my mind to the truth of your Word. My resurrection in Christ is life
abundantly. My body reflects healing restoration and life flowing energy.
My thoughts reflect your love to others. My emotions reflect the Light of
your Love. My words bring forth a harvest of your goodness.

# APRIL 24

We often
relate to one
another with the
hidden purpose
of maintaining our own
self-protected degree
of comfort, while
avoiding whatever
interaction we perceive
to be threatening.

When he has brought out all his own, he goes on ahead of them, and his sheep follow him because they know his voice. But they will never follow a stranger; in fact, they will run away from him because they do not recognize a stranger's voice.

John 10:4-5

Lord, you are Completeness. I live complete in Christ who came to give life and give it abundantly. I open my mouth to you and let out a lungful of praise for life in Christ Jesus. I no longer live behind walls, masks or pretense because I rest by faith in the love poured out for me at the cross. I live clothed in righteousness. I put on the garments of praise. I put off shame, guilt, and condemnation as I drink in the truth of your Word. I see the drops of Jesus' blood as those that shout your love for me. I see your knowing the number of hairs on my head as your wondrous care for me. I see your provision of grace that supplies all my needs in Christ Jesus as more shouts that ring in my ears telling me of your great and immeasurable love for me. Your perfect love casts out all fear. In Christ, I am loved, complete and fully accepted. I live for your approval and not the approval of others. I am secure in your everlasting promises that watch over me. I rest in Christ and live in the freedom of his spirit. My heart writes a song of continual praise. Inhale my worship and exhale your glory. You are worthy to be praised. Thank you.

# APRIL 25

When we incubate
in our pain
and brood
over our troubles,
despair is hatched.

I'm feeling terrible—I couldn't feel worse! Get me on my feet again. You promised, remember? When I told my story, you responded; train me well in your deep wisdom. Help me understand these things inside and out so I can ponder your miracle-wonders. My sad life's dilapidated, a falling-down barn; build me up again by your Word. Barricade the road that goes Nowhere; grace me with your clear revelation. I choose the true road to Somewhere, I post your road signs at every curve and corner. I grasp and cling to whatever you tell me; God, don't let me down! I'll run the course you lay out for me if you'll just show me how.

Psalms 119:25-32 *(The Message)*

Lord, you are Divine Provision. I trust in you to bring all goodness to my life. I choose Christ – the source of life. I live in the freedom of Christ knowing that he is for me so who can be against me. My spirit is alive and whole in Christ. Every cell in my body radiates light, harmony and health. Every organ in my body vibrates with the perfect energy you created in me as I rest in Christ. My mind is in perfect peace as I keep my mind on you. I guard my heart for out of it comes the issues of life. Your Word is life to my spirit and health to my soul. I live in the abundance of Christ. I know peace because the Prince of Peace lives in me. Every day, I write another song of Halleluiah praises to you. My thoughts flow in sweetness as you deepen my understanding of your love for me. With every fiber of my being, I celebrate life in Christ Jesus. Thank you that your mercies are new every morning. Thank you that as I shout, "Grace, Grace" to my mountains you turn them into plains. Halleluiah praises. Nothing compares to you.

# APRIL 26

What we value is far
more lasting that what we
possess and whom
we inspire is far more
important than whom
we impress.

But you are the ones chosen by God, chosen for the high calling
of priestly work, chosen to be a holy people, God's instruments to
do his work and speak out for him, to tell others of the night-and-
day difference he made for you—from nothing to something, from
rejected to accepted.

I Peter 2:9-10 *(The Message)*

Lord, you are everlasting Life. Thank you that in Christ I am chosen
for the high calling of priestly work. In Christ, I am a king and a priest.
Through the supply of grace in Christ, I am a minister of reconciliation.
My words and my actions reflect your goodness and your love to everyone
I meet. What others see is the Christ within me. All that I am rests in your
divine goodness. I radiate beauty because I am a new creation in Christ.
I speak life because you are my life. I live with favor, power and authority
because I am grafted into Christ through Grace. I humbly marvel at the
fullness of the God-head living within me who allows me in the name of
Jesus to take dominion over sickness, disease, poverty, lack and sin. I reign
with advantage and blessing because the resurrection power of Christ lives
in me. Apart from Christ, I can do nothing. All that I am is by the grace
of Christ living in me. My joy pens a song of praise to you throughout
the day. My gratitude sings that songs as my lungs are filled with the life
of Christ now and forever. Thank you for your ever flowing and unending
goodness. Halleluiah praises.

# APRIL 27

The length and
width of our
influence is
dependant
upon the
depth and
height of our
relationship
with Christ.

So we fix our eyes not on what is seen, but on what is unseen, since
what is seen is temporary, but what is unseen is eternal.

2 Corinthians 4:18

Lord, you are Omnipresent. I stand tall before you because I come on
bended knees. I humble myself before you and you lift me up. Apart from
the grace of Christ alive within me, I can do nothing. Thank you for giving
me spiritual eyes of faith to see and understand that Christ Jesus is the
truth, the way and the life. I look through the eyes of faith and know you
are always with me, you'll never forsake me and you'll never leave me. You
hold me now and forever in your unending grip of love as I rest in Christ.
I am strong in the Lord because I rest in Christ. I am hidden with Christ
in God. I live in everlasting praise to you. Words of praise are on my lips
when I arise in the morning. Words of praise pour from my lips at noon
day. Words of praise flow from my lips when I lay my head down to sleep.
I sing praises to you because you are the rock of my salvation. I bless your
name because your name is the name above all names. You are my God. I
am your chosen, blessed and highly favored child. Thank you.

# APRIL 28

Devaluing others lays a
foundation of fear which
provides a place
to build a wall
for a whole
house of
suspicion.

Those who think they can do it on their own end up obsessed with measuring their own moral muscle but never get around to exercising it in real life. Those who trust God's action in them find that God's Spirit is in them—living and breathing God! Obsession with self in these matters is a dead end; attention to God leads us out into the open, into a spacious, free life. Focusing on the self is the opposite of focusing on God. Anyone completely absorbed in self ignores God, ends up thinking more about self than God. That person ignores who God is and what he is doing. And God isn't pleased at being ignored. But if God himself has taken up residence in your life, you can hardly be thinking more of yourself than of him. Anyone, of course, who has not welcomed this invisible but clearly present God, the Spirit of Christ, won't know what we're talking about. But for you who welcome him, in whom he dwells— even though you still experience all the limitations of sin—you yourself experience life on God's terms. It stands to reason, doesn't it, that if the alive-and-present God who raised Jesus from the dead moves into your life, he'll do the same thing in you that he did in Jesus, bringing you alive to himself? When God lives and breathes in you (and he does, as surely as he did in Jesus), you are delivered from that dead life. With his Spirit living in you, your body will be as alive as Christ's!

Romans 8:5-11 *(The Message)*

Lord, you are Righteous. Everything that comes to me is by your Grace and through the gift of life in Christ Jesus. As I focus on and abide with the living Christ within, more love, freedom, grace, joy and life flow from me. I rest in the love of Christ for me and he loves others through me. Christ allows me to pour out his goodness onto others because He has poured his goodness into me. I am chosen of God, holy and dearly loved. I live in the fullness of Christ Jesus. I bathe in your unconditional love. I breathe in your favor with every breath I take. I feast on your Word and it nurtures my spirit. I drink in the living water of Christ Jesus and he quenches my thirst. I walk in your divine strength. I create in your divine inspiration. I plant seeds of love because the love of God in Christ lives in me. Thank you Jesus for bringing forth your abundant harvest of grace through love to all those I met. My lips sing your praises. My soul magnifies you.

# APRIL 29

Since by nature
we resist change,
it often
takes a crisis
to nudge us
towards looking at
and dealing with
wrong beliefs.

In the world you have tribulation *and* trials *and* distress *and* frustration; but be of good cheer [take courage; be confident, certain, undaunted]! For I have overcome the world. [I have deprived it of power to harm you and have conquered it for you.

John 16:33 (AMP)

Lord, you are Supreme. You are the same yesterday, today and forever. You are Truth and Light. I rest in and rely on Christ as my provision. Christ is my hope of glory. I live in the resurrection power of Christ and the might of his spirit flows from me. I rest in the strength of Christ and he turns my weaknesses into his strengths. I give thanks in all circumstances because this is your will in Christ Jesus. In Christ, I am more than a conqueror. I welcome your light of grace inviting the spirit of Christ to shine on my wrong beliefs. I quickly confess my shortcomings and thank you for your redeeming grace. I rebuke doubt and hopelessness as a scheme of satan. I hold fast to the truth of your Word confessing it as my weapon of victory. Every event of my life builds upon the last to bring forth your completed blessings that are mine in Christ Jesus. My obstacles are springboards to my next level of victory in Christ Jesus. I put on the garment of praise because I know in Christ I can do all things. I joy in renewing my mind to your Word.

# APRIL 30

A crisis brings us to a crossroad
of identity because our choice
will expose our
values revealing
whether our identity
is based upon
temporal and external things,
or lasting and eternal things.

So that Christ may dwell in your hearts through faith. And I pray that you, being rooted and established in love, may have power, together with all the Lord's holy people, to grasp how wide and long and high and deep is the love of Christ, and to know this love that surpasses knowledge—that you may be filled to the measure of all the fullness of God. Now to him who is able to do immeasurably more than all we ask or imagine, according to his power that is at work within us, to him be glory in the church and in Christ Jesus throughout all generations, for ever and ever! Amen.

Ephesians 3:17-22

Lord, you are Truth. In Christ, I have my being, my purpose and my life. Christ in me brings identity, power and authority for living. I radiate love and joy as I touch the love of Christ inside of me. Divine power is working in me. I am able to do far beyond what I ask or imagine according to the power of Christ at work in me. Every part of my life is flowing with the divine presence of Christ. In Christ, I am filled with the fullness of the God-head-Father, Son and Holy Spirit. I have the mind of Christ. I am reaping a bountiful harvest because I am rooted in Jesus. Evil has no power over me in the mighty name of Jesus. By faith, I have every blood bought blessing of Christ Jesus. Christ has broken the yoke of the powers of darkness. I live in the freedom of God's Grace in Christ Jesus. I take joy and delight in opening my mouth to shout a lungful of praises. Inhale my worship and exhale your glory. I joy in praising you.

## MAY 1

We will stand
as an island
of strength
in a sea of
dismay when we
walk every day
with Jesus.

The LORD himself goes before you and will be with you; he will never leave you nor forsake you. Do not be afraid; do not be discouraged.

Deuteronomy 31:8

Lord, you are Everlasting Supply. You are my shield, my glory and the lifter of my head. You are all around me bringing hope to the inner most parts of my being. You go before me and you are my rear guard. You dance all around me. You lavish your goodness on me in Christ Jesus. My heart soaks up your presence like a sponge drinks in water. You feed my spirit. My soul longs for you. You surround me with favor as a shield. Your mercies are new every morning. My spiritual eyes see your goodness. You bless me with favor. You lavish your blessings with love as you release them to me in Christ Jesus. I am blessed when I come in and blessed when I go out. By faith, every divine promise is mine in Christ Jesus. I am sealed, signed and delivered by the Holy Spirit. Abiding in Christ, I live in the fullness of his joy, his righteousness and his peace. You are the joy of my salvation. I live whole, alive, joyful and complete in Christ Jesus whose grace is sufficient in all things. Thank you that your perfect love casts out all fear. Halleluiah praises.

## MAY 2

When we fail to accept
Christ's finished work of the cross,
we will continue
living life
out of our own
self-sufficiency
and miss
God's gift of
supernatural sufficiency.

So if you're serious about living this new resurrection life with Christ, act like it. Pursue the things over which Christ presides. Don't shuffle along, eyes to the ground, absorbed with the things right in front of you. Look up, and be alert to what is going on around Christ—that's where the action is. See things from his perspective. Your old life is dead. Your new life, which is your real life—even though invisible to spectators—is with Christ in God. He is your life. When Christ (your real life, remember) shows up again on this earth, you'll show up, too—the real you, the glorious you. Meanwhile, be content with obscurity, like Christ.

Colossians 3:1 5 *(The Message)*

Lord you are Creator. Thank you for resurrection life in Christ Jesus. I have all the fullness of Your life living on the inside of me. Your Grace is an open flood gate which sustains and empowers me. In Christ I am one with the Father and He is one with me. I am one with my undivided love and undivided joy. Kingdom love flows through me through the living Christ within. I pour love onto others because love lives in me. Every portion of Divine Goodness comes to me in an uninterrupted steam of supply. I am blessed and highly favored. I am free. I live as a child of the King. I am the righteousness of God in Christ Jesus. Thank you.

# MAY 3

The truth of God's Word,
rooted in our spirit, confessed out our mouth
and appropriated by faith, will be
applied by the
Holy Spirit
to make freedom an
experiential reality
in our everyday living.

To you, O God, belong the greatness and the might, the glory, the victory, the majesty, the splendor; Yes! Everything in heaven, everything on earth; the kingdom all yours! You've raised yourself high over all. Riches and glory come from you, you're ruler over all; You hold strength and power in the palm of your hand to build up and strengthen all. And here we are, O God, our God, giving thanks to you, praising your splendid Name.

1 Chronicles 29:11

Lord, you are Victory, Splendor and Greatness. I marvel at your majesty. Your glory is wrapped around creation. From the heights of the tallest mountain to the depths of the deepest ocean your signature of wonder is everywhere. You created me in your image and breathed your life into me. I live today and everyday alive unto you in Christ Jesus. My mouth is an open vessel of praise and thanksgiving. As I feast on your Living Word, I am awestruck by the love you have for me. Through my faith in Christ, you have lifted me into your presence seated with Christ Jesus. Unexpected doors fly open and unexpected favor pours forth in unexpected ways under your perfect grace wrapped in unending love. You order my steps by your divine Grace. I am your workmanship created for good works in Christ Jesus. I am your righteous, holy and blameless child through the blood of Christ. Thank you for creating me for the praise of your glory.

# MAY 4

When we fail to personally realize
the freedom, love and acceptance
given to us by Christ
at the cross, we will experience a
continuation of *inter*personal
conflicts, *intra*personal
rejections, and a confused
identity based on
behavior that will never
satisfy and will continue
to invite the same traumas
into our presence that
we experienced in the past.

So now Israel, what do you think God expects from you? Just this:
Live in his presence in holy reverence, follow the road he sets out
for you, love him, serve God, your God, with everything you have
in you, obey the commandments and regulations of God that I'm
commanding you today—live a good life.

Deuteronomy 10:12-13

Lord, you are Alpha and Omega. You are my beginning and my end.
Apart from abiding in Christ, I can do nothing. With Christ, all things are
possible. I yield myself to you. You hold my life in your hands. You know
all things and see all things. For you, there is no past, present and future.
You see all things from the perspective of eternity. You knitted me together
in my mother's womb. You predestined my steps before the foundation of
the world in Christ Jesus. I humble myself before your throne of grace and
find mercy in my time of need. I open myself to and receive your divine
healing by faith. I invite your wisdom to search and permeate every area
of my life. I receive help from those you bring into my life. I confess what
needs confessing, I grieve what needs grieving and I forgive what needs
forgiving. As I abide in Christ he is transforming me from the inside out.
I am firmly rooted, built up, established in my faith and overflowing with
gratitude. My heart shouts your praise. You are worthy to be praised.

# MAY 5

The more we face our
shortcomings and bring them
to the light
of God's grace,
the more loving,
free and empowered
we will live.

So keep at your work, this faith and love rooted in Christ, exactly
as I set it out for you. It's as sound as the day you first heard it from
me. Guard this precious thing placed in your custody by the Holy
Spirit who works in us.

2 Timothy 1:13-14

Lord, you are pure endless Love. All goodness is an overflow of your love.
I live rooted in Christ. He brings about all that you have created for me
to be and do. In Christ, my scars become stars, shining hope to others. In
Christ, I can advance against a troop and scale any wall. My failures or
the failures of others against me pale in comparison of your love for me.
In quietness, I rest in the Christ living inside of me. My spirit is fed and
my soul finds rest in Christ Jesus. My faith and trust grow in the fertile
ground of your faithful and everlasting Promises. I gratefully and joyfully
receive every blood bought blessing of Christ. I drink in every promise as a
refreshing cold glass of water on a hot summer day. No matter where I am
or what is happening all around me, I rest in Christ Jesus where all things
are possible through him. I walk through the valleys of my life unafraid
because your Righteous Right hand upholds me. You give me vision as if
I were standing atop a towering mountain. You are my God. I am your
child. Thank you.

# MAY 6

When we run
from our
shortcomings,
we leave
God's gift of
forgiveness unopened.

But with you there is forgiveness, so that we can, with reverence, serve you.

Psalm 130:4

Lord, you are the source of forgiveness. I am cleansed by the blood of Jesus. In Christ, I live holy and blameless. I am the Righteousness of God in Christ Jesus. No condemnation, guilt or shame abides in me. I forgive others as I ask you to go to and though my hurt. Your grace takes my hurt, heals it and returns the gift of peace to me. I am free to live, free to give and free to be all you have divinely ordained. Joy rises up in me like rushing water against the rocks, as I flow in your uninterrupted favor. Thank you for wrapping me in your love as you nudged me to lay down my offenses, cast the weight on you and release those I held captive. As I brought my darkness to your light, your strength was my strength. Receive my shouts of praise as I gratefully thank you for revealing to me that my sinful actions were directly related to my wrong mindset of victimization. In you, Jesus I am not a victim, I am victorious. As the cross demonstrates you paid my sin debt in full, you have shown me that forgiveness releases the debt that an offender can never repay. You satisfy my longing and need for love and approval. Your love is pure and lasting. I receive the fullness of your joy with thanksgiving. My soul magnifies you.

# MAY 7

> Relying on our own
> self-efforts to bring
> inner change
> will only tighten the
> chains of bondage
> already wrapped
> around our souls.

Jesus said, "You're absolutely right. Take it from me: Unless a person is born from above, it's not possible to see what I'm pointing to—to God's kingdom."

John 3:3

With your very own hands you formed me; now breathe your wisdom over me so I can understand you. When they see me waiting, expecting your Word, those who fear you will take heart and be glad. I can see now, God, that your decisions are right; your testing has taught me what's true and right. Oh, love me—and right now!—hold me tight just the way you promised. Now comfort me so I can live, really live; your revelation is the tune I dance to.

Psalm 119:73-78 (MSG)

Lord, you are Abundance. You have fashioned me with your masterful hands before the foundations of the world. My life is hidden in Christ Jesus who is my life. Apart from Christ, I can do nothing. All of my self-efforts are as filthy rags. I wear the robe of righteousness in Christ because your grace has supplied it and your love crafted its design. Christ Jesus turns my weaknesses into his strengths. I rest in his provision and gratefully glory in his goodness. Your wisdom has shed light on my powerlessness apart from you. Through your grace, I see that my self-efforts are only fleshly attempts to relieve the tension arising from my deepest hurts. I yield myself to Christ the healer asking him to go to and through my hurts. I cast my burdens on you Jesus and thank you for touching my hurts with your love and filling me with your peace. Releasing what you never intended for me to carry frees me to receive the fullness of your love and share your love with others I meet. My spirit joys in you. Thank you.

# MAY 8

Genuine inner growth is not
perfected behavior;
it's a deepening
awareness of our
weaknesses,
our sins, our needs
and a growing
awareness that we
are not self-sufficient.

Good friend, take to heart what I'm telling you; collect my counsels and guard them with your life. Tune your ears to the world of Wisdom; set your heart on a life of Understanding. That's right—if you make Insight your priority, and won't take no for an answer, searching for it like a prospector panning for gold, like an adventurer on a treasure hunt, Believe me, before you know it Fear-of-God will be yours; you'll have come upon the Knowledge of God.

Proverbs 2:1-5 *(The Message)*

Lord, you are Divine Provision. Thank you for drawing my eyes away from this world and to life in the spirit. By faith, I am one with the spirit of Christ Jesus. Jesus' words of, "Apart from me, you can do nothing," have made it clear that all my self-efforts will not change my behavior or bring forth the fruits of love, joy, peace and righteousness. You are the source of these fruits. I bear these fruits in Christ. I yield my prideful flesh to your Grace. As Christ has imparted new life within, I join with that life abandoned to all you have created me to be. I am in unity with the process of change as the Holy Spirit molds me. I am becoming more Christ like every day. As I take my thoughts captive, obediently feasting on your Word, I partake of your divine nature. I rest in Christ Jesus who is the one and only source of inner transformation. My ears long to hear your wisdom. My eyes are fixed on Christ. My soul magnifies you. Inhale my worship and exhale your glory. Receive my thanksgiving as a fragrant offering of your goodness.

# MAY 9

Discovery and
recovery are an
exciting adventure
when surrendered to God.

Trust God from the bottom of your heart; don't try to figure out everything on your own. Listen for God's voice in everything you do, everywhere you go; he's the one who will keep you on track. Don't assume that you know it all. Run to God! Run from evil! Your body will glow with health, your very bones will vibrate with life! Honor God with everything you own; give him the first and the best. Your barns will burst, your wine vats will brim over. But don't, dear friend, resent God's discipline; don't sulk under his loving correction. It's the child he loves that God corrects; a father's delight is behind all this.

Proverbs 3:5-12 *(The Message)*

Lord, you are Creator. Thank you for revealing your hidden treasures as I yield to you in Christ. As I invite your spirit to search me, you bring to mind those areas of my life that long for your touch of healing love and amazing Grace. I joyfully submit to the presence and provision of Christ living in me. Where he leads me and how he enlarges me is an unending supernatural miracle of your manifestation. I open myself to receive all the good that is mine through Christ Jesus. I am created to glorify you and serve others in love. I live in your overflowing abundance and steadfast mercy in Christ Jesus. I marvel at the works of your hands as you have created me as a one of a kind masterpiece to worship you, to praise you and to glorify you. Take your chisel of Grace and chip away at anything which needs shaping for I am overjoyed, honored and humbled to be clay in your hands. I delight in your ways. Every day I am awed by your love for me in Christ Jesus. My praise is a celebration of your wonder. Thank you.

# MAY 10

We miss
the touch of
God's
transforming grace
when we conceal
our lack in the
darkness
of our
souls.

For you were once darkness, but now you are light in the Lord; Live as children of light (for the fruit of the light consists in all goodness, righteousness and truth) and find out what pleases the Lord. Have nothing to do with the fruitless deeds of darkness, but rather expose them. It is shameful even to mention what the disobedient do in secret. But everything exposed by the light becomes visible—and everything that is illuminated becomes a light.

Ephesians 5:8-13

Lord, you are Light. I am a child of the light because Christ Jesus lives in me. My spirit lives in the glory of Christ Jesus who is my light. I renew my mind to the truth of your Word which sheds your light of truth over every area of my life. In your grace, I recognize the fruits of the darkness in my flesh. I live by faith in Christ Jesus. As I walk in the spirit, I do not fulfill the lusts of the flesh. In your strength, I acknowledge my weakness, failures and sins. I humbly lay these at the foot of the cross. I confess what needs confessing, grieve what needs grieving and forgive what needs forgiving. Christ turns my mountains into plains as I shout by faith, "Grace, Grace." Through Christ, obstacles of hindrance are removed by his tender mercy and loving Grace. Resting in your grace is nurturing, nourishing and exciting. I invite your living spirit to change me, mold me and use me. Wash me all over in your living Word as I rest in you. Thank you.

# MAY 11

We grab
hold of our
future
when we
let go of the
pain in our past.

Therefore, if anyone is in Christ, the new creation has come: The old has gone, the new is here! All this is from God, who reconciled us to himself through Christ and gave us the ministry of reconciliation: that God was reconciling the world to himself in Christ, not counting people's sins against them. And he has committed to us the message of reconciliation. We are therefore Christ's ambassadors, as though God were making his appeal through us. We implore you on Christ's behalf: Be reconciled to God. God made him who had no sin to be sin for us, so that in him we might become the righteousness of God.

2 Corinthians 5:17-21

Lord, you are Righteousness. I live covered in your blood bought blessings of provision, supply, joy, peace and righteousness by faith in Christ Jesus. I am accepted in the beloved. I am a new creation and old things have passed away. My position is unchanging as I am signed, sealed and delivered by the Holy spirit. My name is written in the Lamb's Book of Life. The gift of everlasting life is mine by the blood of the Lamb. Christ lives in me and I live in him. My entire being shouts, "Halleluiahs" as my sin debt has been paid in full. The chains of sin that once had the power to hold me in captivity and bondage have been broken by Christ Jesus. My spirit is reborn in Christ. My soul is being renewed every moment of the day. Old habits, old patterns, and wrong beliefs are being changed as I look to, grow in, and yield to Your Word. I am seeing the Kingdom fruit of Christ-likeness in my beliefs, thoughts, perceptions, attitudes, emotions, behaviors and words. My destiny is unfolding in Christ. Thank you for life in Christ Jesus.

# MAY 12

The door
to change opens
from the
inside out
and hinges
on self-reflection.

Are you hurting? Pray. Do you feel great? Sing. Are you sick? Call the church leaders together to pray and anoint you with oil in the name of the Master. Believing-prayer will heal you, and Jesus will put you on your feet. And if you've sinned, you'll be forgiven—healed inside and out. Make this your common practice: Confess your sins to each other and pray for each other so that you can live together whole and healed. The prayer of a person living right with God is something powerful to be reckoned with. Elijah, for instance, human just like us, prayed hard that it wouldn't rain, and it didn't—not a drop for three and a half years. Then he prayed that it would rain, and it did. The showers came and everything started growing again.

James 5:13-18 *(The Message)*

Lord, you are Healing Restoration. Thank you for revealing to me that whatever I am holding onto is holding onto me. As I come to your throne of grace to partake of your mercy in my time of need, thank you for the strength of Christ. His presence in me and his grace through me draws me to his truth and his healing. I trust in and rest in Christ to bring his transformation from the inside out. I am open to those you bring into my life to walk with me through my hurts. Everything in my life by your divine design, your perfect timing and your supplying abundance is mine in Christ Jesus. Your promises for me are unchanging and forever settled in Heaven. I lay aside every weight that hinders me. I declare victory over every area of weakness in my flesh in Jesus name. All that you have planned for me, I receive in faith. I walk by faith and not by sight. I expect new fields of divine harvest to open to me and I reap in love and thanksgiving. My Kingdom harvest is abundance. I willingly ask you to search me and bring to the light all that needs Your touch of healing love. I live in the abundance of Christ Jesus. Thank you.

# MAY 13

Knowing mere words
from the Bible
won't change us,
but yielding to
what it
says will.

My goal is that they may be encouraged in heart and united in love, so that they may have the full riches of complete understanding, in order that they may know the mystery of God, namely, Christ, in whom are hidden all the treasures of wisdom and knowledge. I tell you this so that no one may deceive you by fine-sounding arguments. For though I am absent from you in body, I am present with you in spirit and delight to see how disciplined you are and how firm your faith in Christ is. So then, just as you received Christ Jesus as Lord, continue to live your lives in him, rooted and built up in him, strengthened in the faith as you were taught, and overflowing with thankfulness. See to it that no one takes you captive through hollow and deceptive philosophy, which depends on human tradition and the elemental spiritual forces of this world rather than on Christ.

Colossians 2: 2-8 *(The Message)*

Lord, you are the Living Word. All things were created by you and pass through you. As I look to Christ who is the Way, the Truth, and the Life, he is teaching me his ways, enlightening my spiritual eyes, and expanding my understanding. Your Word is Covenant truth and power. Mountains move as I speak to them by faith in the name of Jesus. Chains of bondage are broken in the name of Jesus. Brokenness is healed in the name of Jesus. My life is rooted and grounded in Christ Jesus who is my supply in all things. I bear Kingdom fruit as I abide in Christ. I am strong in faith. I overflow with praise and thanksgiving. Goliaths fall as I exercise the measure of faith you placed within me at the time of my salvation. I renew my thoughts to the truth of your Word and release their supernatural power to work on my behalf as I send them forth from my mouth by faith. I yield myself to the spirit of Christ living within me to manifest your Covenant promises in my natural circumstances. Inhale my worship. Exhale your glory. Thank you.

# MAY 14

Failure to confess our hurts
grieve our losses,
and forgive our offenders,
hinders our relationships.
Emotional distance follows and that
disconnected part of our souls
will sabotage our choices
and hinder our inner freedom.

Now the Lord is the Spirit, and where the Spirit of the Lord is, there is freedom.

2 Corinthians 3:17

Lord, you are Freedom. I yield myself to Christ who lives in me by faith. I rest in his fullness. I live in his abundance which supplies my needs and transforms my weaknesses into his strength. I fix my eyes on your Word and joy at the honor of spending time with you. Your Word is life to my spirit and health to my soul. I pursue peace because I yield to the Prince of Peace living within. I cast my cares to Christ Jesus and live in the freedom of his finished work on the cross. In Christ, I claim my victory for in him there are no unconquerable obstacles. I am quick to forgive others because you have taught me there is power in peace. I release my offenders by the Grace of Christ because your spirit has revealed to me that forgiveness releases the debt that my offenders can never repay. I pray for my offenders and ask that you bring kingdom enlightenment to them and cover them with your love. I set my affections on things above and not on things of the earth. I bathe myself in your Word and live refreshed and renewed. I glory in your unending goodness. My lips sing your praises. My soul magnifies you. Thank you.

# MAY 15

Love,
forgiveness,
and truth are
impeded when we
deceive ourselves
in denial,
clothe ourselves
in unforgiveness
and mask ourselves in
pretense.

"You live in the midst of deception; in their deceit they refuse to acknowledge me," declares the LORD.

Jeremiah 9:6

Lord, you are Truth. Your Word is the mirror which reflects your truth. The sum of your word is truth, and every one of your righteous precepts endures forever. Your Word is a lamp unto my feet and a light that guides my way. Send out your light and your truth from me to others I meet so together we can glorify you. As I look at myself through your Word, I see clearly that Christ is the way, the truth, and the life. In and of myself there is no good work in me. Seeds of truth planted in love return a harvest of truth and love because they are divinely engineered with your God DNA bringing forth your nature. Thank you for the divine and eternal seed of Christ Jesus. Thank you for the work of the Holy Spirit that directed my life to receive Christ as my Lord and Savior. Thank you for adopting me as your child and allowing me by faith to be a joint heir with Christ Jesus. In Christ, my life is unveiled. Thank you

# MAY 16

Putting on a mask
may cover
what's on the
outside,
but no
mask conceals
what's on
the inside.

An honest witness tells the truth, but a false witness tells lies.

Proverbs 12:17

Lord, you are True and Steadfast. As I look to your Word, my face is unveiled in Christ Jesus and he is transforming me into his same image from glory to glory by his spirit. Christ is the mirror that reflects his nature which is truth. Thank you that in Christ I am loved and acceptable in your sight. Thank you that in Christ I live everyday in his righteousness. Thank you that the knowledge of your truth brings freedom to every part of my life. The fullness of your Spirit living on the inside of me has made me whole. I lay aside my old defense mechanisms to hide my shame, guilt or distorted self value. In you, I have great value that no demon or no person can kill, steal, or destroy. By faith in Christ, I am under no condemnation. I resist the devil and any power of darkness that seeks to devour me and distort your truth. Jesus you are greater than the ruler of this world. I am seated in heavenly places with you where all things are under your feet. No harm and no hindrance comes against your divine design for my life. Thank you.

# MAY 17

When
we lose
something
of value and
do not
grieve,
our hearts
hold onto
the old
attachment
and we get stuck.

Hide your face from my sins; wipe away all my guilty deeds! Create
a clean heart for me, God; put a new, faithful spirit deep inside me!

Psalm 51:9-10 (CEV)

Lord, you are New beginnings. Through life in your son, Christ Jesus, which I live by faith, all barriers vanish and all obstacles disappear. Any perceived benefits that sin attempts to deceive me with pales in comparison to the value my relationship to you. I live washed in the cleansing blood of Christ Jesus. I renounce all pride that would open the door to satan's work of deception. I rebuke all destruction from the gates of my heart in the name of Jesus. I have perfect confidence which is abounding faith in Christ that he will supply all my needs according to his riches in glory. My spirit writes a symphony which Christ Jesus directs as my life overflows with a melody of peace, love and joy. I live in the fullness of Christ Jesus. I abide in Christ and he abides in me. I live in the resurrection power of Christ Jesus. Joy unspeakable, Grace abounding, and praise overflows in Christ Jesus who lives within me. I celebrate life by faith in Christ. Inhale my worship. Exhale your glory. My lips sing your praises. Thank you.

# MAY 18

What we
choose to
remain tied to
emotionally
will stunt our
growth
spiritually.

I keep my eyes always on the LORD. With him at my right hand, I will not be shaken.

Psalms 16:8

Lord, you are Life. Your love is all around me. I release all in me that needs releasing. Divine gates swing open for my good and your glory as I rest in Christ Jesus. I am strong in courage and bold in faith as your Righteous Right Hand holds me. Although I live in this world, I am not of this world. My life begins and ends with Christ who is the author and finisher of my faith. Christ unifies my spirit to you. Christ is my peace. Christ is my comfort. Christ is my strength. As I yield to Christ within, I am renewed, refreshed and strengthened. As the Holy Spirit transforms me into Christ-likeness, I live empowered to fulfill your calling on my life. My ministry of reconciliation is overflowing with a harvest of love and favor. Christ opens my spiritual eyes to see your vision for my life. In boldness by faith, I step out to lay claim to every portion of my promised land. I reign in Heavenly places under the authority and grace of Jesus Christ. I humble myself before you and you lift me up. Thank You.

# MAY 19

Often
what we
hold
onto tightly,
takes a tight
hold over us.

I say to the LORD, "You are my Lord; apart from you, I have no good thing."

Psalms 16:2

Lord, you are Eternal Supply. Things I can see, hear, touch, taste and smell in the natural are wasting away. You are at work in my life with unexpected people, at unexpected times, and with unexpected wonders. I open myself as I yield to Christ Jesus to receive all of your goodness brought forth by faith in him. I take hold of the kingdom alive within and step out courageously to stake my claim for Christ while I praise you and serve others. Lord, you are my stronghold. I lay hold of your Grace-filled Goodness by faith. As your child living under Grace, I am whole. Worldly chains in my carnal nature are broken as I abide in Christ. The new nature I have in Christ is manifesting in my beliefs, thoughts, actions and words. I feast at your banquet table of Grace. Every part of my being is nurtured and filled. Your divine plan for my life is unfolding in your timing and in your way. I stand on my faith confessions of your living Word and you are faithful to bring your supernatural forth in natural manifestations. You are glorious and worthy to be praised. Thank you for loving me.

# MAY 20

When we lay our hurts
at the feet of Jesus
and those He brings
into our lives,
we position
ourselves
for the process
of transformation
and healing
that ultimately
brings completion
to and freedom from
our past hurts.

Jesus said, "The Father is with me. I've told you all this so that trusting me, you will be unshakable and assured, deeply at peace. In this godless world you will continue to experience difficulties. But take heart! I've conquered the world."

John 16:32-33

Lord, you are Unshakeable. All that has happened in my history is a springboard to my future harvest because of who I am in Christ Jesus. Just like the new green sprouts that burst forth in springtime, my soul is bursting forth with new life. I look at my circumstances with the joy of the Lord. I taste and see that you are good. I marvel in humility and thanksgiving at the wonder of how I am created in your image. I trust in you. My lips sing your praises. By your mercy, you have taken every burden I have cast on Christ Jesus and he has inscribed his mark of love on my heart. I live amazed at your immeasurable love. I live awed by your tender mercies. I live overjoyed that you have provided a way through your love for me as demonstrated in Jesus giving his all for me to redeem me. I am a new creation in Christ Jesus. In him, the new has come and the old has passed away. Thank you that as I spend time with you, you hear me and talk with me. Thank you that as I renew my mind to your Word that you deliver its truth from my spirit to my soul. I open my mouth and shout out lung-filled praises to you. Thank you.

# MAY 21

Unresolved
anger holds
seeds
that
take
root
in
bitterness.

Don't grieve God. Don't break his heart. His Holy Spirit, moving
and breathing in you, is the most intimate part of your life, making
you fit for himself. Don't take such a gift for granted. Make a clean
break with all cutting, backbiting, profane talk. Be gentle with one
another, sensitive. Forgive one another as quickly and thoroughly as
God in Christ forgave you.

Ephesians 4:30-33 *(The Message)*

Lord, you are Lasting Forgiveness. I lay my hurts before your throne of
Grace because I do not want the seed of anger to take root. You O Lord,
are good and forgiving, abounding in steadfast love to all who call upon
the name of Jesus. In my human weakness, I do not have the ability to
remove the pain of offense. I choose to yield myself to Christ, the Forgiver,
and ask him to release his supply of grace in me and through me and with
his strength I can respond to your command to forgive others as you have
forgiven me. Thank you for taking my burden and filling me with your
peace. The power of your blood that forgave me of my sin debt holds the
power of forgiveness as I abide in you. My mind is being renewed in your
Word. Offenses have no hold over me as I realize that their power comes
from an unmet need in myself. I ask the Holy Spirit to search me and
make clear my need so I can humble myself and receive your supply. I do
not need approval or agreement from another to know I am deeply loved
and greatly valued. In you, I am judged righteous in Christ. Regardless of
another's behavior, I see others through your eyes as deeply loved, valued
and created in your image.

# MAY 22

We find
freedom when
we choose
to own
what
is hindering
us.

Therefore, since we are surrounded by such a great cloud of witnesses, let us throw off everything that hinders and the sin that so easily entangles. And let us run with perseverance the race marked out for us, fixing our eyes on Jesus, the pioneer and perfecter of faith. For the joy set before him he endured the cross, scorning its shame, and sat down at the right hand of the throne of God. Consider him who endured such opposition from sinners, so that you will not grow weary and lose heart.

Hebrews 12:1-3

Lord, you are Freedom. My eyes are fixed on Jesus who is the pioneer and perfecter of my faith. I rest in Christ Jesus as I run my race of life. I cast down worldly and fleshly obstacles as I send forth your Word from my lips. Your Word is life and power in my life. Thank you Jesus that your blood has paid the price once and for all for my freedom. No weapon formed against me can prosper as I abide in you by faith. I have been delivered from the domain of darkness and transferred into the kingdom of Christ in whom I have redemption and the forgiveness of sin. Thank you Jesus that you are my high priest and no temptation comes to me that you have not broken the power over. As you are transforming me into your divine nature, I open every part of my being to honestly acknowledge all that you reveal I need to release to you. You open my eyes to see clearly and my heart to receive fully. I take upon my life the yoke and burden of Christ Jesus. I cast my cares on you and live in freedom. Thank you.

# MAY 23

A wrong belief,
an attitude,
a judgmental look,
or unspoken gratitude
may all be
considered small items
with large consequences.

Mortals make elaborate plans, but God has the last word. Humans are satisfied with whatever looks good; God probes for what is good. Put God in charge of your work, then what you've planned will take place. God made everything with a place and purpose; even the wicked are included—but for judgment. God can't stomach arrogance or pretense; believe me, he'll put those upstarts in their place. Guilt is banished through love and truth; Fear-of-God deflects evil. When God approves of your life, even your enemies will end up shaking your hand; Far better to be right and poor than to be wrong and rich. We plan the way we want to live, but only God makes us able to live it.

Proverbs 16:1-9 *(The Message)*

Lord, you are Sovereign. Your will and your plans are lasting and eternal. You loved me enough to bind yourself to your Covenant promise that you will never leave or abandon me. You loved me enough to save me by the blood of Christ Jesus. You loved me enough to give me every spiritual blessing in Christ Jesus. You loved me enough to create me in your image and breath life into me by your spirit. You loved me enough to remove my sin as far as the east is from the west. You loved me enough to accept my faith in the righteousness of Christ as my own. You loved me enough that every detail of my life is in motion under your supplying Grace. I am approved in Christ who lives in me. I plan my steps and you direct the way. I am chosen, blessed and highly favored in Christ Jesus. I live in humble adoration of your majesty, your wonder and your power. In You Jesus, I have obtained an inheritance, having been predestined according to your purpose. You work all things according to the counsel of your will. All things work together for my good because I am called according to your purpose. Halleluiah praises.

# MAY 24

We were created
for God's pleasure
and His glory,
but we will sink
into a state of
perpetual
self-centeredness
if we refuse to
humbly bow
before Him.

My help and glory are in God—granite-strength and safe-harbor-God—So trust him absolutely, people; lay your lives on the line for him. God is a safe place to be."

Psalm 62:8-9 *(The Message)*

Lord, you are the one Eternal Ruler. The heavens and the earth reflect your glory. I stand on my knees in humble adoration of you. You have created me in your image and given me dominion over the earth. You have told me to be fruitful and multiply. You have divinely set in motion the order, structure and harvest of every seed I plant by faith. Thank you for creating me, saving me, providing for me and saving me in Christ Jesus. Apart from Christ living in me, I have nothing of value in my self-efforts to offer you. I yield myself to Christ and gratefully receive his goodness. I am what I am by your Grace. You are my provision, my comfort, my defender, my strength and my healer. Every morning and throughout the day, my spirit draws life from you. My soul magnifies you name. I joy in yielding myself to Christ and resting in his finished works as he supplies all my needs according to his riches in glory. Your endless and immeasurable love brings me to my knees where I raise my hands in praise. Thank you.

# MAY 25

No matter
what our
present
circumstances,
God will
have the
last word.

That at the name of Jesus every knee should bow, in heaven and on
earth and under the earth, and every tongue acknowledge that Jesus
Christ is Lord, to the glory of God the Father.

Philippians 2:10-11

Lord, You are worthy of Praise. In and through You all things come to
pass. I bow before you overjoyed in your love as your continual good comes
to me in Christ Jesus. Your mercy is new every morning. You rule over
heaven and earth and yet your eyes are watching over me. Your Word is
life, everlasting Truth and Covenant promises that in Christ supplies me
and covers me. I live in grateful thanksgiving knowing that whatever I ask
by faith in the name of Jesus according to your will is mine. By humility
and the fear of the Lord blessings of riches, honor and life are mine. I
am your workmanship, created in Christ Jesus for good works, which you
preordained that I should walk in them. All that I am and all that I do is
through your Grace. Apart from Christ Jesus, I cannot create works that
glorify you. Apart from Christ, I cannot love or forgive others. Apart from
Christ, there is no good works in my flesh. Apart from Christ, I cannot
overcome in my own strength. You are my God. I am your beloved child.
Thank you.

# MAY 26

We often
follow
through
with what
we're
accountable to.

Jesus said, "If you were really blind, you would be blameless, but since you claim to see everything so well, you're accountable for every fault and failure."

John 9:41 *(The Message)*

Lord, you are Justice. I answer to you. As I live connected to the Christ within, I set my mind on the true, just and pure things of the Kingdom. I speak truth because truth lives in me. I love justice because you are just. I seek purity because you are pure in every way. The doors of Heaven open to me in the name of Jesus. I live accountable to my right of a royal inheritance in Christ. When Christ was crucified, I was crucified with Him. I was resurrected in him when he was resurrected. I am seated with him in Heavenly places. I reign with Christ sharing his Heavenly inheritance. I live free of condemnation. The blood of the Lamb is sprinkled on Heaven's mercy seat. I am accepted and loved. I live in the fullness of Christ and reflect his love in me to those around me. I move in the expanding waves of love and creativity as the Master lives within me. As I walk in faith, every good favor is mine. I am a child of the King. I am a citizen of Heaven. I am a child of the Living God. My lips sing your continual praises.

# MAY 27

As long
as we're only
interested in
being heard,
we'll likely miss
what's really being said.

Because if you confess with your mouth "Jesus is Lord" and in your heart you have faith that God raised him from the dead, you will be saved. Trusting with the heart leads to righteousness, and confessing with the mouth leads to salvation.

Romans 10:9-10 (CEV)

Lord, you are Eternal life and Infinite Wisdom. Confessing your Word in faith releases you to work in my life. My ears are quickened and attuned to your perfect harmony. My ears hear and my will follows the perfect Shepherd which is Christ in me the hope of glory. I am an anointed sheep in your flock. You are the door for immediate and endless supply. I yield to Christ and he supplies all my needs according to his riches in Glory. As I abide in Christ, I live in his fullness. Christ is my supply. His love is my purpose. His mercy is my hope. His forgiveness is my life. Nothing or no one can remove, hinder or interfere with the divine design for my life. Your eternal and living Word feeds my spirit and brings life to my soul. Your faithfulness endures forever. My heart writes a song of joy and my lips sing your praises. You are my God and I am your child. Thank you that as I draw near to you, you draw near to me. Thank you for being unending love, immeasurable supply and eternal life in Christ Jesus. Glory Halleluiah.

# MAY 28

Surface arguments
often come
from deeper
unmet
relational
needs.

Watch out for people who try to dazzle you with big words and intellectual double-talk. They want to drag you off into endless arguments that never amount to anything. They spread their ideas through the empty traditions of human beings and the empty superstitions of spirit beings. But that's not the way of Christ. Everything of God gets expressed in him, so you can see and hear him clearly. You don't need a telescope, a microscope, or a horoscope to realize the fullness of Christ, and the emptiness of the universe without him. When you come to him, that fullness comes together for you, too. His power extends over everything.

Colossians 2:8-10 *(The Message)*

Lord, you are Truth. You control my destiny and rain down blessings over me as I yield to Christ who lives in me. In Christ, all my needs are met through your endless supply of Grace. I live with a fullness of joy and a bounty of hope. Your aliveness within me is your divine presence and your provision for my every need. My value, worth and purpose come from abiding in, leaning on and trusting Christ. You have predetermined my kingdom destiny in Christ Jesus. I celebrate the finished work of Christ Jesus on the cross as my death and my resurrection. In Christ, I live, breathe and move. You are more beautiful than words can describe. Praise and thanksgiving are on my lips throughout each day. I live expectantly knowing that you will lavish your love upon me. I abide in the fullness of Christ and bear kingdom fruit that is lasting and eternal. I glory in your wonder. I kneel amazed in your presence. I marvel at your limitless love for me. I applaud your majesty. You are worthy to be praised. Shouts of Halleluiah are on my lips.

# MAY 29

The music
for the dance
of conflict
plays off our
differences with another,
but the melody
becomes a song
when we write it
together.

With your very own hands you formed me; now breathe your wisdom over me so I can understand you. When they see me waiting, expecting your Word, those who fear you will take heart and be glad. I can see now, God, that your decisions are right; your testing has taught me what's true and right. Oh, love me—and right now!—hold me tight! just the way you promised. Now comfort me so I can live, really live; your revelation is the tune I dance to. Let the fast-talking tricksters be exposed as frauds; they tried to sell me a bill of goods, but I kept my mind fixed on your counsel. Let those who fear you turn to me for evidence of your wise guidance. And let me live whole and holy, soul and body, so I can always walk with my head held high.

Psalms 119:73 *(The Message)*

Lord, you are perfect Harmony. You are the music my soul dances to. You know me inside and out. You created me in all your wisdom and beauty. All that is mine in Christ Jesus flows to me and through me. Divine love warms and lights everything it touches as I live in Christ. I am blessed and highly favored by you, my Creator. No person, or no power of darkness can block or interfere with the perfect love I have in Christ Jesus. The chains of bondage once around me by the power of sin have been loosed once and for all in Christ Jesus, my Savior, my Lord and my friend. I abide in Christ and his refection is the life that others see. As I keep my mind on you, you lead me in your truth. You reveal your hidden treasures of the kingdom, as I seek you. Nothing or no one compares to being in your presence. My spirit is alive and my soul is stirred as I spend time with you. As I confess your Word from my mouth, you are true in your faithfulness to perform it.

I live in your kingdom harmony of righteousness, love and peace because your grace has introduced me to the author of those blessings – Christ Jesus. Thank you.

# MAY 30

Conflict can be
a temporary barrier
or a permanent
wall depending
upon your perception.

Therefore let us stop passing judgment on one another. Instead,
make up your mind not to put any stumbling block or obstacle in
the way of a brother or sister.

Romans 14:13

Lord, you are perfect Love. In your divine mind, there are no lost
opportunities or closed doors. I look to your Word to open the eyes of
my heart where your Truth and your Grace always reveal light. Doors I
closed in my past to hold pain in are now open to the light of your Love.
As I yield to Christ, walls I built around my hurts come tumbling down.
I break every unequal yoke in the name of Jesus. Every burdensome stone
is released from my life in the name of Jesus. I view conflict as a way to
hear someone else's need and share your love. I look at others through the
eyes of Christ. In Christ, I am divinely sensitive to other's needs whether
expressed clearly and openly or subtly and quietly. I see all those I meet as
divine treasures created in your image. I honor others as your masterpiece.
I build others up through words of encouragement and the love I share
comes from the never ending supply of Christ living inside me. I love
others with the same love Jesus has for the Father and lavished upon me.
Thank you.

# MAY 31

When we honor and
value others
as God's Masterpiece,
we are much less
threatened
by the differences
that hold the power
to feed our own
defensiveness.

Real wisdom, God's wisdom, begins with a holy life and is characterized by getting along with others. It is gentle and reasonable, overflowing with mercy and blessings, not hot one day and cold the next, not two-faced. You can develop a healthy, robust community that lives right with God and enjoy its results only if you do the hard work of getting along with each other, treating each other with dignity and honor.

James 3:17 *(The Message)*

Lord, you are Wisdom. I am free to live as the person you created me to be because Christ lives within me. The grace of Christ Jesus equips me with every good thing to do the work which you have called me to do. I overflow in his love and mercy. I use my words to build others up. I use my mouth as a vessel of service to others in the love of Christ. I renew my mind with the truth of your Word, casting down vain imaginations and every high thing that exalts itself against the knowledge of God, and bringing into captivity every thought to the obedience of Christ. I cast my burdens on Christ so they do not take root in my life and weigh me down distracting and hindering me from fulfilling my ministry of reconciliation. I yield myself to Christ Jesus and his authority as head of my body. I see my life as a gift to be treasured and poured out in honor of your unending love and abounding grace. I yield the pieces of my life to the altar of your grace and wait expectantly as you knit them together in divine order and your sovereign will.

# JUNE 1

Humility is a
powerful force;
the virtual
foundation
of
miracle
working
love.

Be completely humble and gentle; be patient, bearing with one
another in love. Make every effort to keep the unity of the Spirit
through the bond of peace. There is one body and one Spirit, just as
you were called to one hope when you were called; one Lord, one
faith, one baptism; one God and Father of all, who is over all and
through all and in all.

Ephesians 4:2-6

Lord, you are Sovereign Creator. All of creation holds the mark of your
Spirit. Everything created is done in your perfect nature and your wondrous
love. I relate to all of your creation with humility and honor. I love what
you love, seek what you seek and preserve what you preserve. Your divine
order is established in my mind, body, and affairs. As I rest in the peace of
Christ, miracles and wonders unfold all around me. I radiate your divine
love and peace because I am one in spirit with Christ Jesus. The love I
radiate to others is an overflow from Christ living in me. As I partake
of his divine nature, I reflect his nature. I honor others as Christ honors
me before the Father. I forgive others as the blood of Christ has released
me. I value others because Christ values me. I refrain from judging others
because I was not given the authority to pass judgment on another's value
and worth who like me was created in your image. I choose to walk in love
because love unleashes your uninterrupted grace towards me. Thank you.

# JUNE 2

Eyes that refuse
to look are far
more blind than eyes
that cannot see.

This day I call the heavens and the earth as witnesses against you that I have set before you life and death, blessings and curses. Now choose life, so that you and your children may live and that you may love the LORD your God, listen to his voice, and hold fast to him. For the LORD is your life and he will give you many years in the land he swore to give to your fathers, Abraham, Isaac and Jacob.

Deuteronomy 30:19-20

Lord, you are All-Seeing. You sent Jesus Christ for the world to see your immeasurable love. You offered your Covenant of Grace through Christ Jesus for me to personally receive your uninterrupted flow of love. Tears flow from my eyes as I see how much you loved me that you would wrap yourself in flesh and walk among mankind. Every drop of holy and blameless blood shed by Christ Jesus shouts your love for me. I choose to embrace your gift of life in Christ by faith. When I asked Jesus to be my Lord and Savior, you placed the fullness of your living spirit within me. You wrote my name in the Lamb's book. You seated me in heavenly places with Christ Jesus. I am accepted and beloved. I am a child of royal inheritance. In Christ, I am invited into your throne room of grace where I feast with you and drink living water. There is nothing or no one who compares to you. My spirit is filled with new life in Christ. My spirit radiates a continuous melody of praise to you. My soul magnifies your name. Thank you.

# JUNE 3

Often when
we concede
the war,
we win
the
battle.

What causes fights and quarrels among you? Don't they come from your desires that battle within you? You desire but do not have, so you kill. You covet but you cannot get what you want, so you quarrel and fight. You do not have because you do not ask God. When you ask, you do not receive, because you ask with wrong motives, that you may spend what you get on your pleasures.

James 4:1-3

Lord, you are Peace. I have peace in Christ Jesus who is the Prince of Peace as my thoughts rest on you. I abide in Christ resting in his provision for my every need. Christ fills my spirit with his grace and love. His grace and love spills over onto those I meet. Thank you Jesus that you came to give me life and give it abundantly. Thank you for teaching me that things of this world and things of this flesh will never meet my need for love that you fill completely. You are working all things together for my good. Every day, I write another chapter of Hallelujah praises to you for you have rewritten the text of my life. Each day, I joy in my spirit as you teach me how to take hold of all you have done for me. I am the expression of your fruits of the spirit because I abide and you supply. I live in and rely on Christ to radiate his love to others through me. Preferences in my flesh are the embodiment of my beliefs, perceptions, attitudes, thoughts, emotions, words and actions. Your Word brings peace to my soul as I plant its seeds of truth in my heart. I yield "my way" to you, the "High Way." My soul magnifies your name. Thank you.

# JUNE 4

Every
moment
is a gift
from God;
unwrap them
and enjoy
the
wonder.

For in him all things were created: things in heaven and on earth, visible and invisible, whether thrones or powers or rulers or authorities; all things have been created through him and for him.

Colossians 1:16

Lord, you are Master Creator. All things seen and unseen are yours. Nothing happens that you do not see. I release the living Christ in me to unwrap your hidden wonder living on the inside of me. The fullness of the God-head, Father, Son and Holy Spirit lives within me. The mystery and wonder of your imparting the full measure of yourself within me is beyond my comprehension. My response to your immeasurable love is to fall to my knees in humble adoration. My spirit overflows with life. My soul leaps with unending joy. You unwrap another layer of your untold wonders and abundant blessings as I seek you. Joy unspeakable floods my life as I feast on your Word. Throughout each day, I celebrate my abundant life in Christ Jesus. I lift my hands and open my mouth to honor you with praises. You are worthy to be praised. I worship you in spirit and truth. Inhale my worship and exhale your glory. My tongue will speak of your righteousness and praise you all day long. Glory Halleluiah and unending praise. Thank you.

# JUNE 5

Peace with
God and
ourselves
allows us to
have more
balanced
expectations
towards others.

Remind the people to be subject to rulers and authorities, to be obedient, to be ready to do whatever is good, to slander no one, to be peaceable and considerate, and always to be gentle toward everyone. At one time we too were foolish, disobedient, deceived and enslaved by all kinds of passions and pleasures. We lived in malice and envy, being hated and hating one another. But when the kindness and love of God our Savior appeared, he saved us, not because of righteous things we had done, but because of his mercy. He saved us through the washing of rebirth and renewal by the Holy Spirit, whom he poured out on us generously through Jesus Christ our Savior, so that, having been justified by his grace, we might become heirs having the hope of eternal life.

Titus 3:1-7

Lord, you are the Master Gardener. Everything you created operates on seed principle. You planted your seeds of love in Christ Jesus when you offered your love through him to be my harvest of salvation. By faith in Christ, I plant seeds of love and grace. The harvest you bring to me and through me in Christ is beyond description. I joy in sharing your harvest of love with others by loving and serving them. I joy in celebrating your grace which empowers and enables me to love others, encourage others and forgive others with the same measure that you have given to me. In you, I look at others as your divine creation worthy to be honored just as you have honored me. Thank you for teaching me to look to you to meet my needs and not others. You are the only one who knows me inside and out. You know the purpose you created me for before the foundation of the world and you bring that purpose to pass as I rest in Christ. No one else sees or knows me like you do. I am an open vessel to your blessings and divine favor.

# JUNE 6

Focusing
on our
weaknesses
only increases
them and
hinders
the power
of God
from changing them
into strengths.

For the foolishness of God is wiser than human wisdom, and the weakness of God is stronger than human strength.

1 Corinthians 1:25

Lord, you are Pure Wisdom and Endless Strength. You never faint or grow weary. Your understanding is unsearchable. You give power to the weak and those who have no might you increase their strength. I yield to Christ who lives within me. I cast my cares on him and live free by the strength of his Grace. My faith in Christ stirs up remembrance after remembrance that as I rest, he supplies. I joy in abiding in Christ expectantly thrilled much as a young child opening a gift to see how he works all things out for my good. I marvel at how his abounding supply is never ending and never failing to meet my needs in ways beyond my imagination. My spirit, one with the Spirit of Christ, dances in perfect harmony to the music of life even if the song is not pleasant to my ears, because I know that as I sing a song of praise, my words of faith unleash my risen Lord to release his supernatural provision over my natural circumstances. Your goodness astounds me. What a privilege to shout a lungful of praise to you. Thank you.

# JUNE 7

Being upset
internally will
contribute
to our
being
upset
externally.

You will keep in perfect peace those whose minds are steadfast, because they trust in you. Trust in the LORD forever, for the LORD, the LORD himself, is the Rock eternal.

Isaiah 26:3-4

Lord, You are Righteousness and Peace. I wear the crown of righteousness by faith in Christ Jesus. Peace umpires my spirit and overflows into my soul as I think on you. I have peace because Christ Jesus, the Prince of Peace lives in me. I pursue peace with others regardless of their response to accept or reject me. I cast my cares on Christ Jesus because he cares for me. I align my thoughts with the truth of your Word asking you to take your truth and mold and shape me into your likeness. I speak words of blessing over my offenders and forgive quickly because I desire that no one or nothing hinders your flow of Grace in my life. Thank you for revealing to me that my love walk is not about my self-effects, but completely a reflection of who you are in me. I believe and receive everyone of your promises as truth. I rest in Christ as the Rock of my salvation. Agitations, frustrations, and situations pale as I yield them to you and wait expectantly knowing you will work all things together for my good. Thank you.

# JUNE 8

God's Grace
is his
permanent
eraser
for all our
messes.

Through whom we have gained access by faith into this grace in which we now stand. And we boast in the hope of the glory of God.

Romans 5:2

For it is by grace you have been saved, through faith—and this is not from yourselves, it is the gift of God—not by works, so that no one can boast. For we are God's handiwork, created in Christ Jesus to do good works, which God prepared in advance for us to do.

Ephesians 2:8-10

Lord, you are Grace. In your love for me, you lavish Grace upon me in Christ Jesus. As a new creation in Christ, my spirit is alive unto Christ. Christ's blood has redeemed me from eternal separation and covers me with his strength, his identity, his authority and his victory. Nothing from my past has the power to overcome, overtake or hinder me from all that is mine as I abide in Christ Jesus. I live in awe of the privilege you have given me to confess Jesus as my Lord and Savior. You have redeemed me from the darkness. I am a child of the Light. Your Grace is like a waterfall that rushes over me, refreshes me and restores me. For you, O Lord, are good and forgiving, abounding in steadfast love to all who call upon the name of Jesus. When I come before your throne of Grace to repent, you are faithful and just to remove my sins as far as the east is from the west. Your Grace wrapped in your love does not condemn me. My praise is resounding and my joy complete. My soul magnifies your name. Thank you.

# JUNE 9

God's
Word
is
His
blueprint
for
our
best.

God means what he says. What he says goes. His powerful Word is sharp as a surgeon's scalpel, cutting through everything, whether doubt or defense, laying us open to listen and obey. Nothing and no one is impervious to God's Word. We can't get away from it—no matter what.

Hebrews 4:12-13 *(The Message)*

Lord, you are Limitless Wisdom. I have joy in making an apt answer, and a word spoken at the right moment. Your Words of life live in me and flow from me. I welcome and receive your Word as living instruction, divine wisdom, loving correction and life to my spirit. I celebrate your goodness as I feast on your Word. All the blessings and covenant promises of your Word are "yes and amen" by faith in Christ Jesus. I quiet my soul as I come before your throne of Grace expecting and waiting to hear your voice. I open myself to hear as I open your Word. I receive the riches of Heaven that are mine by Christ Jesus. Your vastness, yet your personal realness, to invite me into fellowship with you in Christ Jesus is overwhelming. As I confess your Word from my lips, you are watching over it to perform it. As your Word examines my heart, I humbly and joyfully submit my life to you desiring you to shape and mold all that needs shaping and molding. I am your vessel shaped by you and poured out for others. Thank you.

# JUNE 10

Listening
is a
gift
you can
give to
others
at any
time.

Now then, my children listen to me; blessed are those who keep my ways.

Proverbs 8:32

Listen to advice and accept discipline, and at the end you will be counted among the wise.

Proverbs 19:20

Lord, your voice commands heaven and earth. Your Word is full of your nature, your will and your life giving words. Spending time with you in worship and reading your Word is abounding joy. Nothing or no one compares to you. You feed my spirit as I feast on your Word. My faith is stirred because faith comes by hearing and hearing by the Word of God. Your Promises are the mold into which I pour my prayers. To fellowship with you in prayer is to praise, rest, abide and yield to Christ who is my life. My constant desire to spend time with you pales in comparison to your love, your majesty and your gift of life in Christ Jesus. I am faithful because you are worthy. I love because you first loved me. I am whole because you saved me by faith in Christ Jesus. Your will is unfolding in every area of my life. As I abide in and cling to Christ Jesus, I bear much fruit. My eyes look to you from where my help comes. Every blood bought blessing of Christ Jesus is mine by faith. Thank you for loving and saving me. Receive my praises.

# JUNE 11

When we
value others
like God
values
others,
our joy
overflows.

May the God of endurance and encouragement grant you to live in such harmony with one another, in accord with Christ Jesus that together you may with one voice glorify the God and Father of our Lord Jesus Christ.

Romans 15:5-6 (ESV)

Lord, you are Pure Love. You are good to me and supply all my needs according to your riches in Glory in Christ Jesus. I rejoice in you and exult in hope as you grow my faith and fulfill the desires of my heart. I live, breathe, move and yield to Christ Jesus who lives within me. I am the extension of your loving nature. The joy I share with others is your overflow of joy in me. The love I share with others spills out to others from your inflow of love in me. The sparkle in my eye comes from being the apple of your eye. I live in the same resurrection power that raised Jesus from the dead. No matter what comes against me I have victory through the power of the blood of the Lamb and the word of my testimony. I rise every day and live every moment alive in Christ and thankful for his Grace which supplies all my needs. You are my God and I am your chosen, accepted and beloved child. All the blessings Christ restored to me at the cross flow in uninterrupted measure. I joy in renewing my mind to the truth of your Word. Halleluiah praise.

# JUNE 12

Whatever has been
exposed to the
light of love
can be healed.

Let no debt remain outstanding, except the continuing debt to love
one another, for whoever loves others has fulfilled the law.

Romans 13:8

Because a loveless world," said Jesus, "is a sightless world. If anyone
loves me, he will carefully keep my word and my Father will love
him—we'll move right into the neighborhood! Not loving me
means not keeping my words. The message you are hearing isn't
mine. It's the message of the Father who sent me.

John 14:23-24 *(The Message)*

Lord, you are Unconditional and Unending Love. Your love for me held
Jesus to the cross. As I look to your Word, I see that love never gives up,
it's not self-centered, it's not demanding, it doesn't strut or walk around
with a swelled head. It doesn't fly off the handle in judgment or criticism.
Your love keeps no score card of mistakes. Your love holds the invitation
of your immeasurable goodness. Your love lives in the light as you are in
the light. I am a vessel of love filled with Christ Jesus that pours out in
service to others for your glory. Apart from Christ living in me, I have
no ability to love as Christ loved. Thanksgiving and praise well up in my
heart as I thank you for revealing to me that my life has been predestined
before the foundations of the world. Joy abounds and overflows because
you redeemed me from the pit of hell, quickened my spirit alive unto
Christ and supply all my needs according to your riches in glory in Christ
Jesus. You supply and simply ask me to believe and abide. Thank you for
life in Christ.

# JUNE 13

When love
is the song
you dance
to, life
will be full
of wondrous
harmony.

Therefore, as God's chosen people, holy and dearly loved, clothe yourselves with compassion, kindness, humility, gentleness and patience. Bear with each other and forgive one another if any of you has a grievance against someone. Forgive as the Lord forgave you. And over all these virtues put on love, which binds them all together in perfect unity.

Colossians 3:12-14

Lord, You are perfect Love. I put on your love and clothe myself with behavior marked by mercy, kindness, compassion and patience. I am gentle and forbearing with others for it is your love that is perfecting me in all things. I reflect the love of Christ to others because as I yield to his presence within so his love is unleashed to those around me. His love permeates my heart and nourishes my soul. My thoughts, my words and my actions are an extension of your loving nature. I renew my mind to the truth of your Word and as my mind believes my will conceives. I guard my love walk because you have shown me that your love, your peace and your grace work together. I love others because you have first loved me. I forgive others in the supply of your grace because you have forgiven me. I dance to the unforced rhythms of grace as I humbly follow the lead of Christ. I build others up in your love recognizing every person is fashioned by your Hands and worthy of honor and respect. Thank you.

# JUNE 14

Taking offense
often diminishes
when we
give up
trying to read
the mind of others.

All praise to the God and Father of our Master, Jesus the Messiah! Father of all mercy! God of all healing counsel! He comes alongside us when we go through hard times, and before you know it, he brings us alongside someone else who is going through hard times so that we can be there for that person just as God was there for us. We have plenty of hard times that come from following the Messiah, but no more so than the good times of his healing comfort—we get a full measure of that, too.

2 Corinthians 1:3-5 *(The Message)*

Lord, you are Healing Counsel. I receive revelation and direction from the Holy Spirit living in me which is the wonder of the spirit of Christ Jesus within. As I rest in Christ, out of my innermost being flows springs and rivers of living water. My ears are attentive to your Godly counsel. My spirit is open to your leading. Your wisdom living inside me guides me in divine discernment. I go where you tell me to go and do what you tell me to do. I listen faithfully for your voice and humbly receive your instructions. I am a Kingdom child. You are my shield withholding no good thing from me as I walk blameless in Christ Jesus. In Christ, I am righteous, holy and blameless. In Christ, I see those I meet as your wondrous accepted and beloved creation. My words speak of your love and grace. They are like healing salve. My actions reflect the love of Christ. As I see myself in you, I look at others differently. Every moment in the day, my desire is to reflect your goodness. My lips sing Your praises. Thank you.

# JUNE 15

When we
look for the
good in
others,
we very
often find it.

So let's agree to use all our energy in getting along with each other. Help others with encouraging words; don't drag them down by finding fault. You're certainly not going to permit an argument over what is served or not served at supper to wreck God's work among you, are you? I said it before and I'll say it again: All food is good, but it can turn bad if you use it badly, if you use it to trip others up and send them sprawling. When you sit down to a meal, your primary concern should not be to feed your own face but to share the life of Jesus. So be sensitive and courteous to the others who are eating. Don't eat or say or do things that might interfere with the free exchange of love.

Romans 14:19-21 *(The Message)*

Lord, you are Divine Peace. Yielded to Christ my source, I can see beyond my natural sight. I see hurting hearts where I can share your unending love and mercy. As I live yielded to you, I am a vessel that pours out your healing Grace which sets captives free and heals the broken-hearted. Those you lead me to are the remnant you have divinely assigned to me by your will. My words of encouragement are sweet like honeycomb because your love to me is sweeter than anything I know. My hands are blessed to do your works. My thoughts are divinely led to birth your anointed creativity. My words are reflections of your truth. My spirit lives in the newness of life Christ Jesus has given me. Nothing or no one can hinder your divine inheritance for my life. Christ is my source. My life is covered by his Grace and Truth anointed with your favor. My lips praise you from whom all blessings flow. Halleluiah praises that I am your child living in anointed favor with every blood bought blessing of Christ. Thank you.

# JUNE 16

Our words
can write
a symphony
of harmony
in the
hearts of
others.

Do not let any unwholesome talk come out of your mouths, but only what is helpful for building others up according to their needs, that it may benefit those who listen.

Ephesians 4:29

Love from the center of who you are; don't fake it. Run for dear life from evil; hold on for dear life to good. Be good friends who love deeply; practice playing second fiddle.

Romans 12:9-10 *(The Message)*

Lord, you are Harmonious Peace. Out of the fullness of my heart, my mouth speaks words that build others up and glorify you. From the storehouse of your good treasures, Christ in me has given me his abundant love to overflow as encouragement to those around me. Obedience and humility are fertile ground that nourish the seeds of love in my heart. My spirit dances in the wonder of your limitless love. I love you and serve others with an abundant passion not in my own strength or ability but because of the supply of Grace in the person of Christ Jesus who lives within. My desire to be a mirror that reflects your love is a humble and simple way I can honor you for loving me enough to die on my behalf, pay my sin debt in full, invite me into intimate fellowship and supply all my needs. I am an open vessel for the genuine love of Christ living within me. In and through Jesus, I am authentic, genuine and real. I serve others with gladness. Inhale my worship and exhale your Glory. Thank you for loving me.

# JUNE 17

Even when we
feel alone,
we
never
really
are.

If you love me, show it by doing what I've told you. I will talk to the Father, and he'll provide you another Friend so that you will always have someone with you. This Friend is the Spirit of Truth. The godless world can't take him in because it doesn't have eyes to see him, doesn't know what to look for. But you know him already because he has been staying with you, and will even be in you! I will not leave you orphaned. I'm coming back. In just a little while the world will no longer see me, but you're going to see me because I am alive and you're about to come alive. At that moment you will know absolutely that I'm in my Father, and you're in me, and I'm in you.

John 14:15-20 *(The Message)*

Lord, you are Omnipresent. There is no place I can go or hide where your eyes are no watching over me. You know the number of hairs on my head. You saw me before the foundation of the world. You are my shield, my fortress, my strong tower, my defender, my provider, my refuge, my hope, my life, my grace and my salvation. I have access to the blessings of every divine promise you have spoken in your Word in Christ Jesus. Resting in Christ fills my spirit with life and my soul with joy. Your Word has told me to be anxious for nothing but in everything by prayer and petition with thanksgiving to let my requests be made know to you. As I lean on, trust in, and yield to Christ, he is my peace that surpasses all comprehension and guards my heart. I set my mind on what is true, what is honorable, what is right, what is pure, what is lovely, and what is of good repute. I join with my spirit that desires to sing your praises day and night. I put on the garments of praise and stand amazed at your goodness. Thank you.

# JUNE 18

We worship
God
with our best,
when we surrender
all of ourselves.

Whoever does not take up their cross and follow me is not worthy of me. Whoever finds their life will lose it, and whoever loses their life for my sake will find it. Anyone who welcomes you welcomes me, and anyone who welcomes me welcomes the one who sent me.

Matthew 10:38-40

Lord, you are Worthy. My spirit joys in worshiping you. My soul magnifies you. Worshipping you is as effortless and natural as breathing. When my eyes open each morning, my greatest desire is to bring you glory. Throughout the day, I sing songs of thanksgiving to celebrate your incredible and immeasurable wonder. My mind dances as I mediate on your goodness and feast upon your Word. You have poured abundant life into me by faith in Christ Jesus. I am a citizen of heaven. I am a child of the King. I long to offer you my best as I clothe myself with humility and obedience. I am chosen, loved and highly favored. My soul is preserved in tranquility as I look to and rest in Christ. I clothe myself with humility toward others for you oppose the proud, but give grace to the humble. Your Word is my victorious weapon against satan. My praise is my shout of thankfulness from knowing that with Christ in me he will make a way where there seems no way. Halleluiah Praises for evermore. Inhale my worship. Exhale your glory.

# JUNE 19

Love
that holds
the greatest
power
of witness
makes room
for the
brokenness
in all of us.

The Lord longs to be gracious to you; he rises to show you compassion. For the Lord is a God of justice. Blessed are all who wait for him!

Isaiah 30:18

As a father has compassion on his children, so the Lord has compassion on those who fear him.

Psalm 103:13

Lord, you are Divine Healer. You are filled with compassion and justice to which no person can fully understand. You created all things and set them in motion. Your love wrapped itself in flesh in Christ Jesus and revealed itself to mankind as Christ Jesus lived on earth. Your love for me and all your divinely created and purposed children is beyond description. Thank you for allowing your loving compassion to live in my life in Christ Jesus. Joy and gratitude spill over into all that I do as I ponder all you have given to me. As I draw near to you, you draw near to me. I receive your new mercies every morning. You renew my strength and restore my soul. Love flows from me like a gentle stream because the wonder of Christ to wonderful for words lives in me. You are my hiding place. You protect me from trouble and surround me with songs of deliverance. Your love nurtures and restores me. I feast at your banquet table of grace. I delight myself in Christ and He give me the desires of my heart. Thank you.

# JUNE 20

God
looks at
our hearts.
He already
knows our outside
warts.

No, in all these things we are more than conquerors through him who loved us. For I am convinced that neither death nor life, neither angels nor demons, neither the present nor the future, nor any powers, neither height nor depth, nor anything else in all creation, will be able to separate us from the love of God that is in Christ Jesus our Lord.

Romans 8:37-39

Lord, you are an Inside God. You created me in your perfect image and called me according to your divine purpose. I am your masterpiece, uniquely called, equipped to live in your Light and fashioned to receive every blessing wrapped in your love. I walk in your love fed by your divine Grace of Christ Jesus. Your love sustains me, upholds me and radiates from me to others. No lack in the natural hinders me from walking in the miracle of life Christ Jesus has given me. No powers of darkness or no one can separate me from your Love. I am your workmanship, created in Christ for good works. I am the Righteousness of God in Christ. I am chosen, holy and dearly loved. I am an expression of the life of Christ. I clothe myself with compassion, kindness, humility, gentleness, patience and love. I radiate the love of Christ living within me to all those I meet. I am a child of the King gratefully and joyfully resting in the abundance of Christ and yielding to him. Thank you for wrapping your love in Christ. Halleluiah praises.

# JUNE 21

God's
presence
is always
something
we humbly
enter.

Shout for joy to the LORD, all the earth. Worship the LORD with gladness; come before him with joyful songs. Know that the LORD is God. It is he who made us, and we are his; we are his people, the sheep of his pasture. Enter his gates with thanksgiving and his courts with praise; give thanks to him and praise his name. For the LORD is good and his love endures forever; his faithfulness continues through all generations.

Psalm 100:1-6

Lord, you are Majesty and Worthiness. I come into your presence with humble thanksgiving and your courts with praise. I am wonderfully and fearfully made in your image. Christ Jesus is my shepherd and I am a sheep in his divine flock. You have set your kingdom in divine motion with sowing and reaping. You have completed the seed of life in your Word. Every promise of your word is supernatural seed that brings forth your faithful and intended harvest. I sow praise to you because every fiber in my being longs to praise you. Your love is overwhelming and your goodness unlimited. You work all things together for my good and for your glory. I put on and wear the garment of praise to humble myself and reverence your unfathomable majesty. Nothing or no one compares to you. I joyfully bathe in your anointing as the unity of praise covers my very being and divinely lights my pathway. I harvest the fruit of joy as I rest in your gift of life in Christ Jesus. I praise you for your faithfulness. I praise you for eternal life and grace provision this side of heaven. I praise you in the sanctuary of my spirit where you abide in Christ Jesus. Thank you for creating me in your love. My lips will forever sing your praises. Thank you.

# JUNE 22

God's presence brings a
steady stream of joy,
a constant rush of hope,
an unending flow of truth,
an unmatched love
and an everlasting peace.

May the God of hope fill you with all joy and peace as you trust in him, so that you may overflow with hope by the power of the Holy Spirit.

Romans 15:13

You make known to me the path of life; you will fill me with joy in your presence, with eternal pleasures at your right hand.

Psalm 16:11

Lord, you are Joy, Hope, Truth, Love and Peace. Your unmatched love provides me access to the vinedresser who is Christ Jesus who brings the fruits through me as I yield to him. You make know to me the path of life in Christ Jesus. Your love for me through Christ brings forth your eternal pleasures from your right hand which is where Christ is forever seated. I have every spiritual blessing in heavenly places in Christ Jesus. I wait expectantly to receive all the good you have for me. Christ is my endless supply. My steps are anointed. My way is sure. In Christ, I conquer and have victory. People, circumstances and powers of darkness cannot kill, steal or destroy your divine design for my life. Pain may rock the boat of my soul, yet my peace remains. My hope is in you. In the name of Jesus, you have given me the right to take authority over sin, sickness, devils, demons and my natural circumstances. As I confess your Word over my life, you are watching over it to bring your supernatural manifestations into my natural circumstances. You can change minds and change hearts. Thank you for provision in Christ Jesus.

# JUNE 23

As
long
as we
are making
excuses,
we will
avoid seeking
solutions.

For since the creation of the world God's invisible qualities—his eternal power and divine nature—have been clearly seen, being understood from what has been made, so that people are without excuse. For although they knew God, they neither glorified him as God nor gave thanks to him, but their thinking became futile and their foolish hearts were darkened.

Romans 1:20-21

Lord, you are Lasting Freedom. As I look in the mirror of your Word, it reflects your nature. I am clay in your hands to be molded by you as you see fit. I gratefully and humbly yield to your shaping because you love me completely and only desire to lavish upon me your goodness. Apart from you there is no goodness in me. You bring divine light to my unperfected flesh, as I abide in Christ Jesus. I make Righteous choices because Christ lives in me. You deliver me out of all my afflictions. I anchor my beliefs and sift my thoughts according to the Truth of your Word. I run to you and not away from you humbly accepting the invitation of my Lord and Savior to cast my cares on him and go free. I marvel at Christ Jesus like a young toddler jumping for joy. As I look to you, your love brings completion to every divine intention and perfects me in Christ. The more I seek you, the more I find you. I draw near to you and you draw near to me. I am Your child. You are my God. My lips sing your praises. Thank you.

# JUNE 24

In God's
economy,
expressing
mercy and love
does not depend
on a circumstance,
a schedule,
or the response
of another.

A new command I give you: Love one another. As I have loved you,
so you must love one another.

John 13:34

Lord, You are Pure Love and Lasting Mercy. I love others through the
divine nature of Christ Jesus living in me. My focus is glorifying you and
serving others. I see with the eyes of Christ which reveals that every part
of your creation is worthy of love and honor. My supply of love and mercy
pours forth on everyone I meet, and depends on Christ alive in me. I
am an open vessel holding the richness of your wonder. My love for you
fuels my love for others. I radiate your love as I yield myself to Christ. I
clothe myself with behavior marked by love, mercy, patience, forgiveness,
hope and kindness. I am gentle, kind and forbearing with others. I view
differences or grievances as an opportunity to share the love of Christ with
others. As I walk in love, I glorify you. As I abide in Christ Jesus and yield
to him, I see more clearly the weight of offense is not a burden I choose
to carry. I cast my cares on Christ, so I am free to love deeply and forgive
quickly. My life is wrapped in the love of Christ and his provision.

## JUNE 25

God
will invade
our space
every time
we invite
him to share it.

God can do anything, you know—far more than you could ever imagine or guess or request in your wildest dreams! He does it not by pushing us around but by working within us, his Spirit deeply and gently within us.

Ephesians 3:20-21 *(The Message)*

Lord, you are Immeasurable. You created me in your image and gave me free will. You have told me I have the choice between life and death and between blessings and curses. You have called upon heaven and earth to witness my choice. You have instructed me on which choice to make and that is life. I have chosen life in Christ Jesus. When he stood at the door of my life and knocked, I opened the door and invited him to live within me. When I call upon his name, you answer me. When I seek you, I find you. I live holy and blameless in Christ Jesus. By faith, Christ imparted his nature and his complete abundance to meet my every need. Christ has invited me to cast my cares on him because he cares for me. By faith, every blood bought blessing of Christ Jesus lives within me waiting for me to take hold by faith in his resurrection power and wait expectantly as he lights my way. I live as your unfolding masterpiece abiding in Christ who brings his nature and provision to me and through me. Thank you.

# JUNE 26

A genuine
longing for God
starts in a
heart that has
realized it beats
only because
God allows it to.

"Oh yes, you shaped me first inside, then out; you formed me in my mother's womb. I thank you, High God—you're breathtaking! Body and soul, I am marvelously made! I worship in adoration— what a creation! You know me inside and out, you know every bone in my body; You know exactly how I was made, bit by bit, how I was sculpted from nothing into something. Like an open book, you watched me grow from conception to birth; all the stages of my life were spread out before you, The days of my life all prepared before I'd even lived one day.

Psalm 139:13-16 *(The Message)*

Lord, You are the Creator and Order of all life. I live in and flow through with you in Christ Jesus. You are my beginning and my end. In Christ Jesus, my hunger is nourished and my thirst is quenched. You knew me before the earth was formed. You knitted me together fearfully and wonderfully in my Mother's womb. The hairs on my head are numbered. You called me according to your divine purpose. You are my unending supply. You know my thoughts before I speak. You are higher than any other. I am sheltered in your righteous presence. As I abide in Christ Jesus, thanksgiving floods my spirit and spills over into my soul. Your Word tells me of your amazing grace that saved me and your matchless love that laid out every salvation detail. No words are adequate to describe your wonder. To rest and abide in Christ Jesus, the King of Kings, where I am chosen, loved and accepted is beyond amazing. Thank you for being my creator who daily raises your chisel to chip away and reveal the masterpiece you see in me.

# JUNE 27

Those internal
buttons we
allow others to
push in us are often
the same ones
that need
fine tuning
through
self-reflection.

It's easy to see a smudge on your neighbor's face and be oblivious to the ugly sneer on your own. Do you have the nerve to say, 'Let me wash your face for you,' when your own face is distorted by contempt? It's this I-know-better-than-you mentality again, playing a holier-than-thou part instead of just living your own part. Wipe that ugly sneer off your own face and you might be fit to offer a washcloth to your neighbor. "You don't get wormy apples off a healthy tree, nor good apples off a diseased tree. The health of the apple tells the health of the tree. You must begin with your own life-giving lives. It's who you are, not what you say and do, that counts. Your true being brims over into true words and deeds.

Luke 6:41-45 *(The Message)*

Lord, you are an Eternal Mirror. Search me and know my heart. See if there are any hurtful ways in me and lead me into your everlasting Kingdom. Christ wiped away my shadows and smudges at the cross. The Grace of Christ Jesus feeds my spirit and showers my soul. Daily his new mercies blossom in my soul. Your Word is an eternal mirror. As you open my eyes, I see more and more of my imperfections, wrong beliefs and fleshly behaviors. Your Word is the mirror that reflects your nature and your way. I renew my mind to your Word and you are changing me from the inside out. I lay my weaknesses before your throne of Grace and see them turned into strengths in and through Christ. Since there is no good thing in me, I cannot do enough or quit enough to change myself. I confess when I mess up and gratefully receive your forgiveness. As I abide in Christ, he abides me. Christ in me is the hope of glory. You are my God supplying all my needs according to the riches in glory in Christ Jesus. Thank you.

# JUNE 28

We will
live in the
ocean of
abundance
when we see
God as our
inexhaustible
supply.

You can be sure that God will take care of everything you need, his generosity exceeding even yours in the glory that pours from Jesus. Our God and Father abounds in glory that just pours out into eternity. Yes.

Philippians 4:20 *(The Message)*

Lord, you are Everlasting Supply. Your Grace is sufficient to meet every need now and forever. I rest in your provision and receive your inexhaustible supply of Grace by faith in Christ Jesus. All that you have created me for unfolds in the abundance of Christ Jesus. Nothing comes my way that blocks or hinders my harvest in Christ. My life is rooted and grounded in Christ. His abundance resides in me and pours out from me. Your Glory pours through Christ living in me. The Light that is shining from me is your Light. Your presence is what others see in me as I honor them by love in words and service. Your Living Water is a river that never runs dry. You quench the thirst of my soul. You are the King of Kings and the Lord of Lords. You are able to do exceedingly abundantly above all that I can ask or think according to the power that works within me. In Christ, I live abundantly. I open my mouth to you and let out a lungful of praises. My soul magnifies you. You are so worthy of praise. Unending Halleluiah. Thank you.

# JUNE 29

We often attract
what
we fear most,
because we often
find what we're
expecting.

For the Spirit God gave us does not make us timid, but gives us
power, love and self-discipline.

2 Timothy 1:7

There is no fear in love. But perfect love drives out fear, because
fear has to do with punishment. The one who fears is not made
perfect in love. We love because he first loved us. Whoever claims
to love God yet hates a brother or sister is a liar. For whoever does
not love their brother and sister, whom they have seen, cannot love
God, whom they have not seen. And he has given us this command:
Anyone who loves God must also love their brother and sister.

1 John 4:18-21 *(The Message)*

Lord, you are Unconditional Love. Every good thing is lining up in my life
according to your divine presence. In Christ, you have granted me life and
favor. Your providence preserves my spirit. I walk by faith and not by sight.
Your divine presence lights my path by the Holy Spirit. You have given
me a spirit of power, love and a sound mind. I have the mind of Christ as
I join with the Christ within. I am a new creation. I renew my thoughts
with your Word. My regenerated self, created in the image of Christ rules
my spirit. The Love of Christ in me replaces the old fears. I am accepted,
reborn and redeemed in the beloved. I am alive and free to love as Christ
loved. I renew my mind to the truth of your Word and marvel at your
unconditional love for me. I am a Kingdom child created, molded, saved
and empowered by Grace. In Christ, I am free to be all you created me to
be. I live in the abundant supply of Christ Jesus. Your perfect love casts out
all fear. It is your love that is perfect. Thank you.

# JUNE 30

What
we do
to others
we are
likely
doing
to ourselves.

Here is a simple, rule-of-thumb guide for behavior: Ask yourself what you want people to do for you, then grab the initiative and do it for them. Add up God's Law and Prophets and this is what you get."

"Don't look for shortcuts to God. The market is flooded with surefire, easygoing formulas for a successful life that can be practiced in your spare time. Don't fall for that stuff, even though crowds of people do. The way to life—to God!—is vigorous and requires total attention.

Matthew 7:12-14 *(The Message)*

Lord, you are Unending Love. Thank you for giving me access to your throne of Grace by faith in Christ Jesus. His transforming love is changing me from the inside out. I reach out to others in a boldness and love that is far bigger than my flesh. I am one with my undivided good nurtured by Eternal love. I give my undivided attention to the Christ within me for out of my heart comes the issues of life. Your authentic, unconditional love living in me is the love I share with others. You are the source of the encouraging and uplifting words I speak. I am filled with the divine nature of Christ. Peace lives in my heart because I abide in the Prince of Peace. I feast on your Word meditating on it and humbly asking the Holy Spirit to search me and reveal those areas of my life that do not line up with your Word. I open myself to you in humility. I do not desire to close myself off to you in pride. I share the gift of peace in my heart with those I meet. Your abundance blesses my life. Thank you for abundance of life in Christ Jesus.

# JULY 1

Sometimes
we have to
block our outer
ears to hear
with our inner ones.

Wise men and women are always learning, always listening for fresh insights.

Proverbs 18:15 *(The Message)*

Lord, you quicken my ears to hear. By faith, my ears are attuned to your faithful guidance. I follow you as a sheep follows its Shepherd. Christ Jesus is my Eternal Shepherd. I quiet my soul by stepping away from the noise of the world to spend time with you. You speak in the quietness of my spirit. You speak to me through your Word. Your Word comes alive as I meditate on it. Thank you for watching over your Word to perform it. As I seek your kingdom and your Righteousness, you add all things to me. Your unending favor abides in me as I abide in Christ. Every aspect of my divine call is unfolding. I am drawn to your goodness and held to you by the love of Christ in me. I am open to receive all that you have for me. I gratefully receive the abundance of Christ by faith. Christ in me is the hope of Glory. I praise you with abounding thanksgiving. My lips delight in singing your continual praises. My soul magnifies you.

# JULY 2

Every problem
in relationships
stems from the
wrong view of love.

Let no debt remain outstanding, except the continuing debt to love
one another, for whoever loves others has fulfilled the law.

Romans 13:8

You, my brothers and sisters, were called to be free. But do not use
your freedom to indulge the flesh; rather, serve one another humbly
in love.

Galatians 5:13

Lord, you are Perfected and Endless Love. In Christ, I am free from the
penalty of sin and its power. I am free from the law of self-works and
performance. Living, creating and fulfilling my needs comes by resting in
Christ. I yield to Christ in me who loves others through me. Christ has
imparted his eyes to me to see others as your divine masterpiece. As I look
through the eyes of Christ within, I can see others offense as a cry to be
heard in love and a wondrous opportunity for me to make the choice to
share you with them. Even when other's actions do not line up with my
expectations or your Word, I can love deeply and forgive quickly because
Christ's nature lives in me. I see unresolved offense as an obstacle to my
love walk that hinders my relationships and blocks the flow of your Grace.
I choose to confess what needs confessing, grieve losses that need grieving
and forgive what needs forgiving not by my willpower or fleshly strength,
but through the Grace of Christ Jesus who lives in me and flows through
me. Thank you.

# JULY 3

Everything God
tells us to do
is a
benefit to ourselves
and a blessing
to others.

For the LORD gives wisdom; from his mouth come knowledge and understanding. He holds success in store for the upright, he is a shield to those whose walk is blameless, for he guards the course of the just and protects the way of his faithful ones.

Proverbs 2:6-8

Lord, you are Sovereign. Creation testifies to your order, your aliveness and your amazing wonder. I joy in feasting on your Word which feeds my spirit and brings order to my soul. Thank you for allowing me the honor of confessing your Word in faith and waiting expectantly while you perform it. Thank you that all your promises are "yes and amen" in Christ Jesus. As I plant the seeds of your Word in my spirit and renew my mind to your Word, Christ is bringing forth his fruit from me. Every seed planted in faith, brings a harvest of glory to you and a blessing to others and myself. I am destined for great works because the great "I AM" lives in me. The exchange of his blood for my sin debt and his life for my sin penalty has been completed. Thank you that in Christ Jesus sin no longer has dominion over me because I am under Grace and not under the law. I reap the fruits of his spirit which are love, peace, joy, forbearance, kindness, goodness, faithfulness, gentleness and self-control. I rest in Christ. I live in Christ. Thank you.

# JULY 4

The world
loves demotion.
God loves
promotion.

His mercy extends to those who fear him, from generation to generation. He has performed mighty deeds with his arm; he has scattered those who are proud in their inmost thoughts. He has brought down rulers from their thrones but has lifted up the humble.

Luke 1:50-52

Lord, you are high above all things, Creator, and giver of all life. In Christ, I am high and lifted up. Your divine spirit gives me wisdom and elevates me to safe and blessed places. You are my God, my refuge, my fortress and my safe dwelling. No power can come against the divine plan for my life. No weapon formed against me can prosper as I plead the blood and declare your Word. Every tongue that rises up against me, you will condemn. I live in complete and total victory steadfast, immovable, abounding in the work of Christ and knowing that my labor is not in vain. I abide in Christ and triumph as a trophy of His victory. I joy in the matchless fellowship with my Savior. I joy with humble gratitude and passionate thanksgiving for Christ Jesus, my Lord who is, who was, and who is to come. I speak peace to the storms the world loves to bring upon me for the Prince of Peace lives in me. I live established in Christ Jesus. Halleluiah.

# JULY 5

Every outer manifestation of power
comes from inner purity,
and only God
is qualified
to perform
such a splendid
miracle.

For no matter how many promises God has made, they are "Yes" in Christ. And so through him the "Amen" is spoken by us to the glory of God. Now it is God who makes both us and you stand firm in Christ. He anointed us, set his seal of ownership on us, and put his Spirit in our hearts as a deposit, guaranteeing what is to come.

2 Corinthians 1:20-22

Lord, you are a Covenant Miracle working God. All that I am comes from you. You created me in your image. You saved me from eternal death by the blood of Christ Jesus. You supply all my needs according to your riches in glory in Christ Jesus. You are a Covenant Miracle working God. No one or nothing compares to you. The miracle of Christ imparting his righteousness to me is a miracle beyond description. Christ has anointed me, set his seal of ownership on me, and put his Spirit in my heart as a deposit, guaranteeing my inheritance. I serve you with gladness and honor. I love in the fullness of Christ. I bear kingdom fruits as I abide in Christ, the Vinedresser. Every moment is filled with the wonder of your presence. Every breath I take is life and joy in Christ. Your divine power has granted me all things that pertain to life and godliness. I receive your precious and great promises as I partake of your divine nature that lives in me. Thank you for creating me, loving me, and saving me. I joy in Jesus, my Lord and Savior.

# JULY 6

The world's economy
is my way
*or* the highway.
God's economy
is My Way
*is* the
High Way.

Jesus said, "I am the way, and the truth, and the life. No one comes to the Father except through me."

John 14:6

And a highway will be there; it will be called the Way of Holiness; it will be for those who walk on that Way. The unclean will not journey on it; wicked fools will not go about on it.

Isaiah 35:8

Lord, you are the High Way. The love of Christ poured out for me, his righteousness imparted to me, and his grace that supplies my every need by faith is more than I can comprehend. My way in Christ is the High Way as I abide in him. I reach my destination and high calling because Christ leads the way. My path is unobstructed by the power of your Spirit living in me and lighted by your Word. You are faithful and just watching over your Word to perform it in my life. There is no obstacle to great for you to conquer. You are my God. I am your child. The evil one does not hinder me as I confess your Word and plead the blood. I am raised up with Christ and seated in Heavenly places. Thank you for unveiling the light of your truth, so I could humbly choose Christ and live forever empowered and expectant of eternal glory. I open my mouth and let out a lungful of praises. Thank you for new life, new birth and new identity in Christ Jesus.

# JULY 7

When we are
crucified and
identified
with Christ,
our ego
joys in taking
a back seat.

What actually took place is this: I tried keeping rules and working my head off to please God, and it didn't work. So I quit being a "law man" so that I could be God's man. Christ's life showed me how, and enabled me to do it. I identified myself completely with him. Indeed, I have been crucified with Christ. My ego is no longer central. It is no longer important that I appear righteous before you or have your good opinion, and I am no longer driven to impress God. Christ lives in me. The life you see me living is not "mine," but it is lived by faith in the Son of God, who loved me and gave himself for me. I am not going to go back on that. Is it not clear to you that to go back to that old rule-keeping, peer-pleasing religion would be an abandonment of everything personal and free in my relationship with God? I refuse to do that, to repudiate God's grace. If a living relationship with God could come by rule-keeping, then Christ died unnecessarily.

Galatians 2:19-21 *(The Message)*

Lord, you are Divine Provision. You are Sovereign God. There is no other higher than you. Thank you for revealing to me that Christ is the Way, the Truth, and the Life. My attempts to do good and be good through my own sweat have left me in a tale spin. I accept the truth of your Word that teaches me that apart from Christ I can do nothing. My efforts are in vain. My pride comes before my fall. My self righteousness is like filthy rags. Your love has opened my eyes to see that you created me to glorify you and serve others. I gave up the right to myself when I accepted the amazing grace you offered me in Christ Jesus to save me, redeem me, and create me anew. In Christ, my works are a natural outflow of his inflow within. I am not bound by empty religion based on man-made philosophy. I live in your redeeming Grace. My lips sing your praises. In Christ, I am alive now and forever. Thank you for placing your love within me in Christ Jesus. I live overflowing and satisfied in his goodness. Yielding to you is a joy.

# JULY 8

Through the Grace
of God,
life flows in
abundance producing
lasting peace,
immeasurable love
and indescribable joy.

Through Him also we have [our] access (entrance, introduction) by faith into this grace (state of God's favor) in which we [firmly and safely] stand. And let us rejoice and exult in our hope of experiencing and enjoying the glory of God.

Romans 5:2 (AMP)

Lord, you are Grace which supplies. Thank you for Christ Jesus who is my overflowing supply and my constant abundance. Christ has torn the veil of sin that once separated me from you. He is the door that I humbly enter into your presence. The joy of Christ living within me is my strength. The Grace of Christ Jesus is his presence and his unending supply to meet all my needs. Christ has given me the keys of Heaven. I am seated in heavenly places with him fully clothed in his righteousness and wearing the crown of victory which he has placed on my head. His blood shed for me shouts your love for me which is to wonderful for words. I sing unending praises because I am the apple of your eye. I am a constant wonder in your making as the Holy Spirit molds and shapes me. I am a vessel of Christ's divine love pouring out from the abundance of Christ within. Life, peace, love and joy are mine as I abide in Christ and he abides in me. My lips sing your praises. My soul magnifies you name. Every breath I take is an offering of praise.

# JULY 9

The world says you
have to do to
be....
God says you
have to be
to do.

You did not choose me, but I chose you and appointed you so
that you might go and bear fruit—fruit that will last—and so that
whatever you ask in my name the Father will give you.

John 15:16 (TNIV)

Lord, you are Unending Provision. I lived for a season in the noise of
the world, attempting to produce fruit, and meeting my needs through
pride and works. Your love and amazing grace has removed the blinders
from my eyes showing me clearly that I was not created to produce fruit,
but to bear fruit in Christ Jesus. I joy in resting in, abiding in, relying on
and trusting in Christ who knows and supplies my every need. I celebrate
your goodness from the first steps I take each morning that all you have
created me for and called me to is complete in Christ Jesus. I delight in
declaring your promises over my life, mixing them with faith, and waiting
expectantly as you fulfill them way beyond my wildest imaginations. My
hands are blessed to bring forth your fruit as I offer them to you. My mind
is blessed to bring forth your seeds of creativity as I abide in Christ. I rest
in the finished work of the cross. In Christ, you make known to me the
path of life. I joy in your wonder. My labor is to rest in Christ. My work is
to yield to Christ.

# JULY 10

Authentic rejoicing
always comes
from God's
genuine Grace.

Also at that time, people will say, "Look at what's happened! This is our God! We waited for him and he showed up and saved us! This God, the one we waited for! Let's celebrate, sing the joys of his salvation. God's hand rests on this mountain!

Isaiah 25: 9-10 *(The Message)*

Lord, your Grace is Unending Supply. Every part of your creation sings of your glory. You created my mouth as a vessel of praise. The shouts of praise indwelling my spirit and sent forth from my lips hold your glory light and your creative energy to change what receives it. You created my body to house your glory. I joyfully and freely lift up my hands to praise your wonderful and holy name. You created my spirit to worship you in spirit and in truth. I bless you at all times for you are worthy to be praised. Every melody that forms in my spirit is sent forth for your praise. My confessions of your Word hold within them the sounds of victory that are sent forth by my lips in faith to bring forth your victory and defeat every enemy that attempts to kill, steal and destroy your will in Christ Jesus for my life. You have revealed your love for me and redeemed me by the blood of the Lamb. I have every blood bought blessings of Christ Jesus living in me and watching over me. My response is to praise you forevermore. Glory Halleluiah.

# JULY 11

We have right
standing with
God
because we bowed
our knees before
Jesus.

Whatever God has promised gets stamped with the Yes of Jesus.
In him, this is what we preach and pray, the great Amen, God's Yes
and our Yes together, gloriously evident. God affirms us, making us
a sure thing in Christ, putting his Yes within us. By his Spirit he has
stamped us with his eternal pledge—a sure beginning of what he is
destined to complete.

2 Corinthians 1:20-22 *(The Message)*

Lord, you are the one and only High God. Your greatness is above
anything I could ever think, dream or imagine. Thank you for revealing
to me that my greatest standing comes on bended knees before Christ
Jesus. I humbly receive the steady, unbroken flow of divine goodness of
Christ living in me. I am your loved, chosen and adopted child redeemed
by the blood of Christ Jesus. I am a co-heir with Christ. My supply for
every need in my life comes by faith in Christ Jesus. No weapon formed
against me can prosper. I resolve to stand firm on the Rock of Christ
as I live in faith. I have been delivered out of the dominion of darkness
and transferred into your kingdom of Light. In Christ, I have forgiveness
of sins, a new spirit nature, and an eternal inheritance. I live as a new
creation empowered to fulfill the divine appointments of my life in Christ.
I am alive in Jesus, called according to your purpose to do his good works.
Thank you for putting your "Yes" within me in Christ Jesus. Halleluiah
praises now and forevermore.

# JULY 12

When we are bold
enough to step out in
faith and
wise enough to
welcome the Spirit
of Truth,
we are in for a
spirit filled adventure.

By entering through faith into what God has always wanted to do for us—set us right with him, make us fit for him—we have it all together with God because of our Master Jesus. And that's not all: We throw open our doors to God and discover at the same moment that he has already thrown open his door to us. We find ourselves standing where we always hoped we might stand—out in the wide open spaces of God's grace and glory, standing tall and shouting our praise.

Romans 5:1-2 *(The Message)*

Lord, you are the Door of Truth. I open the door of my heart to Christ Jesus and joyfully receive his abundance. You have inscribed on my heart the truth of who you are and your plan for me which is abiding, yielding, and resting in Christ Jesus. You have created me, redeemed me and supplied my every need in Christ Jesus. Apart from Christ, my self efforts are dust particles in the wind. I know, believe, claim and accept the love and grace of Christ living in me by faith. I live redeemed, healed, delivered, prosperous, successful, protected, joyous, sealed, safe, assured and eternally saved in Christ Jesus. I joyfully receive your divine favor and endless blessings in Christ Jesus. Thank you that as I step out in faith and submit to the truth of the Spirit that your love for me allows me to discover you have already thrown open every door to me. Living in relationship to you by the spirit is amazing. You are my God. I am your child. Thank you.

# JULY 13

zzzz

If you want to
wear the crown
of life,
then lay
down the pride of life.

For the LORD takes delight in his people; he crowns the humble with victory.

Psalm 149:4

Now this I know: The LORD gives victory to his anointed. He answers him from his heavenly sanctuary with the victorious power of his right hand.

Psalm 20:6

Lord, you supply my eternal crown. I kneel before Christ Jesus who wore the crown of thorns so that I might wear the crown of life in him. I glorify your risen son, the Holy One who overcame death and imparts to me your righteousness. My spirit in union with Christ shouts continual praises for according to your great mercy, you have caused me to be born again to a living hope through the resurrection of Jesus Christ from the dead, to an inheritance that is imperishable, undefiled, and unfading, kept in heaven for me, who by your power has guarded me through faith for a salvation ready to be revealed in the last time. Your goodness multiplies in me by the full measure of the God-head that's alive within me. I joy in yielding to the Holy Spirit to mold and shape me into Christ-likeness. Every fiber of my being rises up to sing your praises. A new song of celebration for your goodness and your abounding Grace in Christ Jesus leaps from my lips throughout the day. Your gift of life in Christ writes every new song. Thank you.

# JULY 14

To cross
the finish line,
you have to
keep moving
your feet.

Do you see what this means—all these pioneers who blazed the way, all these veterans cheering us on? It means we'd better get on with it. Strip down, start running—and never quit! No extra spiritual fat, no parasitic sins. Keep your eyes on Jesus, who both began and finished this race we're in. Study how he did it. Because he never lost sight of where he was headed—that exhilarating finish in and with God—he could put up with anything along the way: Cross, shame, whatever. And now he's there, in the place of honor, right alongside God. When you find yourselves flagging in your faith, go over that story again, item by item, that long litany of hostility he plowed through. That will shoot adrenaline into your souls!

Hebrews 12:1-3 *(The Message)*

Lord, you are life and purpose. I run the race before me with boldness, confidence and victory in sight because Christ has already provided the victorious way by the cross. I am able by faith in Christ to put one foot in front of another by his strength. I am reinforced with divine power in my spirit by Christ living in me. I am deeply rooted in love, founded in security and destined to triumph. I receive his miracle working power of abundance in praise and with thanksgiving. I am blessed and highly favored as Christ lives in me and his blessings overflow to me. You make known to me the path of life; in your presence there is fullness of joy; at your Right hand where Christ Jesus sits are pleasures forevermore. Sound the trumpet of victory. Beat the drums of perfect timing. Unleash the fanfare of celebration because every step I take I celebrate the abundance of Christ Jesus alive in me. Halleluiah victory. Halleluiah thanksgiving.

# JULY 15

Baptism in Christ
is not just washing us up;
it's also dressing us up
in a robe of
righteousness and inviting
us to the
King's House
to partake of His banquet feast of grace.

Whoever believes and is baptized will be saved, but whoever does not believe will be condemned.

Mark 16:16

God made him who had no sin to be sin for us, so that in him we might become the righteousness of God.

2 Corinthians 5:21

Lord, you are Holy and Righteous. Thank you for your amazing love which in Christ Jesus saved me through your gift of amazing Grace. Knowing that Christ exchanged my filthy rags of self-righteousness stained by sin with his robe of righteousness sends me to my knees in humble gratitude. Your love for me held Christ Jesus to the cross. I live as a joint heir with Christ united in one spirit. I am redeemed and forgiven all my sins. I live with no condemnation. I am complete in Christ. I come boldly before your throne of Grace in the name of Jesus and whatever I ask according to your will I receive. I live in freedom and joy. I am confident that Christ will complete the good works he started in me. I live in joyous praise and thanksgiving. I worship you with gladness and thanksgiving. Thank you for saving me by your love and supplying me in your Grace. I live forever free in Christ Jesus. My being radiates thanksgiving to you.

# JULY 16

God adopted us
in Jesus
for the sole purpose
of spoiling
us with
His love.

This resurrection life you received from God is not a timid, grave-tending life. It's adventurously expectant, greeting God with a childlike "What's next, Papa?" God's Spirit touches our spirits and confirms who we really are. We know who he is, and we know who we are: Father and children. And we know we are going to get what's coming to us—an unbelievable inheritance! We go through exactly what Christ goes through. If we go through the hard times with him, then we're certainly going to go through the good times with him!

Romans 8:15-17 *(The Message)*

Lord, you are Life. As my spirit is one with you in Christ Jesus, your love, your peace and your righteousness supply me. Your have revealed to me through your living Word that I am your loved, chosen and adopted child. Your spirit testifies with my spirit that I am your child. I am your workmanship. Every day is a new day to rejoice and exalt in my hope of experiencing and enjoying your presence. I rest in Christ Jesus my Lord and Savior and his grace supplies my every need according to his riches in glory. All that you purposed for me before the foundation of the world is unfolding in and through the grace of Christ Jesus. Trials and tribulations of this world pale in comparison to my inheritance in you. No weapon formed against me shall prosper. You have overcome the power of sin and I live loosed from the bondage of sin. I live by faith in Christ as a child of the light. Nothing or no one compares to you. My lips joy in singing your praises. You are worthy to receive glory, honor and praise. Thank you Halleluiahs.

# JULY 17

The ground
at the foot
of the cross is level
because it's where
Jesus invites
us to come just as we are.

This is how much God loved the world: He gave his Son, his one and only Son. And this is why: so that no one need be destroyed; by believing in him, anyone can have a whole and lasting life. God didn't go to all the trouble of sending his Son merely to point an accusing finger, telling the world how bad it was. He came to help, to put the world right again. Anyone who trusts in him is acquitted; anyone who refuses to trust him has long since been under the death sentence without knowing it. And why? Because of that person's failure to believe in the one-of-a-kind Son of God when introduced to him. "This is the crisis we're in: God-light streamed into the world, but men and women everywhere ran for the darkness. They went for the darkness because they were not really interested in pleasing God. Everyone who makes a practice of doing evil, addicted to denial and illusion, hates God-light and won't come near it, fearing a painful exposure. But anyone working and living in truth and reality welcomes God-light so the work can be seen for the God-work it is.

John 3:16-21 *(The Message)*

Lord, you are Light, Resurrection, and Life. As I abide in Christ, my spirit rests in his perfect harmony. I am whole in Christ. I am redeemed in Christ. I am restored in Christ I am forgiven in Christ. I am provided for in Christ. I am protected in Christ. I am defended in Christ. You fill my mind with creative and prosperous ideas. I receive your overflowing love through Christ that blesses me and everyone I meet. Your blessings fill my very being with the glory light of Christ and attracts to me all your goodness that is mine in Christ Jesus. I live in the light as Christ is the Light. My spirit is forever blessed with the grace of Christ in me. I live forevermore making melody in my heart. Thank you Jesus for giving and bringing life to my spirit. Thank you Jesus for living within me where your fullness of spirit flows uninterrupted to my soul as I yield to, abide in and rest in you. I receive your love with gladness and thanksgiving. Halleluiah praises.

# JULY 18

When we are
on fire for
God,
we allow
His Spirit
to refine us like gold.

I know how great this makes you feel, even though you have to put up with every kind of aggravation in the meantime. Pure gold put in the fire comes out of it proved pure; genuine faith put through this suffering comes out proved genuine. When Jesus wraps this all up, it's your faith, not your gold, that God will have on display as evidence of his victory.

1 Peter 1:6-7 *(The Message)*

Lord, you refine my life like gold which is your righteousness. You stir my heart with the unending fire of your love to be all you have predestined me to be. Your power flows to me in a steady, unbroken and ever-increasing flow as I yield to Christ within. Through your faithfulness, I know I am always taken care of and have everything that you have purposed for me to have. I rest in the abundant supply of Christ. When trouble comes against me, you strengthen and protect me in Christ. My faith and the presence of Christ in me brings every aspect of my life to be as a trophy of your goodness. I rejoice in your never ending mercy and steadfast love. No power of darkness or no one can hinder or gain victory over the living power of Christ living in me and through me. You silence my enemies and close the mouths of any hindrances. You are great and worthy to be praised. My lips shout praises with each lungful of breath I take. My spirit sings your praises. My soul magnifies your name. Every fiber of my being resonates in your love.

# JULY 19

Anytime we're
down and out,
we can come to
Jesus
and be
High
and
LIFTED
UP.

Cast your cares on the LORD and he will sustain you; he will never let the righteous be shaken.

Psalm 55:22

For even if the mountains walk away and the hills fall to pieces, my love won't walk away from you, my covenant commitment of peace won't fall apart. The God who has compassion on you says so.

Isaiah 54:10 *(The Message)*

Lord, you are Never-ending Provision. You are the firm foundation on which I stand. Nothing of the flesh or nothing of this world provides and meets my needs like Christ who lives in me. I cast my burdens on Christ and live in his freedom. I stir up my faith as my lips speak your living Word. I am not shaken by things my eyes can see. I rest in Christ and the faith of his provision knowing that all things work together in Christ Jesus for my good. I believe in your everlasting love and your faithfulness to perform your Word as I confess it from my mouth. I live in your divine protection. I overcome by the word of my testimony and the blood of the Lamb. You are my ever present help in times of trouble. Christ is the Rock on which I stand. I joy in knowing that Christ in me is the hope of glory. I rest in Christ having yoked myself to him by faith. Thank you for loving me, saving me, and supplying me. My soul flows in union with my spirit.

# JULY 20

Deception
usually
involves
just an
ounce of
truth.

What this adds up to, then, is this: no more lies, no more pretense. Tell your neighbor the truth. In Christ's body we're all connected to each other, after all. When you lie to others, you end up lying to yourself.

Ephesians 4:25 *(The Message)*

Lord, you are Truth and Light. In you, there is no false thing and no darkness. I live connected to your truth and your light by the life-giving spirit of Christ who is truth and light living in me. The Holy Spirit inscribes your truth on my life as I feast on your Word. As I yield to Christ, he brings forth his nature through me. I abide and he supplies. My soul nature desires to run away and hide my weaknesses in darkness where they remain covered in shame and guilt. Thank you Jesus for nailing my shame and guilt to the cross. As I take my thoughts captive to the obedience of Christ, he unleashes his nature in my spirit and it overflows to my soul nature transforming me from the inside out. My thoughts take hold of the glorious wonder that I am chosen, loved and completely accepted in Christ Jesus. With my needs supplied in Christ, I cease to toil through my own efforts and find no need to cover up or make excuses for my weaknesses. I confess my weaknesses to you and ask the Christ in me to replace them with his strength. I bear kingdom fruit as I abide by faith in Christ Jesus. I live yielded and transparent in your light of truth.

# JULY 21

God
gives us the address
of eternity and
allows us the choice
to accept it.

It wasn't so long ago that you were mired in that old stagnant life of sin. You let the world, which doesn't know the first thing about living, tell you how to live. You filled your lungs with polluted unbelief, and then exhaled disobedience. We all did it, all of us doing what we felt like doing, when we felt like doing it, all of us in the same boat. It's a wonder God didn't lose his temper and do away with the whole lot of us. Instead, immense in mercy and with an incredible love, he embraced us. He took our sin-dead lives and made us alive in Christ. He did all this on his own, with no help from us! Then he picked us up and set us down in highest heaven in company with Jesus, our Messiah. Now God has us where he wants us, with all the time in this world and the next to shower grace and kindness upon us in Christ Jesus. Saving is all his idea, and all his work. All we do is trust him enough to let him do it. It's God's gift from start to finish! We don't play the major role. If we did, we'd probably go around bragging that we'd done the whole thing! No, we neither make nor save ourselves.

Ephesians 2:1-9 *(The Message)*

Lord, you are Life Eternal. I have already arrived at Heaven's door by faith in Christ Jesus who has saved me, redeemed me and supplies my every need. Heaven's eternal address is forever in my spirit and etched in thanksgiving in my mind. No words can frame the wonder of your amazing Grace in Christ Jesus. Your love is more wonderful than I can comprehend. I am redeemed, sealed and marked for Eternal life by the Holy Spirit and through the blood of Jesus. By faith, my name is written in the Lamb's book. In Christ, I live, breathe, move and have my being. I joyfully run to your love and hide myself in your supplying Grace. The works of my hands are blessed. I live fully equipped and humbly yielded to your divine plan for my life which is abiding in Christ and yielding to his works through me. My lips sing your praises. My thoughts celebrate your never-ending goodness as I consider the wonder of your love. Halleluiah.

# JULY 22

God's love placed in us
by faith in Christ Jesus
will not satisfy us
until we are so filled
with him that our love
flows back to him in return.

Be good to me, God—and now! I've run to you for dear life. I'm hiding out under your wings until the hurricane blows over. I call out to High God, the God who holds me together. He sends orders from heaven and saves me, he humiliates those who kick me around. God delivers generous love, he makes good on his word.

Psalms 57:1-3 *(The Message)*

Lord, you are Omnipresent. Your eyes are forever on me. Your generous love delivers and protects me through the grace supply of Christ Jesus. Christ is my strength. As I abide in him by faith his perfect love casts out all fear. Christ has given me his authority to declare victory over the powers of darkness by his name, his blood and his Word. In Jesus name, I trample on serpents and scorpions, and over all the power of the enemy and nothing shall by any means hurt me. I put on the full armor of God by faith in Christ Jesus and hold my peace which enfolds me in his rest. No weapon formed against me shall prosper. I fix my eyes on Christ Jesus who is the author and finisher of my faith. Nothing comes against your divine assignment for my life. All things are working together for my good. The doors of your favor are opened to me by the Grace of Christ Jesus and delivered in his love for me. I rejoice in all circumstances for this is the will of God in Christ Jesus. I cast my cares on Christ and live in freedom, joy and love. Thank you.

# JULY 23

Faith in Jesus
will always express
itself in relational love,
and each
expression of love,
will open us
to another step of
amazing
blessing.

I suspect you would never intend this, but this is what happens. When you attempt to live by your own religious plans and projects, you are cut off from Christ, you fall out of grace. Meanwhile we expectantly wait for a satisfying relationship with the Spirit. For in Christ, neither our most conscientious religion nor disregard of religion amounts to anything. What matters is something far more interior: faith expressed in love.

Galatians 5: 4-6 *(The Message)*

Lord, you are Perfect Unconditional Love. Your divine activity and divine love are operating in every area of my life as Christ in me brings forth your will through me. The divine plan of my life manifests as it is bathed in your love. I live in the realm of the extraordinary because you have gifted me with your extraordinary presence of the spirit of Christ living in me. As I praise you and confess your Word, you unleash your supernatural over my natural circumstances. No self-effort and no work of mankind compares to your grace supply. Your divine energy is at work all around me. Angels surround me and keep my foot from being dashed against a rock. I look to, trust in and rely on Christ Jesus. Your goodness and mercy hunt me down all the days of my life. My heart sings your praises. In Christ, my joy is complete. You are my God. I am your child. Thank you Lord, that daily you bless me with favor. Your love for me releases your life in me.

# JULY 24

Where there is a struggle
in making our head
to heart
connection,
there is likely an
emotional disconnection
that is short
circuiting the process.

Thank you! Everything in me says "Thank you!" Angels listen as I sing my thanks. I kneel in worship facing your holy temple and say it again: "Thank you!" Thank you for your love, thank you for your faithfulness; Most holy is your name, most holy is your Word. The moment I called out, you stepped in; you made my life large with strength.

Psalm 138:1-3 *(The Message)*

Lord, you are wholeness and clarity. Search my heart by the Holy Spirit. I open myself and yield to his truth. Where he shows me there are beliefs, thoughts, perceptions, attitudes and unresolved emotions waiting to receive your touch of love and release, I ask you to make them clear to me. Hold nothing back Lord as I ask you to shape and mold me into Christ-likeness. I ask the supplying Grace of Christ to empower and strengthen me to confess what needs confessing, grieve what needs grieving and forgive what needs forgiving. I humbly receive the spirit of truth to search me and bring truth to where truth needs to be. You have created me for the praise of your glory and I see clearly now that holding onto unresolved pain keeps me stuck in the pride of life. Your truth replaces my wrong beliefs about myself and others. I renounce all ungodly thought patterns and belief systems in the name of Jesus. I renounce all fear, unbelief and doubt in the name of Jesus. In Christ, I am a new creation. Thank you for replacing the old mindsets with the truth as I renew my mind to your living Word. Your truth sets me free in Christ Jesus.

# JULY 25

When we live
in bondage
to the should'a,
could'a, would'a,
and if only's,
the grip of our past
threatens the freedom
of our present
and sabotages
the possibilities
of our future.

Therefore, there is now no condemnation for those who are in Christ Jesus, because through Christ Jesus the law of the Spirit who gives life has set you free from the law of sin and death.

Romans 8:1-2

Lord, you are Total Acceptance. Self-condemnation is a thing of the past as I live chosen, blessed, highly favored and completely loved in Christ Jesus. Rejection is a scheme of satan to steal, kill and destroy my identity in you. I resist the devil in Jesus name and the sword of the spirit and he has to flee. I live alive and in perfect union with you through Christ who has torn the veil of sin that separated me from you. Your goodness and mercy aggressively hunts me down by your love and overtakes me every day showering me with unexpected blessings in unexpected ways. I see my past as a stepping stone to my future. I joy each morning in the abundance of your new mercies. I renew my mind with the truth of how you see me in Christ. I am a new creation. I take my everyday, ordinary life—my sleeping, eating, going-to-work, and walking-around life—and yield it before you as a fragrant offering of humility. Praise and thanksgiving pour forth from every part of my being. I abide in Christ who is my life. Praises.

# JULY 26

We reach the finish
line when we enter
the race
and
we finish the race
only when
we start
in the first
place.

Do you not know that in a race all the runners run, but only one gets the prize? Run in such a way as to get the prize. Everyone who competes in the games goes into strict training. They do it to get a crown that will not last, but we do it to get a crown that will last forever.

I Corinthians 9:24-25

Lord, you are Alpha and Omega, the beginning and the end. I enter the race you have set before me in joyful expectation because you are my personal trainer. You knitted me together in my Mothers' womb and created me with an expected outcome. The ministry of reconciliation you have called me to is a race I start and finish by faith in Christ Jesus. No obstacle can hinder me from claiming the trophy of Eternal Life in Christ as you complete the work of the Father in me. Your hedge of protection is all around me. Your living power is inside me as I abide in Christ. My sufficiency is Christ sufficiency. As I exercise the creativity, the gifts and the talents you placed in me in Christ, his wonders of glory manifest through me. Everyday I wear your crown of victory in humble adoration of your limitless goodness. You have already moved Heaven and earth for me. I wear the Crown of Christ with praise and thanksgiving. I receive the prize that is before me with joy and gladness. Hallelujah praises. Every breath I take, reflects your wonder.

# JULY 27

Each of us
is God's original
masterpiece,
fashioned by His Hand,
and purposed by His Divine Plan.

And even the very hairs of your head are all numbered. So don't be afraid; you are worth more than many sparrows.

Luke 12:7

For we are God's handiwork, created in Christ Jesus to do good works, which God prepared in advance for us to do.

Ephesians 2:10

Lord, you are the Master Potter. You fashioned me by your hands and breathed life into me. In Christ Jesus, I am one with you in spirit. I am a chosen vessel, an eternal treasure and an endless wonder fashioned in your image. Never has there been and never will there be another like me. You have created me with a hope and a future completing my life before the foundation of the world. I joy in your immeasurable love for me. You enable me to fulfill all you have called me to with Christ living on the inside of me. I am alive in Christ now and forevermore. I joy in spending time with you. My relationship with you in Christ is the greatest treasure of my life. I feast on your Word which nourishes my spirit. I sit before your banquet table of grace dressed in the royal righteousness of Jesus and grateful you have chosen me to feast with you.

# JULY 28

Inner freedom
unfolds as it is
watered in love,
grounded in hope
and
rooted in faith.

My beloved friends, let us continue to love each other since love comes from God. Everyone who loves is born of God and experiences a relationship with God. The person who refuses to love doesn't know the first thing about God, because God is love—so you can't know him if you don't love. This is how God showed his love for us: God sent his only Son into the world so we might live through him. This is the kind of love we are talking about—not that we once upon a time loved God, but that he loved us and sent his Son as a sacrifice to clear away our sins and the damage they've done to our relationship with God.

1 John 4:7-10 *(The Message)*

Lord, you are Pure Love. Wrapping flesh around the Word, Christ Jesus and sacrificing him once and for all at the cross to pay my sin debt in full is the ultimate expression of your love. And you didn't stop there. In Christ, you have supernaturally made me one with him in spirit. I am a new creation. With Christ living in me by faith, he manifests your love to me and through me to those around me. Apart from abiding in Christ, I have no capacity to love you, myself or others. When I look at others through the "eyes of Christ," I see them as God's masterpiece. Your love allows me to accept those who disappoint me by no longer requiring them to satisfy me, leaving me free to love them, to reach towards them for their sake, without having to protect myself from feeling disappointed by their response to me. The nurture and care I share with others is the overflow of the nurture and care of Christ in me. In Christ Jesus, all things are possible. Thank you.

# JULY 29

We're never alone;
the Lord is always
upholding the righteous.

Be strong and courageous. Do not be afraid or terrified because of them, for the LORD your God goes with you; he will never leave you nor forsake you.

Deuteronomy 31:6

For the eyes of the Lord are on the righteous and his ears are attentive to their prayer, but the face of the Lord is against those who do evil.

1 peter 3:12

Lord, you are Omnipresent. I am strong and of good courage because Christ lives within me. There is no place I can go that you are not beside me. You will never leave me or forsake me. I trust and cling to your faithfulness. I rest in Christ rooted by faith in him abiding in him as my way, my truth, and my life. When I experience feelings of fear, I stir up your faith living in my spirit and cast in down with the truth of your living Word. Your perfect love casts out all fear. You save me from every evil attack and bring me safely into your heavenly kingdom. You are near to the broken-hearted and save the crushed in spirit. In Christ, I live in abundant peace and reassurance. When I call upon your name, you answer me. As I draw near to you, you draw near to me. Your Spirit renews my strength when the winds of adversity blow. No storm, no obstacle, no threat and no enemy can stand against the provision of your Grace. In Christ, my steps are ordered, sure and clear. I am more than a conqueror in Christ Jesus. I live abundantly in Christ.

# JULY 30

The sunrise marks
the dawning
of a new day
and
Jesus
marks the
dawning of a
new life in
every heart.

For if we have been united with him in a death like his, we will certainly also be united with him in a resurrection like his.

Romans 6:5

Therefore, if anyone is in Christ, the new creation has come: The old has gone, the new is here!

2 Corinthians 5:17

Lord, you are newness of life. By the blood of Jesus, my spirit is alive unto You. I have every spiritual blessing in Heavenly places through Christ. I have resurrection and new life because the blood drops Jesus shed had my name on them. I receive your blessing of salvation and redemption by faith with joy and thanksgiving. As a new creation, I receive all the blessings, authority, identity, power, gifts, enablement's and favor through Christ Jesus. My soul aligns to your finished work of the cross as I renew my mind with your Word and abide in Christ Jesus. I love to spend time with you, worship you and listen for your voice. My relationship with you is greater than any others. All that I am is by your Grace in Christ Jesus. I am free and forgiven in Christ. I am filled with the precious Holy Spirit who lives in me to complete the work of Christ. In Christ, my joy is complete. My lips sing Your praises. My lungs inflate to praise you.

## JULY 31

Since we did not
create the laws
governing the
universe,
we can not
play the
game of life
according
to our own
rules.

In the beginning was the Word, and the Word was with God, and the Word was God. He was with God in the beginning. Through him all things were made; without him nothing was made that has been made. In him was life, and that life was the light of all mankind. The light shines in the darkness, and the darkness has not overcome it.

John 1:1-5

Lord you are Divine Order. You created me in your image to glorify you, to worship you and to rule and reign in submission to you. You are Sovereign. You created Christ as the head of your body of believers. Like the Godhead is Father, Son, and Holy Spirit you created me as triune being–Spirit, soul, and body. My spirit is alive unto you in Christ Jesus. I worship you in spirit and in truth. I am ruled by my spirit yielded to Christ who lives within me. As I spend time with you, feast on your Word, and abide in Christ by faith, you make known to me the hidden treasures of the kingdom. Your spirit through the Holy Spirit teaches, guides and corrects me in your love. I live joyfully submitted to your kingdom order where love abounds, peace abides and righteousness lives. Spending time with you is refreshing like the mist rebounding off a gentle water against my face on a hot summer day. My soul aligns to your goodness. Thank you.

# AUGUST 1

Only
God
can turn
our scars
into stars.

Therefore, if anyone is in Christ, the new creation has come: The old has gone, the new is here! All this is from God, who reconciled us to himself through Christ and gave us the ministry of reconciliation: that God was reconciling the world to himself in Christ, not counting people's sins against them. And he has committed to us the message of reconciliation. We are therefore Christ's ambassadors, as though God were making his appeal through us. We implore you on Christ's behalf: Be reconciled to God.

2 Corinthians 5:17-20

Lord, you are Divine Transformation. I receive your gift of life in Christ Jesus with overflowing joy and wondrous awe. The lashes you took which tore your flesh made a way for my healing to be complete in you. You received the thorn of crowns, a symbol of mockery and shame, and exchanged it for a crown of righteousness which you have placed on my head by faith. You shed your holy blood and offered your sinless life in exchange for my sin tainted nature. Every day from the moment of my salvation in Christ Jesus is a new and wondrous day. I am free from condemnation. I do not bear the weight of shame and guilt. You are my saving God who daily bears the burden of life. In response to your love for me, your forgiveness of me and your sacrifice for me, I desire to honor you, worship you and serve you in my thoughts, words, and deeds. Just as Christ freely forgave my offense, I quickly forgive others of offense. I draw a line in the sand of my mind and purpose that no person or no offense is worth taking my time and attention away from you. I live in peace. My thoughts glory in your goodness. Thank you.

# AUGUST 2

Brokenness
is the fertile
soil in our
hearts
where the
harvest of
healing
originates.

The righteous cry out, and the LORD hears them; he delivers them from all their troubles. The LORD is close to the brokenhearted and saves those who are crushed in spirit. The righteous person may have many troubles, but the LORD delivers him from them all.

Psalm 34:17-20

Lord, you are Divine Healer. Your love for me, your provision for me, your healing for me and your supply for me has already been demonstrated at the cross. I glory in Christ Jesus who is my Lord, my Savior, my Redeemer and my Friend. Thank you for revealing to me that no matter what circumstance arises you are watching over me, protecting me, defending me and empowering me through the Grace of Christ Jesus who supplies me. I open my mouth with shouts of praise in all circumstances because Christ in me is greater than any mountain that stands before me. Knowing by faith that the strength of Christ and his measure of faith in me is sufficient to bring victory over every battle, wraps me in your peace. Resting and abiding in Christ by faith, I lay hold of every good thing that is mine by divine right. I confess your Word over my circumstances and joyfully wait as you unleash your supernatural faithfulness into my natural circumstances. I live in Christ peace, Christ rest, and Christ provision. Thank you.

# AUGUST 3

Grieving is the
gift of healing
we give
to ourselves
as we touch
those needs we
discover
were left unmet
by others.

The LORD confides in those who fear him; he makes his covenant known to them. My eyes are ever on the LORD, for only he will release my feet from the snare. Turn to me and be gracious to me, for I am lonely and afflicted. Relieve the troubles of my heart and free me from my anguish.

Psalm 25:14-17

Lord, you are Ever lasting Comfort. Thank you for supplying your unending supply of love in Christ Jesus. Thank you for releasing his love in my spirit to overflow to those places in my soul where unmet expectations of others left me hurt and bruised. I bring my hurts to you. I humble myself before you. I receive the healing and freedom that Christ desires to give me as I yield to him. I rest and joy in your unending love. I surrender myself in transparency before you. You turn my mourning into joyful dancing. You take away my clothes of despair and clothe me with joy. I sing your praises. You are the lifter of my head. Your love bathes me with hope. I live, breathe and have my being in Christ. Thank you Jesus that you came to heal the broken hearted. You came to set the captive free. Thank you Jesus that when I release you always supply. Thank you for allowing me to cast my cares on Christ Jesus and live free and empowered in him.

# AUGUST 4

We often don't realize
how much
anger and sadness
are living in our
hearts until we make
the choice
to walk through
the events
that birthed
those emotions.

Get rid of all bitterness, rage and anger, brawling and slander, along with every form of malice. Be kind and compassionate to one another, forgiving each other, just as in Christ God forgave you.

Ephesians 4:31-33

Lord, you are Love and Peace. Thank you for your Word that has revealed the truth to me that apart from you I can do nothing. Thank you that as I abide in Christ who lives in me, he brings his nature of love and peace through me. Thank you for teaching me that my life in Christ is all about you and not about me. Thank you for your living Word which guides and corrects me. Search me Holy Spirit and show me where I need to release my demanding self-centeredness that fuels anger. Shine your divine light on those areas of pride that fuel unrest. Enlarge my territory as I partake of the divine nature of Christ Jesus who lives in me. My flesh has been crucified with Christ and it is not I who live, but Christ who lives in me. I bathe in your goodness as I spend time with you. By faith in the supplying Grace of Christ Jesus, I confess what needs confessing, grieve what needs grieving and forgive what needs forgiving. I bear the fruits of love and peace as I abide in Christ and he abides in me. Thank you for transforming grace alive in me.

# AUGUST 5

Grieving brings to
light the brokenness
that needs to be
illuminated and loved,
and the loss
that needs to be
uncovered and
healed.

Who through faith are shielded by God's power until the coming of the salvation that is ready to be revealed in the last time. In all this you greatly rejoice, though now for a little while you may have had to suffer grief in all kinds of trials. These have come so that the proven genuineness of your faith—of greater worth than gold, which perishes even though refined by fire—may result in praise, glory and honor when Jesus Christ is revealed.

1 Peter 1:5-7

Lord, you are Freedom. You created me with the gift of tears to release my pain. Each tear that falls is an exchange of my pain for your healing. I draw near to you and you draw near to me. I offer you praise and thanksgiving for life and provision in Christ Jesus who knows how to make a way where there seems no way. As I come to drink from your unending supply of living water, I yield myself to your love and declare that by the stripes of Jesus I am healed. I trust Christ to release his healing grace already available to me in my spirit, purposing it to flow into every area of my soul that longs for release. I gratefully receive those you are bringing into my life to serve me in your love. I seek your healing truth. I forgive those who have injured me. I yield to you and declare not my will but your will be done. I declare no offense will separate me from your love or hinder your flow of Grace. I look to you in all things and gratefully rest in your supply.

# AUGUST 6

Forgiveness opens our
heart to God's healing Grace,
as we yield
ourselves in obedience
to His supply.

If you, LORD, kept a record of sins, Lord, who could stand? But with you there is forgiveness, so that we can, with reverence, serve you. I wait for the LORD, my whole being waits, and in his word I put my hope.

Psalm 130:3-5

We love because he first loved us. Whoever claims to love God yet hates a brother or sister is a liar. For whoever does not love their brother and sister, whom they have seen, cannot love God, whom they have not seen. And he has given us this command: Anyone who loves God must also love their brother and sister.

1John 4:19-21

Lord, you are Forgiveness. You wrapped your love for me in Christ Jesus whose sacrifice for my sin debt is paid in full. You have removed my sin as far as the east is from the west. I honor his sacrifice by faith in Christ as his Grace in me works through me to forgive others as I have been forgiven by you. As I release the debt I perceive others owe me through offense, I invite Christ to fill that empty place with the fullness of his love. I am a willing vessel molded and shaped by abiding in Christ. In your Grace, the gates of blessing swing wide open for my good. I take off my garments of shame, guilt and judgment. I clothe myself in the Righteousness of Christ and reflect his love. As I renew myself in the Truth of your Word, Christ changes me. I rid myself of all such things as these: anger, rage, malice, slander and filthy language from my lips. I am not quickly provoked in my spirit, for anger resides in the lap of fools. I know a gentle answer turns away wrath. I live in Christ accepted, blessed and loved. Christ is my provision. Thank you.

# AUGUST 7

Whatever keeps us
emotionally tied to the past
will keep us
mentally bound in the present.

The LORD confides in those who fear him; he makes his covenant known to them. My eyes are ever on the LORD, for only he will release my feet from the snare. Turn to me and be gracious to me, for I am lonely and afflicted.

Psalm 25:14-16

Lord, you are Life. I humble myself before you and abundantly receive your transforming Grace by faith in Christ Jesus. The Word of Christ Jesus has shown me that the knowledge of the truth will set me free. Jesus is the Word. Jesus is the Truth. Jesus is the fullness of all wisdom and knowledge. You have deposited the full measure of your abundance in me by faith in Christ Jesus. Desiring to live in the truth and freedom of Christ, I yield myself to the voice of the Holy Spirit to search me, mold me, chasten me and correct me. You have revealed to me that to be changed from the inside out means to yield myself to Christ, to rest in him, to feast on his Word and to drink in his living water of truth. Thank you for showing me that I have no power to change myself. Thank you for revealing that my labor is to rest and yield to Christ who lives within. I lay aside my way and choose the High Way. I live in the abundance of Christ Jesus.

# AUGUST 8

When we look within ourselves honestly,
our awareness of weaknesses, failures,
motives and desires increase,
moving us to the only ONE
who can change our weaknesses into strengths,
transform our failures into triumphs,
mold our motives into Kingdom purposes,
and renew our desires with lasting hope.

Don't fool yourself into thinking that you are a listener when you are anything but, letting the Word go in one ear and out the other. Act on what you hear! Those who hear and don't act are like those who glance in the mirror, walk away, and two minutes later have no idea who they are, what they look like. But whoever catches a glimpse of the revealed counsel of God—the free life!—even out of the corner of his eye, and sticks with it, is no distracted scatterbrain but a man or woman of action. That person will find delight and affirmation in the action.

James 1:22-25 *(The Message)*

Lord, you are Truth. I seek your truth and open myself to your Word of truth by faith in Christ Jesus. I joy in spending time in your Word where I meet you for intimate fellowship. You have told me in every way to acknowledge you and you will make straight my path. You have told me to love others and forgive others as you have loved and forgiven me. You have unveiled your love language and it is submission and obedience. You have told me to choose my words carefully because they have the power of life and death. You have told me to walk by the spirit and I will not fulfill the lustful desires of the flesh. You have told me to resist the devil and he will flee. You have told me I more than a conqueror in Christ Jesus and in him all things are possible. Thank you for revealing your truth and allowing me to see clearly that Christ is the Truth who lives in me supplying your Grace, bringing forth your will and manifesting your life in every area of my life. Apart from Christ, I can do nothing. You are the God of transformation.

# AUGUST 9

Every day we
are a
mirror
that reflects
the
Lord
of our life.

Dear friend, do not imitate what is evil but what is good. Anyone
who does what is good is from God. Anyone who does what is evil
has not seen God.

3 John 1:10-12

Lord, you are an Eternal Mirror. As I look into the mirror of your Word,
you nurture and feed my spirit. My spirit is one with you by faith in Christ
Jesus. As I abide with Christ and yield to his spirit living in me, the wind of
the Holy Spirit scatters Gods reflections whereby faith in Christ I can take
hold of his truth. I submit my soul to the spirit of Christ living within. For
the spirit sounds out all the deep things of God. I quiet my soul to rest in
the peace of Christ Jesus and to hear his voice. As I walk in the spirit, I do
not fulfill the lusts of the flesh. As I abide in Christ, I reflect his goodness,
his love and his grace. My words and my actions reflect the Light of Christ
as I renew my mind to your Word. My failures are transformed in the
abundance of his loving forgiveness. I submit my will to God's will and
look at myself through the reflection of your Word casting down wrong
beliefs and vain imaginations and replacing them with your truth. I am
what I am by the Grace of God in Christ Jesus. My soul is yielded to you.
Thank you.

# AUGUST 10

God will
deliver us
*In*
our trials
though He may
not move us
*Out*
of them.

The Lord will rescue me from every evil attack and will bring me safely to his heavenly kingdom. To him be glory for ever and ever. Amen.

2 Timothy 4:18

Lord, you are Eternal Supply. I am sealed by the Holy Spirit guaranteeing my inheritance unto eternal life. I am greatly blessed, chosen, highly favored and deeply loved. Your hedge of protection is before me, behind me and all around me. You have delivered me out of the dominion of darkness and transferred me into your kingdom of Light. I am redeemed by the blood of Jesus. I stand firm in faith against every evil attack that comes against me. In faith, I confess the name of Jesus and the power of his blood delivers my victory. My weapons are those of limitless power. I gird my waist with your truth. I put on the breastplate of righteousness. I shod my feet with peace. I quench the fiery darts of wickedness with faith. I wear the helmet of salvation. I carry the sword of the Spirit as your Word. I dress myself in garments of praise and thanksgiving for nothing is impossible of Christ Jesus. I live for and glory in you. Thank you.

# AUGUST 11

God's Word richly reveals
the Christ
who can change us,
the Savior
who can free us,
the Friend
who can help us,
the Source
who can empower us,
and
the Light
who can lead us.

Through him all things were made; without him nothing was made that has been made. In him was life, and that life was the light of all mankind. The light shines in the darkness, and the darkness has not overcome it.

John 1:3-5

Don't be deceived, my dear brothers and sisters. Every good and perfect gift is from above, coming down from the Father of the heavenly lights, who does not change like shifting shadows. He chose to give us birth through the word of truth, that we might be a kind of first fruits of all he created.

James 1:16-18

Lord, you are Creator. You spoke all things into being by your spirit. Heaven and earth reflect the brushstrokes of your majestic and unmatched glory. Nothing or no one escape your eyes or your knowledge. Thank you for creating me in your image and bringing resurrection life to my spirit by faith in Christ Jesus who is my Lord and Savior. Thank you for his transforming Grace that is molding me minute by minute and day by day into your predestined masterpiece. Thank you for giving me a faithful and trusted friend in Christ who will never leave me or forsake me. Thank you for your saving Grace which is Christ Jesus who supplies all my needs according to his riches in glory. The fiber of my being radiates with praise and thanksgiving. Halleluiah praises.

# AUGUST 12

Once a
Goliath comes,
we no
longer
remain a
Shepherd boy.

Every God-begotten person conquers the world's ways. The conquering power that brings the world to its knees is our faith. The person who wins out over the world's ways is simply the one who believes Jesus is the Son of God.

1 John 5:4 *(The Message)*

Lord, you are Conquering Power. Thank you Lord, for your faithfulness. Thank you for hearing the prayers of the righteous. I wear the robe of righteousness because your love gifted it to me in the righteousness of Christ Jesus. My strength comes from the hope and expectation I have in Christ. I stand firmly rooted in Christ Jesus. I give myself fully to the work you have called me to do, knowing your perfect will is directing and protecting me. I speak to mountains in the name of Jesus and they move. All things must bow at his holy feet. I conquer the powers of darkness in the name of Jesus. No weapons formed against me shall prosper. No giant in the natural is greater than Christ Jesus who lives in me. As you send rain to water the earth, your Word quenches my thirst. I plant seeds of faith and claim my surplus of prosperity by faith. Christ is my unfailing and unending source and I live in the glory of his riches. I fill my lungs with a breath of gratitude and shout your praises forevermore. I am created for the praise of your glory.

# AUGUST 13

God created us as seed and
He gave us a free will to
choose where, when,
and how we plant.
Sowing is taking
a piece of the
present, and throwing it
to our future.
If we rape our seed of
expectation through unbelief,
God has no authority to
multiply it.

Remember this: Whoever sows sparingly will also reap sparingly, and whoever sows generously will also reap generously. Each of you should give what you have decided in your heart to give, not reluctantly or under compulsion, for God loves a cheerful giver. And God is able to bless you abundantly, so that in all things at all times, having all that you need, you will abound in every good work.

2 Corinthians 9:6-9 *(The Message)*

Lord, you are the Master Gardener. I plant your Word in my spirit watered by faith and wait expectantly for a bountiful harvest. I harvest in faith because you are able to do exceedingly and abundantly more than I could ever ask, dream or image according to the power that is at work in me. Thank you that Christ Jesus is the living resurrection power at work in me. Every seed I plant, rooted in your love brings kingdom fruit. I bear the fruit of Christ as I abide in Him by faith. He brings the Father's will forth to manifest in my natural circumstances. Christ fills my storehouses. My cup overflows through his divine supply of Grace. I gratefully desire to honor the abounding goodness of all God has given me by sowing Christ' love and grace to those I meet. I serve others joyfully as a living testimony to the goodness of the one true God who created me, redeemed me and abundantly provides for me. Your goodness is beyond words.

## AUGUST 14

We
faith out
what
we
faith in

The apostles said to the Lord, "Increase our faith! He replied, "If you have faith as small as a mustard seed, you can say to this mulberry tree, 'Be uprooted and planted in the sea,' and it will obey you.'

Luke 17:5-7

Do not be deceived: God cannot be mocked. A man reaps what he sows. Whoever sows to please their flesh, from the flesh will reap destruction; whoever sows to please the Spirit, from the Spirit will reap eternal life.

Galatians 6:7-8

Lord, you are Unending Supply. You have filled my life with the seed of life by faith in Christ Jesus. You increase my faith as I hear your Word. Christ has given me a glimpse of the revealed counsel of God – the free and abundant life of rest in him. As I water the seed of Christ planted in me, I reap an unlimited harvest of blessing. Every tender shoot of my life takes root through Christ. I sow to the Spirit as your Word nourishes me. I have the authority of Christ to speak his Word over my circumstances by faith and wait expectantly as he manifests the Father's faithfulness. In faith, I believe my rewards are more bountiful than anything I could ever imagine. Everything that is mine in Christ Jesus, I claim with thanksgiving. Nothing interferes with every portion of goodness that you pour into me. Eternal provision flows to me in an uninterrupted supply in Christ Jesus. Halleluiah praises. I glory in your wonder. Thank you.

# AUGUST 15

Faith
looks up for
transformation;
worry looks around
for complication;
sorrow looks back
for speculation;
Jesus is the only
Restoration!

May the God of hope fill you with all joy and peace as you trust in him, so that you may overflow with hope by the power of the Holy Spirit.

Romans 15:13

Do not be anxious about anything, but in everything, by prayer and petition, with thanksgiving, present your requests to God. And the peace of God, which transcends all understanding, will guard your hearts and your minds in Christ Jesus

Philippians 4:6-7 (NIV)

Lord, you are Faithful Provision. My faith is rooted in Christ and my life unfolds by his Grace. I overflow with hope by the power of the Holy Spirit. I overflow with joy and peace because Christ who lives in me is my source of joy and peace. I yield to Christ within gratefully and full of thanksgiving as he completes the will of the Father in me and through me. Christ is the health of my countenance. My eyes are fixed on Christ. My spirit is alive and nourished by Christ. I humbly bring my requests before your throne of Grace where Christ is seated at your right hand making intercession for me. I abide in, rely on and trust in the abundance of Christ who knows my need before my expression of it leaves my tongue. My light affliction which is but for a moment works for me a far more exceeding and eternal weight of glory. Pursuing peace is an opportunity to praise Christ who is the Prince of Peace alive within me. Thank you.

# AUGUST 16

We are a
promise
in the garden
of Heaven,
the harvest
is rich,
and
Jesus
is the Master Gardener.

Your righteousness, God, reaches to the heavens, you who have done great things. Who is like you, God? Though you have made me see troubles, many and bitter, you will restore my life again; from the depths of the earth you will again bring me up.

Psalm 71:18-20

Lord, you are Eternal Hope. I am redeemed by the blood of the Lamb, Jesus. I give thanks for my eternal home of hope and the wonder of living life empowered and provided by you this side of Heaven. I humbly marvel at your love for me. You have determined that I have great worth and immeasurable value. You saw me before the foundations of the world. You saw me crucified and risen with Christ. I glory in your wonder. I celebrate your love in Christ Jesus who is my source and supply in all things. You have created me, redeemed me and supplied me in Christ Jesus. I live by faith and in thanksgiving knowing that you will never leave me or forsake me. Your feed me with your Word. You supply me by Grace. The only labor you have called me to is to trust, rest and abide in your Word. You have even given me a measure of faith to take hold of your goodness. Thank you for growing my faith as I abide in you. My response to your overwhelming love is to fall to my knees and shout, "Praise you, thank you, unending halleluiah's."

# AUGUST 17

Godly change requires
we put away pretension
and denial and invite Christ
into our fears, our hurts,
our resentments
and our self-protective motives
where he can heal them
and we emerge changed.

But whenever anyone turns to the Lord, the veil is taken away. Now the Lord is the Spirit, and where the Spirit of the Lord is, there is freedom. And we all, who with unveiled faces contemplate the Lord's glory, are being transformed into his image with ever-increasing glory, which comes from the Lord, who is the Spirit.

2 Corinthians 3:16-18

Lord, You are freedom and life. As I yielded to Christ to save me, I yield to him to supply me. My life in Christ is life in the spirit. I yield my will to you and allow Christ to be my divine wisdom. I am spirit led because I am one in the spirit of Christ. I have freedom because Christ has removed the veil that once separated me from you. I live no longer separated from you by sin, but alive to you in Christ Jesus. I no longer live with the sin consciousness of shame and guilt. My mind is fixed on Christ who is life and peace. I joy in renewing my mind with the truth of your Word which feeds my spirit. I take my thoughts captive to the obedience of Christ Jesus. I cast down those thoughts that do not line up with the truth of your Word and replace them with your truth. I behold the glory of Christ and allow the Holy Spirit to search me, teach me and correct me. I boldly confess what needs confessing, grieve my hurts and allow Christ to bring his healing and transformation in and through me. Thank you for transforming truth in Jesus.

# AUGUST 18

When we sow
in anger
there is strife.
When we sow
in pride
there is destruction.
When we sow
in love
there is life.

The lives of good people are brightly lit streets; the lives of the wicked are dark alleys. Arrogant know-it-alls stir up discord, but wise men and women listen to each other's counsel.

Proverbs 13:9-11 *(The Message)*

The mouth of the righteous is a fountain of life, but the mouth of the wicked conceals violence. Hatred stirs up conflict, but love covers over all wrongs. Wisdom is found on the lips of the discerning, but a rod is for the back of one who has no sense. The wise store up knowledge, but the mouth of a fool invites ruin.

Proverbs:10:11-14

Lord, you are Grace Revelation. Your Word teaches me that I have authority in Christ in order to bring your will to earth and not to bring my will to pass. You have given me the privilege of loving and honoring others as your divine creation worthy of honor and worth. I desire to treasure and approve what you treasure and approve. When I accepted Christ Jesus as your offering of complete and total love for my sins, I relinquished my self-rights. As I abide in, yield to and lean on Christ, He releases the manifold grace of God to meet my needs. You have shown me that no good thing is of the flesh. Your grace has broken the power of sin over me once and for all. I reckon myself dead to sin and alive unto God in Christ Jesus. My walk is one of life in the spirit governed by love. I offer peace and forgiveness to others as Christ offered these gifts to me. I look at others through the eyes of Christ as valued and worthy of honor. As you do not condemn me, I do not condemn others. I joy in my relationship with Christ. Thank you.

# AUGUST 19

The same God
that created life in you
can be trusted
with all your details.

Again, truly I tell you that if two of you on earth agree about anything they ask for, it will be done for them by my Father in heaven. For where two or three gather in my name, there am I with them.

Matthew 18:19-20

Lord, you are Faithful. As I draw near to you, you draw near to me. You fulfill the desires of my heart as I abide in Christ Jesus. You are my hope, my life and my God. As I seek, I find and as I knock, you open the door. You hear and answer the prayers of the Righteous. I am righteous in Christ. I join with other believers casting my cares on Christ Jesus and speaking your Word over my life. I delight in spending time with you and thank you for inviting me to come boldly before your throne of grace to find help in my time of need. In my life giving relationship with Christ, you provide your grace for my need in the moment. Your Grace flows in my spirit in a steady unbroken, ever increasing stream of divine wonder, supply and miracles. I plant my seed of faith the size of a mustard seed and watch expectantly as you bring an abundant harvest. Rest, order and peace flow to me through your Grace. Obstacles diminish from my pathway as I rest in Christ. He guides and provides. I trust in, rely on and abide in Christ. My lips sing your praises.

# AUGUST 20

We soar
to new
heights
when
we rest on
the wings of love.

Your righteousness is like the highest mountains, your justice like the great deep. You, LORD, preserve both people and animals. How priceless is your unfailing love, O God! People take refuge in the shadow of your wings. They feast on the abundance of your house; you give them drink from your river of delights. For with you is the fountain of life; in your light we see light. Continue your love to those who know you, your righteousness to the upright in heart.

Psalm 36:6-10

Lord, You are Righteousness. Through your great love for me, Christ has imparted his righteousness to me. The gift of right standing with you is something that no action of mine could ever bring to pass. I receive your gift with overwhelming joy and respond in praise and thanksgiving. I soar because you are the wings of love that carry me. Your manifold grace of Christ Jesus supplies life to my spirit and abundance to my soul. As I hope in you and rest in Christ, my strength is renewed. I take wings as eagles and soar to the heights of all you have called me to do. I run the race you have called me to run without being weary. Every step I take in the natural is anointed, directed and empowered by Christ Jesus who lives in me. Every step I take in faith is destined for my good and your glory. Thank you for your priceless unfailing love. Thank you for Christ Jesus who is the fountain of life. Halleluiah and unending praises.

# AUGUST 21

An offense is not
nearly as powerful
as the underlying need it
uncovers within
ourselves.

If I speak with human eloquence and angelic ecstasy but don't love, I'm nothing but the creaking of a rusty gate. If I speak God's Word with power, revealing all his mysteries and making everything plain as day, and if I have faith that says to a mountain, "Jump," and it jumps, but I don't love, I'm nothing. If I give everything I own to the poor and even go to the stake to be burned as a martyr, but I don't love, I've gotten nowhere. So, no matter what I say, what I believe, and what I do, I'm bankrupt without love. Love never gives up. Love cares more for others than for self. Love doesn't want what it doesn't have. Love doesn't strut, Doesn't have a swelled head, Doesn't force itself on others, Isn't always "me first," Doesn't fly off the handle, Doesn't keep score of the sins of others, Doesn't revel when others grovel, Takes pleasure in the flowering of truth, Puts up with anything, Trusts God always, Always looks for the best, Never looks back, But keeps going to the end. Love never dies. Inspired speech will be over some day; praying in tongues will end; understanding will reach its limit. We know only a portion of the truth, and what we say about God is always incomplete. But when the Complete arrives, our incompletes will be canceled.

1 Corinthians 13:1-10 *(The Message)*

Lord, you are Perfect Love. My flesh battles to be "me first" and yet you have taught me in your Word that my life is not about me, it's about you. As I am a new creation in Christ Jesus by faith, I live by the spirit and do not gratify the desires of the flesh. My spirit rules and reigns in submission to Christ who is the head. In Christ, I am at peace with my past, joyous in my present and secure about my future. I live secure in the knowledge that my value and my worth are not dependant upon who I am or what I think, say, or do. It is based on who I am in Christ Jesus and what He has done for me. I look to Christ living within me to supply all my needs for love and not to other people. I seek truth as I fill my spirit with your truth. I desire intimate fellowship with Christ who is my life and supply. I joyfully and humbly choose you to be first place in every area of my life. I abide in Christ and he abides in me. I celebrate your wonder with thanksgiving.

# AUGUST 22

Truth apart
from
Grace
is judgment.

Don't pick on people, jump on their failures, criticize their faults—
unless, of course, you want the same treatment. That critical spirit
has a way of boomeranging. It's easy to see a smudge on your
neighbor's face and be oblivious to the ugly sneer on your own. Do
you have the nerve to say, 'Let me wash your face for you,' when
your own face is distorted by contempt? It's this whole traveling
road-show mentality all over again, playing a holier-than-thou part
instead of just living your part. Wipe that ugly sneer off your own
face, and you might be fit to offer a washcloth to your neighbor.

Matthew 7:1-6 *(The Message)*

Lord, you are Grace. Grace is the person of Christ Jesus and his provision
to meet my every need. I live in the bounty of your Grace as I spend time
with you, feast on your Word, fellowship with you in prayer and praise and
worship. My hearts desire is to acknowledge you above all else. Each seed I
plant in your loving-kindness is becoming a blessing and a harvest in your
Kingdom. I am filled with your spirit, filled with wisdom, and supplied in
your Grace by faith in Christ Jesus who lives within. I guard my mouth and
renew my mind to the truth of your Word. I am slow to anger as I lay my
pride aside. I acknowledge my self-demanding nature has been crucified
with Christ and no longer has a place in my life. I live as a new creature
with a new nature. The spirit of Christ in me is transforming my wrong
ways of thinking, old habits, strongholds and wrong actions as his love
flows through me. I rejoice in your unlimited mercy. I live in your steadfast
Love. I am transformed in your Grace. Thank you. Glory Halleluiah.

# AUGUST 23

The Spirit
of God
can search
us best
when our
soul is still.

For the Lord gives wisdom, and from his mouth come knowledge and understanding.... Then you will understand what is right and just and fair—every good path. For wisdom will enter your heart, and knowledge will be pleasant to your soul. Discretion will protect you, and understanding will guard you.

Proverbs 2:6,9-11

Lord, you are Wisdom. I live, breathe and have my being in you. I renew my mind as I feast in your Word. You lay up sound wisdom for the righteous. By faith, I wait upon your perfect timing as you work all things together for my good and your glory. The darkness that once lived in me is no more. As I abide in Christ I live in the light as he is in the Light. I am an open vessel for your divine wisdom. Every day you bring new revelations from your Word. No power of darkness, circumstance, words of discouragement, events seen, or not seen in the natural or actions by another can hinder my life of joy in Christ Jesus. Your plan for me is permanent and rooted in faith. I live in joyous victory. My lips mutter your continual praises. You guide me continually, and satisfy my soul with life. I am like a watered garden, and like a spring of water, whose waters do not fail. My cup is full and overflowing. My joy is complete in Christ Jesus.

# AUGUST 24

Our true
character
is revealed
by what
we do behind
closed doors.

This is the verdict: Light has come into the world, but people loved darkness instead of light because their deeds were evil. Everyone who does evil hates the light, and will not come into the light for fear that their deeds will be exposed. But whoever lives by the truth comes into the light, so that it may be seen plainly that what they have done has been done in the sight of God.

John 3:19-21

Lord, you are Pure Light. In you there is no darkness. All that you created came forth from your manifested glory. Your glory is the light, the life, the divine energy that sets all of your creation in motion. My spirit is your candle searching all my inward parts. In your love for me, you have shared your light of glory with me by creating me in your image. Thank you for an open invitation signed by the blood of Jesus to come before your throne of grace throughout every day, share the desires of my heart, praise you, worship you and feast on your Word. Your Word nourishes my spirit which reflects your glory. Your Word is a mirror that reflects the light of your truth. Thank you that your Word is powerful and penetrates my spirit, soul, and body. Your Word reveals to me that I am a child of the light. I live in the light as you are in the light. Your Light leads me into deeper understanding. I take hold of what is valuable to the kingdom and spring forth toward your Light. I hold fast to faith and have a clear conscience. Any old way of darkness in me is freely exposed to your light. Your Word lights my path. Your Word illuminates you.

# AUGUST 25

When we genuinely
confront our fears,
we humble
ourselves before
God's throne
of grace,
because
our fears
often call
for the kneeling
position.

And so we know and rely on the love God has for us. God is love. Whoever lives in love lives in God, and God in them. This is how love is made complete among us so that we will have confidence on the day of judgment: In this world we are like Jesus. There is no fear in love. But perfect love drives out fear, because fear has to do with punishment. The one who fears is not made perfect in love.

1 John 4:16-18

Lord, you are Unfailing Love. I live forever joined to you by faith in Christ Jesus. Your love for me and Jesus' obedience to your will has already demonstrated that while I was yet stained with a sin nature through my inheritance of the first man's sin and living in the grip of its death, Christ Jesus shed his precious and holy blood for me freeing me from the power of sin and the penalty of death. Christ has lifted me to my greatest standing in him. My spirit full of thanksgiving and gratitude finds no other way to say, "Thank you" than to fall to my knees in praise and thanksgiving. Praise you Jesus for demonstrating the perfected love of the Father. I no longer live in fear of abandonment, condemnation, rejection or fear because your perfect love casts out all fear. I abide in Christ who loves me with a pure, unbiased and unconditional love. My receiving the full measure of your goodness has nothing to do with me and everything to do with your precious son, Christ Jesus. My hearts writes a song of unending gratitude. Thank you.

# AUGUST 26

The degree to which
we embrace God's right
to transform our character
into His Son's likeness
determines
the depth of
spiritual awakening
He unfolds
to us.

We do, however, speak a message of wisdom among the mature, but not the wisdom of this age or of the rulers of this age, who are coming to nothing. No, we declare God's wisdom, a mystery that has been hidden and that God destined for our glory before time began. None of the rulers of this age understood it, for if they had, they would not have crucified the Lord of glory. However, as it is written: 'What no eye has seen, what no ear has heard, and what no human mind has conceived' the things God has prepared for those who love him— these are the things God has revealed to us by his Spirit. The Spirit searches all things, even the deep things of God.

1 Corinthians 2:6-10

Lord, you are Sovereign. As master creator, you have the right to reign and rule over the created. You created me in your image to live by the spirit and to rule by the spirit in submission to you. Where the spirit is there is freedom. My spirit once separated from you by sin is now alive to you in Christ. My spirit holds the fullness of the God-head, Father, Son, and Holy Spirit which resides in the temple of my body. I fellowship with you in my spirit. I worship you in spirit and in truth. I hear your voice in my spirit. My carnal mind is unable to grasp how wide and how deep your love is for me for it's logical reasoning and intellect has no way to wrap itself around your greatness. Every day I enter your gates with thanksgiving and your courts with praise. I shout continual "Halleluiah's because you have opened my spiritual eyes to see that nothing or no one compares to you. I joyfully and gratefully humble myself before you and drink in the fullness of every blood bought blessing of Christ Jesus. Thank you awesome God.

# AUGUST 27

Releasing
the power
of the
Holy
Spirit
requires
surrendering
to Jesus.

The Spirit gives life; the flesh counts for nothing. The words I have spoken to you—they are full of the Spirit and life.

John 6:63

Lord, you are Spirit. I am one with you in spirit by faith in Christ Jesus. Thank you for the cleansing blood of Jesus. I live yielded to Christ Jesus as he transforms me into his likeness. I recognize the voice of Christ speaking to me in my spirit by the Holy Spirit. I live blessed, supplied, protected and defended throughout the day as I abide in Christ Jesus. I joy in spending time with you, surrendering myself to you, praising your goodness and living by faith in Christ Jesus. I desire and long to empty myself to make more room for your glory, your wisdom and your provision. All that I am and all that I do is an overflow of Christ Jesus living within. Thank you for the living person of the Holy Spirit that leads and guides me into all wisdom. Thank you for the revelation the Holy Spirit pours out concerning the knowledge of the truth of your Word, the splendor of your nature and the assurance that you are always and forever faithful. I live gratefully surrendered to be examined, molded and shaped. Chisel me all over. Thank you.

# AUGUST 28

Power
always
comes from
plugging
into the
source.

Therefore let all the faithful pray to you while you may be found; surely the rising of the mighty waters will not reach them. You are my hiding place; you will protect me from trouble and surround me with songs of deliverance.

Psalm 32:6-7

Lord, you are Divine Power. The sound of your voice brought forth the manifestation of heaven and earth. You are the source of all divine goodness. Christ Jesus reflected all the goodness of your nature as he obediently carried out your will. I gratefully plug into Christ by faith who is the power source of life. His grace supplies all my needs according to his riches in glory. In Christ, I live in the fullness of every blessing purchased by his blood. No power of darkness, no circumstance, no person and no weakness in my own flesh can short-circuit your love for me or your life in me. Even when I walk in the midst of trouble, you guard me. You rescue me from every evil attack. I have victory over the rulers, authorities and darkness, because the name of Jesus is head of my life and his blood covers me. Every day I celebrate with shouts of praise that your Grace was the manna you sent to your chosen people to meet their needs at their time of need and you give me your same faithful supply. Thank you. You are beyond description.

# AUGUST 29

Once we accept
God's salvation,
His constant
desire is our freedom.
He did not create us to
try and do, but to trust and be.

Christ has set us free to live a free life. So take your stand! Never again let anyone put a harness of slavery on you.

Galatians 5:1 *(The Message)*

So if the Son sets you free, you will be free indeed.

John 8:36

Lord, you are Freedom. You have gifted me with life and the freedom to live it by faith in Christ Jesus. I live in thanksgiving delivered from the power of sin and my sin debt canceled by faith through your Grace. Thank you for teaching me that my life is not about my self-efforts of trying and doing, it's about trusting and abiding in the rest of Christ Jesus who lives in me. The prison bars once holding my spirit captive to death and my soul in bondage to the law have been sprung open by Jesus. Jesus has satisfied your requirements under the law. He exchanged my ungodliness and my unrighteousness for his holiness and his righteousness and imparted them to be through your love for me. I live every moment empowered in Christ living through me. I joy in living in, relating to and growing in Christ Jesus. Nothing or no one compares to my relationship with him. I am free to be, free to live and free to be all you have created me to be as I rest in, rely on, abide in and trust in Christ who is freedom. Christ Jesus is unspeakable joy.

# AUGUST 30

We
surrendered
our rights
to ourselves
when we
accepted
Jesus as Lord
of our
lives.

Then he told them what they could expect for themselves: Anyone who intends to come with me has to let me lead. You're not in the driver's seat—I am. Don't run from suffering; embrace it. Follow me and I'll show you how. Self-help is no help at all. Self-sacrifice is the way, my way, to finding yourself, your true self. What good would it do to get everything you want and lose you, the real you? If any of you is embarrassed with me and the way I'm leading you, know that the Son of Man will be far more embarrassed with you when he arrives in all his splendor in company with the Father and the holy angels. This isn't, you realize, pie in the sky by and by. Some who have taken their stand right here are going to see it happen, see with their own eyes the kingdom of God.

Luke 9:23-27 *(The Message)*

Lord, you are Provision– my beginning and my end. You are my shield and my deliverance. In Christ, I am righteous and free. Nothing can come against the Divine plan you have designed for my life. The desire of my heart is to glorify you. The moment I accepted Christ as Lord and Savior, I was reborn with your nature. My spirit is alive unto you. You have filled me with the fullness of the God-head. The Father has planned and predestined all things created. All plans of the Father have come to complete manifestation in you, Jesus. I have the Holy Spirit who is the person of the God-head that teaches, corrects and guides me into all truth. I surrender all my rights to myself. I empty myself so you can fill me up. I receive your Spirit as a witness to life and truth. I can do all things through Christ who gives me strength. You are my God and I am your child. Shouts of praise are forever flowing from my lips. My life is a continuous adventure of wondrous expectation of your unforced rhythms of Grace. My being explodes with thanks.

# AUGUST 31

When we yield our
desires to God,
we release God
to work
in His way
and in
His timing
for His glory,
for other's benefit
and for our blessing.

God can pour on the blessings in astonishing ways so that you're ready for anything and everything, more than just ready to do what needs to be done. As one psalmist puts it, He throws caution to the winds, giving to the needy in reckless abandon. His right-living, right-giving ways never runs out, never wears out. This most generous God who gives seed to the farmer that becomes bread for your meals is more than extravagant with you. He gives you something you can then give away, which grows into full-formed lives, robust in God, wealthy in every way, so that you can be generous in every way, producing with us great praise to God.

2 Corinthians 9:8-11 *(The Message)*

Lord you are Blessing. Joy greets me at the door of my spirit every morning as I thank you in celebration for your gift of life in Christ Jesus. All of creation reflects the wonder of your majestic glory. Your heart which frames every blessing you display boasts of your beauty, your goodness, your unending love, your unmerited forgiveness and your immeasurable blessings. The center piece of every brushstroke of your hand highlights Christ who is abundant and everlasting life. Words of thanks and gratitude pour from my lips as I humbly receive your bounty of blessing in Christ Jesus. Unexpected blessings flow to me in unexpected ways. I humbly weep in knowing I am your chosen, beloved and accepted child. My lips sing your praises. My heart writes a continuous symphony of harmonious melody as I experience the aliveness of Christ in my spirit. My boast is in Christ Jesus. Thank you. Forever praises.

# SEPTEMBER 1

Often we assume things
without checking the facts,
and then blame others
for the results.

How can you say to your brother, 'Brother, let me take the speck out of your eye,' when you yourself fail to see the plank in your own eye? You hypocrite, first take the plank out of your eye, and then you will see clearly to remove the speck from your brother's eye.

Luke 6:42

You, therefore, have no excuse, you who pass judgment on someone else, for at whatever point you judge another, you are condemning yourself, because you who pass judgment do the same things.

Romans 2:1

The discerning heart seeks knowledge, but the mouth of a fool feeds on folly.

Proverbs 15:13-14

Lord, your Word is an Eternal Mirror. As I look to you, I seek to see others and myself as you see me. The eyes of my heart are open to see you through my surrendered will. Your Word reflects your truth that you have not given me the authority to judge others, but to love them through Christ who lives in me. Only you can see another's heart and only you know their thoughts. Regardless of others words or actions toward me, I choose to value them as you value me and love them as you love me. I trust in the supply of your love Christ imparted to me. I ask you to show me where, when and how I can be a vessel of your love poured out to encourage and serve others. The desire of my heart is to be a mirror that reflects you, the Lord of my life. Apart from being yielded to and abiding in Christ, I do not have the capacity to love as you love. I humbly yield to Christ and he brings forth his nature in my spirit to outward manifestations in my soul. I offer my life to you as a living sacrifice to glorify you, honor you, and love others through Christ.

# SEPTEMBER 2

When we invade
someone else's
territory by taking
responsibility
for them,
we invade their
boundaries
and ultimately
trespass
on their property.

I ask—ask the God of our Master, Jesus Christ, the God of glory—
to make you intelligent and discerning in knowing him personally,
your eyes focused and clear, so that you can see exactly what it is he
is calling you to do, grasp the immensity of this glorious way of life
he has for his followers, oh, the utter extravagance of his work in us
who trust him—endless energy, boundless strength!

Ephesians 1:17-19 *(The Message)*

Lord, you are Wisdom. You know me inside and out. In Christ, I am
greatly blessed, highly favored and deeply loved. Everyone I meet is greatly
blessed, highly favored and deeply loved. I speak favor over others and
release your endless blessings. I see all things and all people through the
eyes of Love and Mercy because Love and Mercy live in me in Christ
Jesus. I honor others with love because like me they have been created in
your image worthy of honor and respect. Your Word has shown me that I
am accountable to you for my thoughts, my words and my actions. Even
as I know you have called me to a ministry of reconciliation, I am a seed
planter by your Grace. I cannot fix or change another. You have given
each of mankind the choice of free will. As I exercise mine by yielding to
and abiding in Christ, I use my words and actions as an encouragement
to others to do the same. I abide in Christ and bear the fruit of Christ-
likeness. I live with endless energy and boundless strength because I live
in Christ. Thank you.

# SEPTEMBER 3

Love always
releases the best
and brings
out the
most.

Watch the way you talk. Let nothing foul or dirty come out of your mouth. Say only what helps, each word a gift.

Ephesians 4:29 *(The Message)*

Watch what God does, and then you do it, like children who learn proper behavior from their parents. Mostly what God does is love you. Keep company with him and learn a life of love. Observe how Christ loved us. His love was not cautious but extravagant. He didn't love in order to get something from us but to give everything of himself to us. Love like that.

Ephesians 5:1-2 *(The Message)*

Dear friends, let us love one another, for love comes from God. Everyone who loves has been born of God and knows God. Whoever does not love does not know God, because God is love. This is how God showed his love among us: He sent his one and only Son into the world that we might live through him. This is love: not that we loved God, but that he loved us and sent his Son as an atoning sacrifice for our sins.

1 John 4:7-10

Lord, you are Immeasurable Love. As I yield to and rest in Christ, I delight and walk in his perfected love. I see others as wonders of your handiwork. I live in the wonder of your extravagant love. I choose in every circumstance to be the love to others that you are to me. Your love flows through me uninterruptedly as I fix my eyes on Christ. Apart from being grafted into Christ by faith, I have no self-made ability to love. I feast on your Word proclaiming its truth that neither death, nor life, nor angels, nor rulers, nor things present, nor things to come, nor powers, nor height, nor depth, nor anything else in all creation, will be able to separate me from the love of

God in Christ Jesus. Thank you for saving me, loving me and supplying me. I live grateful and joyful that Christ who is love lives in me. Thank you for extravagant love in Christ Jesus.

## SEPTEMBER 4

When we reach
out to Jesus,
he will take hold and
never let us down.

Jesus Christ is the same yesterday and today and forever.

Hebrews 13:6-8

And we know that in all things God works for the good of those who love him, who have been called according to his purpose. For those God foreknew he also predestined to be conformed to the image of his Son, that he might be the firstborn among many brothers and sisters. And those he predestined, he also called; those he called, he also justified; those he justified, he also glorified.

Romans 8:28-30

Lord, you are Steadfast. Your Word and your Covenant promises are everlasting. Throughout each day, I marvel at your unending love for me. Your love wrapped flesh around the Word so the Word could wrap love around me. I am overwhelmed by your goodness. Your Grace in the person of Christ Jesus, the Way, the Truth, and the Life, meets my need for love, worth and value. I look to, abide in and rely on Jesus to walk with me through the moments of every day. I praise your goodness when my eyes open in the morning. I feast with thanksgiving on your Word before the sun rises. I ponder your wonder as my thoughts rest on you. I share my thoughts and the desires of my heart knowing you hear them. Thank you for perfecting that which concerns me. I know by faith in Christ Jesus I have every blood bought blessing. I glory in confessing your Word which is your life and your provision in and through me. As I rest by faith in Christ, you bring forth everything that satisfies the righteous desires of my heart. Thank you.

# SEPTEMBER 5

In God's
economy,
loss
is always
gain.

But whatever were gains to me, I now consider loss for the sake of Christ. What is more, I consider everything a loss because of the surpassing worth of knowing Christ Jesus my Lord, for whose sake I have lost all things. I consider them garbage, that I may gain Christ.

Philippians 3:7-8

Lord, you are Divine Supply. I gratefully receive the exchange Christ Jesus made at the cross. My heart spills over in thanksgiving for your endless supply of Grace in Christ Jesus. The depth of your love for me that held Christ Jesus to the cross is immeasurable. In Christ I am redeemed, forgiven and a new creation. I live rooted in Christ and wondrously supplied. Christ is the true and living power within me. All things begin and end with Jesus. I am what I am by the grace of Christ Jesus. I no longer live my way, but yield to the High Way. In Christ Jesus, I am fully equipped to be who you created me to be and do everything you have called me to do. I lose myself in you. You are the Way, the Truth, and the Life. You are worthy to be praised. My cup overflows with joy. Your loving Grace supplies me in Christ sufficiency. I am confident Christ will complete every good work you started in me. My lips sing your praises. Thank you.

# SEPTEMBER 6

God
is our
witness to every
hurt that comes and
every tear that falls.

You have searched me, LORD, and you know me. You know when I sit and when I rise; you perceive my thoughts from afar. You discern my going out and my lying down; you are familiar with all my ways. Before a word is on my tongue you, LORD, know it completely. You hem me in behind and before, and you lay your hand upon me. Such knowledge is too wonderful for me, too lofty for me to attain. Where can I go from your Spirit? Where can I flee from your presence? If I go up to the heavens, you are there; if I make my bed in the depths, you are there. If I rise on the wings of the dawn, if I settle on the far side of the sea, even there your hand will guide me, your right hand will hold me fast. If I say, "Surely the darkness will hide me and the light become night around me," even the darkness will not be dark to you; the night will shine like the day, for darkness is as light to you. For you created my inmost being; you knit me together in my mother's womb. I praise you because I am fearfully and wonderfully made; your works are wonderful, I know that full well. My frame was not hidden from you when I was made in the secret place, when I was woven together in the depths of the earth. Your eyes saw my unformed body; all the days ordained for me were written in your book before one of them came to be. How precious to me are your thoughts, God! How vast is the sum of them! Were I to count them, they would outnumber the grains of sand— when I awake, I am still with you.

Psalm 139:1-18

Lord, You formed every part of my being. I live and move as one spirit with you in Christ Jesus. I submit all of my being to you. I seek you with all that I am. My being rests in the perfection of Christ Jesus as his light streams illumination and his love fills every part of my very being. You keep my heart in perfect peace as I rest in Christ. Circumstances pale in comparison to your divine Goodness. I behold your glory. I praise the works of your hands. My lips sing your praises. My soul magnifies your name. My spirit is alive unto you in Christ Jesus. I humbly and joyfully wear the garments of praise. Be magnified oh great and wondrous God. Thank you.

# SEPTEMBER 7

God's chastisement
seeks to break
our spirit
of rebellion
and
bring us
to a more intimate
relationship
with Him.

No discipline seems pleasant at the time, but painful. Later on, however, it produces a harvest of righteousness and peace for those who have been trained by it.

Hebrews 12:11

My son, do not despise the LORD's discipline, and do not resent his rebuke, because the LORD disciplines those he loves, as a father the son he delights in.

Proverbs 3:11-12

Lord, you are Divine Wisdom. Your Divine Wisdom flows through me to keep me on course with your will. With every beat of my heart, I invite you to search me. I fix my mind on you. I yield to the inner working of the Holy Spirit. I joy in spending time in your Word. I feast on your Word with openness, expectation and submission knowing that your love desires to bless me. I live as one with the spirit of Christ who lives in me. I love spending time in your presence and invite you to wash me, correct me, and grow me into Christ-likeness as only the Holy Spirit can unveil. Your Word is your blueprint for my life. It's your God ordained instruction manual which watches over me with your Covenant promises and comes to life in me through Christ Jesus. I confess your Word as my weapon and my shield. When adversity comes, I respond from your promises. I abide in Christ who is the living and revealed Word forevermore. Thank you.

# SEPTEMBER 8

When God's Word
penetrates to the thoughts
and intents of our heart,
we begin to see more clearly
the ways we violate love.

Do not lie to each other, since you have taken off your old self with its practices and have put on the new self, which is being renewed in knowledge in the image of its Creator. Here there is no Gentile or Jew, circumcised or uncircumcised, barbarian, Scythian, slave or free, but Christ is all, and is in all. Therefore, as God's chosen people, holy and dearly loved, clothe yourselves with compassion, kindness, humility, gentleness and patience. Bear with each other and forgive one another if any of you has a grievance against someone. Forgive as the Lord forgave you. And over all these virtues put on love, which binds them all together in perfect unity. Let the peace of Christ rule in your hearts, since as members of one body you were called to peace. And be thankful.

Colossians 3:9-15

Lord, you are Love. Thank you for teaching me that there is no good thing in my flesh. My flesh operates out of the self-trinity of me, myself and I. My flesh says, "I want it" and my pride says, "I deserve it." In Christ, I live as a new creation with a new nature. My spirit alive unto God in Christ rules over my spirit. I quiet my soul as I rest in Christ and renew my mind to your Word. Thank you Lord, that your Word has everything that pertains to life and godliness defining me and leading me. As I walk in the spirit, I do not fulfill the lusts of the flesh. With my thoughts fixed on Christ and my spirit abiding in him, my works and my actions flow out of his abundance. Thank you Jesus that in you I can press toward the mark of my high calling. Thank you that your presence in my spirit and your supplying Grace enables me to clothe myself with compassion, kindness, humility, gentleness and patience. Thank you for your love which binds all these together. I live in peace as I reflect Christ love to others. Halleluiah praises.

## SEPTEMBER 9

God's love
sees all
His
children
as worthy
of preferential treatment.

Christ arrives right on time to make this happen. He didn't, and doesn't, wait for us to get ready. He presented himself for this sacrificial death when we were far too weak and rebellious to do anything to get ourselves ready. And even if we hadn't been so weak, we wouldn't have known what to do anyway. We can understand someone dying for a person worth dying for, and we can understand how someone good and noble could inspire us to selfless sacrifice. But God put his love on the line for us by offering his Son in sacrificial death while we were of no use whatever to him.

Romans 5:6-8 *(The Message)*

Lord, you are Divine and Pure Love. I marvel at your unending goodness. All that you are and all that you supply springs forth from your love. My joy overflows as I wrap my thoughts around your truth of knowing I am your divinely chosen, completed loved and totally accepted child. Christ has made a way where I could make no way. I live free in Christ, reconciled to you, and wrapped in your Covenant promises. When you look at me you see me in Christ who is holy, blameless and righteous. By faith in the finished works of Christ, I am no longer separated from you by sin. My faith is stirred and my spirit brimming over with exhilaration as I proclaim your truth. I am your workmanship created in Christ Jesus for good works which God prepared beforehand. I am a joint heir with Christ Jesus. I am the head and not the tail. I am above and not beneath. I am blessed in my going out and my coming in. I am born of incorruptible seed. I have a future, a hope and an expected outcome. Never ending thanks Jesus. Unending praises.

# SEPTEMBER 10

God's love
is impartial
with
exception.
No one is
ever left out
who
chooses to
be included.

So that Christ may dwell in your hearts through faith. And I pray that you, being rooted and established in love, may have power, together with all the Lord's holy people, to grasp how wide and long and high and deep is the love of Christ, and to know this love that surpasses knowledge—that you may be filled to the measure of all the fullness of God.

Ephesians 3:17-19

Lord, you are True Love. The gift of life you have given me in Christ Jesus shouts your love for me in the cross. In your vast and immeasurable love, I am filled with your measure of your fullness in Christ as your supplying Grace and steadfast love undergirds my entire being. Thank you that in your love, your divine plan for my life is complete in Christ. Your love holds the abundance by faith in Christ of your provision, your protection, your favor, your wisdom, your righteousness, your joy and your peace. I receive your wondrous gift of life by faith in Christ with a humble heart overflowing with resounding thanksgiving. As I abide in Christ and he in me, I increase, excel and enlarge in my love of you and others. Your love ignites your living Grace within me. I celebrate your love knowing that nothing or no one compares to it. Every blood bought blessing that is mine in Christ Jesus comes through your love. Your gift of love brings me to my knees where I raise my hands and shout your praises. Thank you.

# SEPTEMBER 11

God
wants us to
empty ourselves
so He
can manifest
more of Himself
through us.

This is what the LORD says: "Let not the wise boast of their wisdom or the strong boast of their strength or the rich boast of their riches, but let the one who boasts boast about this: that they have the understanding to know me, that I am the LORD, who exercises kindness, justice, and righteousness on earth, for in these I delight," declares the LORD."

Jeremiah 9:23-24

Lord, you are Life Provision. In Christ, I am a chosen vessel fashioned by your hands and created to glorify you and serve others. You created me as a minister of reconciliation. As I fix my eyes on Christ and abide in his supplying grace, I ask you to enlarge my territory. You are faithful to make my path clear. I desire for your will to be done and not mine. As I spend time in your Word, you fill up my spirit with truth and revelation. I quiet my soul and wait patiently to hear your voice as I praise you and offering thanksgiving to you. I sit before you surrendered and hungry to hear every Word you speak to me. I hunger for your wisdom for there is none that compares to yours. I treasure our time together focused and purposed as a vessel waiting to be filled up so it can be poured out. I thank you that the work that you have created me for and called me to is complete in Christ. I abide in, trust in and rely on Christ to supply his grace to bring your will to complete manifestation in the natural. My lips sing your praises. Thank you.

# SEPTEMBER 12

When we
refuse to take
responsibility
for where we are,
we'll never
arrive at the place
God
wants to take us.

These are all warning markers—danger!—in our history books, written down so that we don't repeat their mistakes. Our positions in the story are parallel—they at the beginning, we at the end—and we are just as capable of messing it up as they were. Don't be so naive and self-confident. You're not exempt. You could fall flat on your face as easily as anyone else. Forget about self-confidence; it's useless. Cultivate God-confidence. No test or temptation that comes your way is beyond the course of what others have had to face. All you need to remember is that God will never let you down; he'll never let you be pushed past your limit; he'll always be there to help you come through it.

1 Corinthians 10:11-13 *(The Message)*

Lord, you are Sovereign God. Nothing escapes your watchful eye. You are creator of all. You know your created inside and out. You know my thoughts before they are formed on my tongue. You know the motives behind my actions. You know when a sparrow falls to the ground. Your Word has revealed that as clay I have no right to talk back to the potter and yet you invite me to share the desires of my heart with you. Thank you for caring about every detail of my life. Thank you for supplying the grace of Christ Jesus, his power, his wisdom, his strength so in Him, I can do all things. I am like a tree planted beside the stream which overflows with fruit. My harvest in Christ is abundant and everlasting. I humble myself before you and you exalt me. I yield my weaknesses to Christ and rejoice as he turns them into strengths for the praise of your Glory. You are my God. I am your child. Worshipping and praising you is the joy of my heart. Thank you.

# SEPTEMBER 13

Whatever we
refuse to
accept by grace
is judged
and
condemned
as pride.

He said to them, "You are the ones who justify yourselves in the eyes of others, but God knows your hearts. What people value highly is detestable in God's sight.

Luke 16:15

Pride goes before destruction, a haughty spirit before a fall.

Proverbs 16:18

For it is not the one who commends himself who is approved, but the one whom the Lord commends.

2 Corinthians 10:18

Lord, you alone are Perfection. The Spirit of Christ in me is perfection. My claim to boast is that of speaking praise about Christ Jesus whose love for me held him to the cross on my behalf. In Christ, I am high and lifted up because he is high and lifted up. My boast of abundant riches and never-ending righteousness is not about me and all about Christ. Christ supplies. I abide in him. I joy in boasting in God's truth which is his nature fully demonstrated in Christ Jesus. Christ has said, "Apart from me you can do nothing." My boast in Christ is comparable to nothing or no one. I scale a wall and declare victory over my adversities because Christ is my supply. I take authority over the defeated kingdom of satan and boast in the name of Jesus as his name, his blood and his Word brings about his victory for me. No weapon formed against me shall prosper in the name of Jesus. I boast in the righteousness Jesus imparted to me because it does not come from my works or the sweat of my brow. I am righteousness unto God in Christ Jesus. My boast every minute of the day is to say, "Thank you, Jesus." I celebrate abundant life in you.

## SEPTEMBER 14

When we choose
to go into
hiding
with our
true selves,
our
false selves
takes over.

Having lost all sensitivity, they have given themselves over to sensuality so as to indulge in every kind of impurity, and they are full of greed. That, however, is not the way of life you learned when you heard about Christ and were taught in him in accordance with the truth that is in Jesus. You were taught, with regard to your former way of life, to put off your old self, which is being corrupted by its deceitful desires; to be made new in the attitude of your minds; and to put on the new self, created to be like God in true righteousness and holiness. Therefore each of you must put off falsehood and speak truthfully to your neighbor, for we are all members of one body.

Ephesians 4:19-25

Lord, you are Unfailing and Living Truth. Your Word is living revealed Truth. Thank you for your Word which holds the truth and the knowledge of your Truth. I joy in renewing my mind to your truth. Thank you for teaching me that what I behold I become. Thank you for revealing to me that what my mind believes my will can conceive. In Christ, I am a new creation and the old self is no longer the reign and rule of my life. I live in the spirit where there is freedom. I listen to my thoughts and take them captive to the obedience of Christ who lives within me. I clothe my thoughts with the truth of your Word and take authority over those thoughts that do not line up with your Word. As I yield to Christ, he manifests truth in me and through me. I live in this world but I am not of this world. The desire of my heart is to honor and glorify you. The cares of this world and the prince of the air try to grab the center stage of my soul by warring in my mind. As I fix my mind on Christ, his peace rules. I fix my eyes on you and lean on your understanding.

# SEPTEMBER 15

Empathy shared
softens hearts
bridging
a connection
at the deepest
level.

Praise be to the God and Father of our Lord Jesus Christ, the Father of compassion and the God of all comfort, who comforts us in all our troubles, so that we can comfort those in any trouble with the comfort we ourselves receive from God. For just as we share abundantly in the sufferings of Christ, so also our comfort abounds through Christ.

2 Corinthians 1:3-5

Let us then approach God's throne of grace with confidence, so that we may receive mercy and find grace to help us in our time of need.

Hebrews 4:16

Lord, you are Compassionate. Your compassion flows out of your love for me and all of your creation. You are the Father of compassion and the God of all comfort. You bore a depth of pain in your spirit beyond my comprehension when Jesus suffered and died for my sin debt. You saw your son fulfilling your will as he was beaten beyond recognition. You felt the agony of every drop of blood that fell on my behalf. No suffering and no temptation has ever occurred that is left hidden to your eyes. You experienced the unfathomable pain of separation when Jesus paid the wages of sin with his death. And yet your love for me was completed at the cross and continues to be lavished on me as Jesus invites me to cast my cares on him and live in freedom. No matter the origin or the degree of my affliction, thank you for promising to never leave me or forsake me. Thank you for promising that your mercies are new every morning. Thank you for promising that in Christ all Grace abounds. I love and comfort others with the love of Christ that is alive within me for where a burden is shared, the weight is divided. Praise God for endless blessings.

# SEPTEMBER 16

Genuine
and lasting change
always occurs in the midst
of a trusting relationship
for that
is the place where
vulnerability embraces
the invitation
of genuine openness.

What a stack of blessing you have piled up for those who worship you, ready and waiting for all who run to you to escape an unkind world. You hide them safely away from the opposition.

Psalms 31:19 *(The Message)*

Lord, you are Trustworthy. You are my refuge, my strength, my fortress, my protector, my defender, my comfort, my strong tower, my shield, my victory, my justice and my dwelling place. You are a Covenant God faithful and true to your Word. Thank you for drawing me to a place in relationship with you where I can come just as I am and know without doubt that I am loved and accepted. Thank you for inviting me to your throne of Grace and allowing me to be seated at the King's table where I partake of your love that Christ serves to me. I am open and vulnerable because I am complete in your love. I love others as Christ loves me. I am covered by your Grace, and wrapped in the glory of Jesus. By faith in Christ and resting in him, every good thing you have ordained for me comes forth. I declare your praises as you have called me in Christ out of my darkness and into his wonderful light. Thank you. Glory Halleluiah.

## SEPTEMBER 17

When we stuff our
unresolved feelings,
we lose touch
with God,
others,
and ourselves.

Therefore humble yourselves [demote, lower yourselves in your own estimation] under the mighty hand of God, that in due time He may exalt you. Casting the whole of your care [all your anxieties, all your worries, all your concerns, once and for all] on Him, for He cares for you affectionately and cares about you watchfully.

I Peter 5:7 (AMP)

Lord, you are Creator. You know every part of me inside and out. Thank you for the open door to your throne of Grace in Christ Jesus. I humble myself before you knowing that you are faithful to your Word and watching over it to perform it. As I confess your Word over my life, it stirs and builds my faith. Thank you for Christ Jesus who brings healing, provision, supply and victory to my every need. I rest in Christ by faith casting my cares, confessing my concerns and thanking him for making a way where the natural tells me there is no way. Search me as I yield to you and bring forth revelation from the truth that is already in me by the finished work of the cross. Test my thoughts for erroneous beliefs, wrongful thoughts, distorted perceptions and ungodly attitudes. Shed your lasting light on the truth I need to see. I receive by faith your healing of emotions I have pridefully carried and nurtured through ungodly mindsets. I release any strongholds that have rooted in my life in the name of Jesus. I open myself to trusted others that you are sending into my life to be your mouthpiece of truth and love. I live in humble gratitude.

# SEPTEMBER 18

To believe we can
make it on our
own is an
arrogant
decision
that cheats
us out
of God's gift of life.

Do not keep talking so proudly or let your mouth speak such arrogance, for the LORD is a God who knows, and by him deeds are weighed.

1 Samuel 2:3

The stuck-up fall flat on their faces, but down-to-earth people stand firm.

Proverbs 11:2 *(The Message)*

Lord, you are Abundance, Freedom and Life. You are a relational God creating me to fellowship with you and others. Your love for me draws me to you and holds me to you in praise and adoration. The abundance of your love for me in Christ Jesus is life-giving and spills over onto those I meet. The glisten in my eyes is because I am the apple of yours. I treasure our quiet time together before each sunrise and throughout the day. You meet me in my spirit where I am alive unto you by faith in Christ Jesus. I guard my relationship with you against the noise of the world that wants to steal my time away from you. I quiet my soul taking authority over its noise by yielding to you through worship and confessing your Word aloud. I fix my eyes on Christ Jesus who is the author and finisher of my faith. I drink in his living water which fills my cup so I can invite others to join me for a thirst quenching drink. As I ponder your Word, my spirit and soul join in a harmonious dance of celebrating your immeasurable wonder. My lips shout your praise.

# SEPTEMBER 19

When we add our
faith, obedience, and humility,
to God's Word,
He multiples it
abundantly.

But even there, if you seek God, your God, you'll be able to find him if you're serious, looking for him with your whole heart and soul. When troubles come and all these awful things happen to you, in future days you will come back to God, your God, and listen obediently to what he says. God, your God, is above all a compassionate God. In the end he will not abandon you, he won't bring you to ruin, he won't forget the covenant with your ancestors which he swore to them.

Deuteronomy 4:29-31

If my people, who are called by my name, will humble themselves and pray and seek my face and turn from their wicked ways, then I will hear from heaven, and I will forgive their sin and will heal their land.

2 Chronicles 7:14

Lord, you are Life. Your Word manifested in Christ Jesus is life. The name of Jesus is above all names. Every knee will bow before Jesus and every tongue confess that he is King of Kings and Lord of Lords. All of creation vibrates with sounds of your glory. I marvel at your wonder. I joy in spending time with you. Your Word is sweet nourishment to my spirit and life to my soul. Thank you for revealing yourself in Christ Jesus. In Christ, I have my being, my purpose and my provision. I have his full provision alive in me by faith. I live in his resurrection power. I take authority over satan and the powers of darkness in the name of Jesus, appropriate his blood by faith and stand on your Word. I yield my needs and openly confess my weaknesses throughout each day and Christ releases his grace to supply my needs and turn my weaknesses into his strengths. I live in amazing wonder. I abide. Christ supplies. My lips sing your praises.

# SEPTEMBER 20

We are able to
extend the
property lines
of our heart
when we allow
God's love
to draw the boundaries

So in Christ Jesus you are all children of God through faith, for all of you who were baptized into Christ have clothed yourselves with Christ. There is neither Jew nor Gentile, neither slave nor free, nor is there male and female, for you are all one in Christ Jesus. If you belong to Christ, then you are Abraham's seed, and heirs according to the promise.

Galatians 3:26-29

Lord, you are Divine Love. I am united to you in love and all that flows from me comes from Christ. I am one spirit with you in Christ Jesus. In Christ, I am your expression of love to those around me. All my being is hidden in Christ. I am overjoyed each day as I picture myself as a little child running excitedly toward your loving arms. Your love defines the boundaries of my heart so the property lines of loving you, others and myself extend far beyond my natural ability to love. In Christ, I am your child who delights in Christ and releases his sweet fragrance of love in every place I go. Christ has seated me in heavenly places with him. I lack for nothing because his provision is more than words can describe. I am identified and clothed with Christ. I see my new nature as a golden glow of His glory that wraps around my being. Thank you Jesus for your love which extends my property lines far beyond my capacity apart from you.

# SEPTEMBER 21

Why do we keep
trying to add to
what Christ Jesus
has already finished?

For it is by grace you have been saved, through faith—and this is
not from yourselves, it is the gift of God— not by works, so that no
one can boast.

Ephesians 2:8-9

Lord, you are Saving Grace. You chose me in Christ Jesus before the
creation of the world to be holy and blameless in your sight. I live in Christ
imparted righteousness. I can't quit enough or do enough to make myself
acceptable, pay my sin debt, relieve my sin consciousness, release myself
from the bondage of guilt and shame, or restore my oneness to God in
my own strength or my own striving. Thank you Jesus that your life giving
blood has set me free once and for all from all man-man philosophies and
empty religion which teaches the law of good works through self effort. I
live by faith under Grace in Christ Jesus. Thank you Jesus for your truth
that nothing good dwells within my flesh. I can will what is right, have the
intention and urge to do right, but I have no power to carry it out apart
from resting by faith in you. I feed my spirit with your Word which is your
truth that renews my mind. I submit to Christ within to bring his life
forth in me and through me. Thank you Jesus that you are the source for
inner transformation. My labor is to rest in your finished work of the cross.
Thank you for loving me, saving me and supplying me.

# SEPTEMBER 22

As we seek
to press into
Christ
and persevere
in faith,
we will walk
and grow in
spiritual awakening.

For the LORD gives wisdom; from his mouth come knowledge and understanding. He holds success in store for the upright, he is a shield to those whose walk is blameless, for he guards the course of the just and protects the way of his faithful ones. Then you will understand what is right and just and fair—every good path.

Proverbs 2:6-9

Lord, you are Spiritual Awakening and life to my Spirit. I am one with you in Spirit and Truth because Christ lives in me who is Spirit and Truth. Spirit means "breath of life". Your spirit called forth creation as you spoke your Word. You have given me your breath of life as I am created in your image. Your breath of life holds your glory which lights my path by faith in Christ Jesus. The spirit of man is the lamp of the Lord, searching all the innermost parts of his being. In Christ, I am a chosen generation, a royal priesthood and a holy nation. I am your workmanship, created in Christ Jesus for good works, which you prepared beforehand for me. Feasting on your Word is life to my spirit. Spending time with you in prayer and worship highlights and defines my very being. I am awestruck by your immeasurable love. I am humbly grateful for your life giving blood of Jesus Christ which saved me and gives me access to every Covenant promise. My spirit dances with joy. My soul magnifies your name. Thank you.

# SEPTEMBER 23

The Holy Spirit invites us to
listen for his voice so we
say
what needs saying,
pray
what needs praying,
and do
what needs doing.

Above all, you must understand that no prophecy of Scripture came about by the prophet's own interpretation of things. For prophecy never had its origin in the human will, but prophets, though human, spoke from God as they were carried along by the Holy Spirit.

1 Peter 1:20-21

Humble yourselves, therefore, under God's mighty hand, that he may lift you up in due time.

1 Peter 5:6

Lord, you are Voice and Life to my spirit. Thank you for inviting me to be still and know that you are God. Thank you that Christ Jesus has completed the way for me to enter your throne of Grace in bold confidence by faith in him. Thank you for creating my spirit with the gift of hearing your voice and following where you lead. Thank you Jesus, for pursing me with your love when I was a lost sheep. Thank you for stretching your hands of Grace towards me, picking me up as a shepherd would a wounded sheep, and placing me on your shoulders to carry me to your healing waters and green pastures of provision. I drink in your living water that quenches my thirst. I feast on your living Word that feeds and nourishes my spirit. Thank you for the Holy Spirit who lives within me guiding me, teaching me, growing me and correcting me. My spirit delights in the aliveness of my spirit unto God by faith in Christ Jesus. I joy in renewing and releasing all the spirit leads me to renew and release. I live in the abundance of Christ Jesus.

# SEPTEMBER 24

Our mind and a parachute
share a common thread.
They both function best
when they're open.

Those who think they can do it on their own end up obsessed
with measuring their own moral muscle but never get around to
exercising it in real life. Those who trust God's action in them find
that God's Spirit is in them—living and breathing God! Obsession
with self in these matters is a dead end; attention to God leads us
out into the open, into a spacious, free life. Focusing on the self is
the opposite of focusing on God. Anyone completely absorbed in
self ignores God, ends up thinking more about self than God. That
person ignores who God is and what he is doing. And God isn't
pleased at being ignored. But if God himself has taken up residence
in your life, you can hardly be thinking more of yourself than of
him. Anyone, of course, who has not welcomed this invisible but
clearly present God, the Spirit of Christ, won't know what we're
talking about. But for you who welcome him, in whom he dwells—
even though you still experience all the limitations of sin—you
yourself experience life on God's terms. It stands to reason, doesn't
it, that if the alive-and-present God who raised Jesus from the dead
moves into your life, he'll do the same thing in you that he did in
Jesus, bringing you alive to himself? When God lives and breathes
in you (and he does, as surely as he did in Jesus), you are delivered
from that dead life. With his Spirit living in you, your body will be
as alive as Christ's!

Romans 8:5-11 *(The Message)*

Lord, you are Abundant Life. All things begin and end with you. My spirit
is one with you in Christ Jesus where your full abundance is available to
me. I renew my mind to the truth of your Word and release your truth
through my confessions and worship with you. My spirit filled with your
truth rules my soul where my mind, my will, and my emotions arise. As
I abide in Christ who is Spirit and Truth, the fullness of your nature
living in my spirit overflows opening and inviting my soul to join in the
celebration of glorifying you. My body joins in the celebration where the

spirit leads and I raise my hands, open my mouth and shout continuous halleluiah's. I am spirit fed and spirit led. Nothing or no one compares to living in the aliveness and freedom of Christ Jesus. Thank you Jesus, that your life giving blood forgives me. Thank you Jesus that your work of the cross is complete. Thank you Jesus for releasing the Holy Spirit who daily unfolds deeper and greater revelations of the Father's love for me. You are joy unspeakable. Thank you.

# SEPTEMBER 25

Our words are
containers of creative power,
as we choose
to be
God's
mouthpiece
to those
around
us.

The Sovereign LORD has given me a well-instructed tongue, to know the word that sustains the weary. He wakens me morning by morning, wakens my ear to listen like one being instructed.

Isaiah 50:4

The tongue has the power of life and death, and those who love it will eat its fruit.

Proverbs 18:21

Lord, you are the Word. You called forth creation by the power of your Word. You have created me in your image and given me the authority in Christ Jesus to call forth his resurrection power over my life circumstances by faith in him. Your Word holds my confessions. You Word has made clear your wisdom for me that the power of blessings and curses are in my tongue. I choose to speak life. My mouth is a well spring of blessing as Christ lives in me. I let no corrupt communication proceed out of my mouth, but only that which is good to the use of edifying, that it may minister grace to those that hear. Your Word is life and a guard over my mouth. I keep watch over the door of my lips. You have given me a well instructed tongue. The words I speak are those that edify and build others up. I see others as created in your image and I value them as you value me. My words are an overflow of your love for me. May the meditations of my heart and the words from my mouth be pleasing to you. Thank you for life in Christ Jesus.

# SEPTEMBER 26

When we feel
overburdened,
we've likely
exceeded
our limits.

Because of the LORD's great love we are not consumed, for his compassions never fail. They are new every morning; great is your faithfulness. I say to myself, "The LORD is my portion; therefore I will wait for him.

Lamentations 3:22-24

Don't fret or worry. Instead of worrying, pray. Let petitions and praises shape your worries into prayers, letting God know your concerns. Before you know it, a sense of God's wholeness, everything coming together for good, will come and settle you down. It's wonderful what happens when Christ displaces worry at the center of your life.

Philippians 4:6-7 *(The Message)*

Lord, you are Grace supply. Thank you Jesus for inviting and allowing me to cast my cares on you and live in freedom and in faith resting in you to supply all my needs according to your riches in glory. Thank you for making a way for me to enter your rest by faith on the day of my salvation. I sustain my rest by faith renewing my mind to your Word and fixing my mind on Christ Jesus who is the Word. Thank you for allowing me to rest by faith in the finished work of Christ Jesus. Thank you for the person of Christ Jesus who is seated at your right hand upholding all things. I live in your kingdom fulfillment by faith. All you have created me for is complete in Christ. Nothing or no one can hinder your favor or your flow of abundant grace to me as I abide in Christ. What you have called me to you supply in Christ Jesus. Thank you for overcoming barriers and obstacles as I rest in you. Halleluiah praises now and forevermore.

# SEPTEMBER 27

As we cultivate
God's Word,
the fruit
of the Spirit
flows
from us.

But what happens when we live God's way? He brings gifts into our lives, much the same way that fruit appears in an orchard— things like affection for others, exuberance about life, serenity. We develop a willingness to stick with things, a sense of compassion in the heart, and a conviction that a basic holiness permeates things and people. We find ourselves involved in loyal commitments, not needing to force our way in life, able to marshal and direct our energies wisely.

Galatians 5:22-23 *(The Message)*

Lord, you are Eternal Seed. When I accepted you as my Lord and Savior by faith, you blessed me with the harvest of eternal life, joy, peace, prosperity, provision and health. In Christ and by faith, I receive the blessings of Abraham over my life. Your Word is kingdom seed. I joy in planting your Word in my heart and watering it with faith. I yield to Christ in me for him to bring forth the harvest of unending blessings. Christ Jesus is the vine and I am the branches. I yield a bountiful harvest as I abide in him. All my energies are divinely anointed. I use my words as seeds of love and encouragement. I release seeds of love through my words and my actions because your spirit alive in me is the source of love. The labors of my hands are too numerous to count as I yield to Christ who lives within me. I live to bring you glory. I live as a surrendered vessel pouring out to others what you have poured into me. I joy in living joyfully, exuberant and expectant. My soul delights in you. My lips sing your praises. Glory Halleluiah.

# SEPTEMBER 28

Others often
examine our
fruit
before
they heed
THE root.

But the fruit of the Spirit is love, joy, peace, forbearance, kindness, goodness, faithfulness, gentleness and self-control.

Galatians 5:22

Lord, you are the Divine Gardener. You planted the Word within me when I accepted Christ by faith. His presence and his full provision live in me now and forevermore. Before Christ became my life, I planted seeds of pride and works in hope that I could produce the fruit of good behavior and acceptance. Your Word has made it clear that no works of the flesh can produce anything of eternal value or eternal measure. You created me to bear fruit. As I yield to Christ as the vine, he bears the fruits of the spirit in me. Only abiding in Christ do I release pure love to build up, joy to unleash light, peace to calm the seas, forbearance to demonstrate patience, kindness to enfold others, goodness to reflect your righteousness, faithfulness to foster inner growth, gentleness to embrace brokenness, and self-control to demonstrate obedience. Christ is my unfailing supply of all good. Doors once closed now open by your Goodness. Impossible channels are unencumbered in your Holy name. The harvest of my hands come in remarkable and unexpected ways as I trust in, yield to and rely in Christ who is my unending source.

# SEPTEMBER 29

We find
peace
when we
pursue
the Prince of Peace.

Because you are my help, I sing in the shadow of your wings. I cling to you; your right hand upholds me.

Psalm 63:7-8

Blessed are those who hunger and thirst for righteousness, for they will be filled.

Matthew 5:6

Turn from evil and do good; seek peace and pursue it.

Psalm 34:4

Lord you are Peace. Jesus is the Prince of Peace that lives in me. The world defines peace as the freedom from disturbance. My peace is within enfolded in my relationship with Christ Jesus. Thank you Lord that your peace has the power to bring forth your authority and your will. Even in the midst of a storm, I can command peace over the waves in your name. I can give thanks in all circumstances because I know you are watching over and protecting the righteous. I give thanks for the peace that passes all understanding as I live in You. You are Sovereign. I live in peace and overflowing blessing. I am a recipient of every spiritual blessing in the heavenly places in Christ Jesus. You are my beginning and end. Your presence in me allows me to be at peace with others. I pursue peace because I pursue my relationship with you and my desire is to be near you. Thank you Jesus. My gratitude overflows. My lips sing your praises. Halleluiah.

# SEPTEMBER 30

The secret
to lasting
joy
is to
walk in love.

My response is to get down on my knees before the Father, this magnificent Father who parcels out all heaven and earth. I ask him to strengthen you by his Spirit—not a brute strength but a glorious inner strength—that Christ will live in you as you open the door and invite him in. And I ask him that with both feet planted firmly on love, you'll be able to take in with all followers of Jesus the extravagant dimensions of Christ's love. Reach out and experience the breadth! Test its length! Plumb the depths! Rise to the heights! Live full lives, full in the fullness of God. God can do anything, you know—far more than you could ever imagine or guess or request in your wildest dreams! He does it not by pushing us around but by working within us, his Spirit deeply and gently within us.

Ephesians 3:14-21 *(The Message)*

But let all who take refuge in you be glad; let them ever sing for joy. Spread your protection over them, that those who love your name may rejoice in you.

Psalm 5:11

Lord, you are Unmatched Love. I live clothed in the garment of praise and humble adoration because your name is wonderful and worthy of praise. Your spirit lives in me. Jesus is transforming me from the inside out. I fling open the door of my heart with thanksgiving and invite you to do your supernatural work changing my natural. As I feast on your Word, your thoughts are becoming my thoughts. As I learn of your gentleness and meekness, I am becoming more gentle and meek. Things I use to deem important pale in comparison with your love for me and the privilege of serving others out of that love. I joy in abiding in Christ and cannot image resting any where else. I live in kingdom grace and light never desiring to go back to the works of the law and darkness. I reap bountifully in love because I live on a first name basis with my supplier. My lips shout your praises. Goodness and mercy follow me all the days of my life. I take in a deep breath to shout a lungful of praise to you. Thank you for abundance in Jesus.

# OCTOBER 1

Self-devaluing ourselves
does not line up
with God's truth.
It's a false pride based in
fear and involves rejection
of what Jesus did for us on the cross.

Summing up: Be agreeable, be sympathetic, be loving, be compassionate, be humble. That goes for all of you, no exceptions. No retaliation. No sharp-tongued sarcasm. Instead, bless—that's your job, to bless. You'll be a blessing and also get a blessing. Whoever wants to embrace life and see the day fill up with good, Here's what you do: Say nothing evil or hurtful; Snub evil and cultivate good; run after peace for all you're worth. God looks on all this with approval, listening and responding well to what he's asked; But he turns his back on those who do evil things.

1 Peter 3:8-12 *(The Message)*

Lord, you are Love. Your perfect love casts out all fear. I am one with your undivided love because I am one by faith in Christ Jesus who is love. I love myself and others with the love of Christ that lives in me. I bathe myself in the truth of your Word which tells me in Christ I am a new creation with a new identity. I am chosen, loved and accepted. I am a branch of the true vine. I am established, anointed and sealed by God. I am a saint. I am righteous. I am holy and blameless. His divine power has given me everything that pertains to life and godliness. I yield to Christ and claim the excellencies of him who called me out of the darkness into his wonderful light. My words and my actions reflect the truth of who I am in Christ as my spirit alive unto Christ speaks them over my life. My words are a symphony of truth that flow from my mind being renewed to your Word. My praise is the finale of thanksgiving that my hearts writes to you. My lips sing a melody of praise for who I am in Christ. My soul magnifies you. Thank you.

# OCTOBER 2

Everything
we do
bears some kind of
fruit.

If you grow a healthy tree, you'll pick healthy fruit. If you grow a diseased tree, you'll pick worm-eaten fruit. The fruit tells you about the tree.

Matthew 12:33 *(The Message)*

I am the Real Vine and my Father is the Farmer. He cuts off every branch of me that doesn't bear grapes. And every branch that is grape-bearing he prunes back so it will bear even more. You are already pruned back by the message I have spoken.

John 15:1-3 *(The Message)*

But blessed is the man who trusts me; the woman who sticks with God. They're like trees replanted in Eden, putting down roots near the rivers—Never a worry through the hottest of summers, never dropping a leaf, serene and calm through droughts, bearing fresh fruit every season.

Jeremiah 17:7-8 *(The Message)*

Lord, you are the Master Gardner. You have created and planted the universe with seed potential. Your divine order and creative motion was set in order when you released the glory of your spirit. Thank you for Christ Jesus who is the true vine. I bear fruit as I abide in Christ. Thank you for loving me enough and caring for me so deeply that you prune me from the inside out. Your ways are higher than my ways. Your thoughts are higher than my thoughts. You see the completed masterpiece you created me to be in Christ Jesus. Blessings of new growth spring forth in me and from me as Christ shapes me into his likeness. Abundant fruit comes from his supernatural supply. I plow in mercy, sow in love and water in faith. I sow the seeds of your Word in my spirit and every part of my being comes alive in Christ. I offer the sacrifice of praise through the fruit of my lips desiring to glorify you in my thoughts, words and actions. I see my words as seeds of encouragement and a reflection of your garden of grace within me. Thank you.

# OCTOBER 3

When we
take a
look at
ourselves,
we can
look at
others
differently.

Do not judge, or you too will be judged. For in the same way you judge others, you will be judged, and with the measure you use, it will be measured to you. Why do you look at the speck of sawdust in your brother's eye and pay no attention to the plank in your own eye? How can you say to your brother, 'Let me take the speck out of your eye,' when all the time there is a plank in your own eye? You hypocrite, first take the plank out of your own eye, and then you will see clearly to remove the speck from your brother's eye.

Matthew 7:1-3

Lord, you are Truth. Your perspective is all knowing and all seeing. Your Word is the light of love that reflects Christ to me and in me. My life is a divinely created vessel for your glory and the service of others through your love. As I abide in Christ the source of love, I reflect his love to others I meet. I see others as divine works of your hands created with worth, value and purpose. Every person I meet is a testimony to your endless wonder. I use my words and actions to build up and encourage others. Regardless of their acceptance or rejection of me, I am firmly grounded in the love Christ has for me and I respond with compassion and kindness towards them. As there is no condemnation in me, I do not condemn others. I recognize that all behavior has meaning regardless of whether I know its meaning. Your Word has clearly revealed and your Grace unfolded that I do not have the right to pass judgment on another's worth or value. I live with my will yielded to grow in Christ. I desire to glorify you. I live to praise you.

# OCTOBER 4

Choices become freedom
when we own
all the aspects
of our identity:
our beliefs,
our perceptions,
our thoughts,
our attitudes,
our emotions,
our actions
and our words.

Since, then, you have been raised with Christ, set your hearts on things above, where Christ is, seated at the right hand of God. Set your minds on things above, not on earthly things. For you died, and your life is now hidden with Christ in God. When Christ, who is your life, appears, then you also will appear with him in glory.

Colossians 3:1-4

Lord, you are Life unlimited. I glory in the marvelous wonder of Christ Jesus transforming my spirit the moment I accepted him by faith as Lord and Savior. Working out my salvation as your Word tells me to do is taking hold of what you have already done within me by renewing by mind and releasing my old mindsets. I am a new creation and the old is passed away. Thank you for loving me enough to save me and for supplying your Grace which has broken the power of sin over me. Thank you for your Word which reveals the truth of your ways. As I renew my mind to your Word and yield myself to Christ, he is bringing into alignment the truth of my new identity. My mind draws on the truth already placed in my spirit by Christ by faith and my soul begins to change as reflected in my beliefs, my perceptions, my thoughts, my attitudes, my emotions, my words and my actions. I love spending time with you, listening to you, worshipping you and opening myself to you. I abide and Christ supplies. Thank you.

# OCTOBER 5

Explore
your beliefs
and open
your world
to a new level of
freedom.

Those who live according to the flesh have their minds set on what the flesh desires; but those who live in accordance with the Spirit have their minds set on what the Spirit desires. The mind governed by the flesh is death, but the mind governed by the Spirit is life and peace. The mind governed by the flesh is hostile to God; it does not submit to God's law, nor can it do so. Those who are in the realm of the flesh cannot please God.

Romans 8:5-8

Do not conform to the pattern of this world, but be transformed by the renewing of your mind. Then you will be able to test and approve what God's will is—his good, pleasing and perfect will.

Romans 12:2

Lord, you are Wisdom. I live alive unto you by faith in Christ Jesus. My spirit is one with your spirit. I renew my mind to the truth of your Word relying on, trusting in and yielding my beliefs and my thoughts to the truth of it. I delight in meditating on your Word, opening myself to you and asking you to search me and bring to light that in my soul that does not line up with my spirit. My soul is the bridge between my spirit and my body. Opening my mind to you is like opening a faucet so water can freely flow. As I renew my mind and believe your Word, my soul agrees with what Christ has already deposited into my spirit. Thank you that as my soul comes into alignment with what is sees in God's spiritual mirror, and takes hold by faith of what Christ has already deposited, my spirit releases truth into my soul. My soul magnifies you rejoicing in the wonder working presence of Christ living in me to bring forth his completed work though me. My body joins in the celebration as shouts of praise pour from my lips. I stand on bended knees and raise my hands to worship and glorify you. You are an awesome God. Thank you.

# OCTOBER 6

We don't have to live by our emotions,
we do have to live with them.
Stuffed emotions remain alive
until the pain that fuels
them is laid at the cross.

Peace I leave with you; my peace I give you. I do not give to you as the world gives. Do not let your hearts be troubled and do not be afraid.

John 14:27

Examine yourselves to see whether you are in the faith; test yourselves. Do you not realize that Christ Jesus is in you—unless, of course, you fail the test?

2 Corinthians 13:5

Lord, you are All Knowing. Your eyes are forever watching over me. Nothing escapes you. Thank you for your Word which is a lamp to my feet and a light to my way. Your Word is freedom and life to my spirit. As I renew my mind to your Word, I submit to you as Jesus did and say, "Not my will, but yours be done." Thank you for unveiling your truth. I draw from the living well of my spirit where Christ lives in completed abundance, and I find rest for my soul. My mind is stirred and drawn to take hold of the fullness of you alive in my spirit. I yield to Christ desiring to know him more. I rest in his presence. I drink his living water. I feast on your Word. I worship in spirit and truth. I allow Jesus to use my surrendered quest as my open invitation for him to work in me. As I examine myself in light of truth, which is Jesus who is the Word, I replace wrong beliefs, false perceptions, ungodly thoughts, and fleshly attitudes which have held my feelings hostage. I willingly yield my brokenness to Jesus who is the all supplying grace to heal what needs healing and supply what needs supplying. Yielding is freedom. Thank you.

# OCTOBER 7

Relational
breakdown
often involves
an issue
of balance
between
nature and nurture.

I urge you, brothers and sisters, to watch out for those who cause divisions and put obstacles in your way that are contrary to the teaching you have learned. Keep away from them. For such people are not serving our Lord Christ, but their own appetites. By smooth talk and flattery they deceive the minds of naive people. Everyone has heard about your obedience, so I rejoice because of you; but I want you to be wise about what is good, and innocent about what is evil.

Romans 16:17-19

We know also that the Son of God has come and has given us understanding, so that we may know him who is true. And we are in him who is true by being in his Son Jesus Christ. He is the true God and eternal life.

1 John 5:20

Lord, You are a God of relationship. Your perfect plan for me centers on my relationship with you in Christ. As I live in Christ, my relationships overflow with your nature of love, forgiveness and hope. Your inflow of love in Christ is my outflow of love to others. I live identified in the righteousness of Christ Jesus. His identity and his life in me draws life to my soul from my spirit complete in him, and enables me to reflect his love to others. I live by the spirit where there is peace and freedom. I am ruled by my spirit and not my flesh. I surrendered my rights to myself when I accepted you as my Lord and Savior. I cast down imaginations, and every high thing that exalts itself against the knowledge of God, and take captive every thought to the obedience of Christ. Thank you for the Holy

Spirit who brings forth the truth you placed in my spirit to my soul where I can share your love and grace with others. I see others as your divine creation and treat them with honor and respect. I abide. Christ supplies. Praise you now and evermore.

# OCTOBER 8

When we
mess up, we can
fess up, and
God will lift us up.
God calls it…
confessing, grieving and forgiving.

Whoever conceals their sins does not prosper, but the one who confesses and renounces them finds mercy.

Proverbs 28:13

If we confess our sins, he is faithful and just and will forgive us our sins and purify us from all unrighteousness. If we claim we have not sinned, we make him out to be a liar and his word is not in us.

1 John 1:9-11

Therefore confess your sins to each other and pray for each other so that you may be healed. The prayer of a righteous person is powerful and effective.

James 5:16

Lord, you are Forgiveness and Restoration. I am blessed because my sins have been forgiven and are remembered no more. With Christ in me, I am compassionate, patient, nonjudgmental, understanding, long suffering and forgiving. I have the mind and heart of Christ. In Christ, I see my relationships through the eyes of his love. No offense comes to me that is too large for your gift of forgiveness in Christ. No wound comes to me that is too large for your love in Christ to offer healing salve. I confess my shortcomings and my weakness quickly because your Word has revealed your love for me and your faithfulness to share your love with me. Your love for me cancelled my debt against you by the shed blood of Jesus at the cross. I cancel the debt owed to me by others through your supply of Grace, Truth, and Love that lives in my spirit. Through the abundance of Christ, his forgiveness in my spirit flows into my soul, as I yield my burdens and my hurts to him. I receive the work of Christ Jesus in thanksgiving. Thank you.

## OCTOBER 9

Each time we take
responsibility
for our own
attitudes,
we gift ourselves
with the treasure
called freedom,
because freedom comes
from the knowledge
of the truth which lives in the light.

If anyone thinks they are something when they are not, they deceive themselves. Each one should test their own actions. Then they can take pride in themselves alone, without comparing themselves to someone else, for each one should carry their own load.

Galatians 6:3-6

Lord, you are Freedom and Truth. As I live in the spirit, I live in freedom. As I abide in Christ, I live in truth. I joy in spending time in your Word which nourishes my spirit and sets the boundaries of truth in my thinking. As I think on your Word which is true and pure, my attitudes reflect the nature of your Word. Your Word is living Grace and living Truth because your Word is Christ Jesus. As I live in Christ, his Spirit brings alignment of my soul with his Spirit alive within me. My labor of working out my salvation is to renew and release as I rest in Christ. Thank you Jesus that you came to give life and give it abundantly. I live in the light as Christ lives in the light. Thank you Jesus for winning the victory for me over the power of sin. I joy in fellowshipping with you, feasting on your Word, casting my burdens on you, sharing my desires with you and resting in your Grace which supplies my every need. I gladly humble myself before you because being lifted up in you is the greatest high ever. I love you Lord. Thank you.

# OCTOBER 10

Bondage to
perfection
is often
rooted in
our fear of
of rejection.

The LORD replied, "My Presence will go with you, and I will give you rest.

Exodus 33:14

But he said to me, "My grace is sufficient for you, for my power is made perfect in weakness." Therefore I will boast all the more gladly about my weaknesses, so that Christ's power may rest on me.

2 Corinthians 12:9

And my God will supply every need of yours according to his riches in glory in Christ Jesus.

Philippians 4:19

Lord, you are Divine Perfection. You order and structure in creation reflects your perfect balance. I live in the perfected identity of Christ Jesus. In Christ, I am holy, blameless and righteous. My identity of perfection is the position you have elevated me to in Christ. Your love for me saved me in Christ Jesus. Your grace in Christ Jesus is his abundance gifted to me by faith. My faith in you through Christ, receives and draws from the abundance Christ died and arose to give me. No behavior or performance of mine can add to or subtract from my perfected identity in Christ. Works of my flesh are works of the law, pride-filled self efforts to do what you have already established, which never bring righteousness and freedom to me. Christ provision draws me to one place and one place only and that is to praise you for lavishing every blood bought blessing of the Lamb upon me. I am chosen and set aside for great works because Christ brings forth his work in me as I rest and abide in him. Thank you for making the way of perfection in Jesus.

# OCTOBER 11

We
wake up
before we
get up.

But everything exposed by the light becomes visible—and everything that is illuminated becomes a light. This is why it is said: "Wake up, sleeper, rise from the dead, and Christ will shine on you.

Ephesians 5:13-14

Lord, you are Light and Truth. Your demonstration of love for my by Jesus paying my sin debt in full opens my eyes to the light that no self-efforts of mine could restore my relationship with you that sin originally separated. Your Word continues to open my eyes that apart from you I can do nothing. I am a child of the light because Christ imparted his life to me. Christ is my hope of glory. My spirit alive unto you through Christ in me is awake to all of your divine Grace and holiness that is mine in Christ. Thank you for enlarging your light, your truth and your love in me every day. Now that I live in the light as Christ is in the light, I no longer desire to return to the darkness. I yield my weaknesses to you and gratefully receive your super abounding grace. I joy in spending time with you and abiding in the fullness of your spirit. No power of darkness, no circumstance and no person can still, kill, or destroy my life in Christ. No weapon formed against me can prosper. My lips sing your praises. I joy in your goodness. Thank you.

# OCTOBER 12

Our buried hurts will be
touched by His Mercy,
cleansed by His Grace,
and healed by His Love
when we bring them
to the light of His
Grace.

So let God work his will in you. Yell a loud no to the Devil and watch him scamper. Say a quiet yes to God and he'll be there in no time. Quit dabbling in sin. Purify your inner life. Quit playing the field. Hit bottom, and cry your eyes out. The fun and games are over. Get serious, really serious. Get down on your knees before the Master; it's the only way you'll get on your feet.

James 4:7-10 *(The Message)*

Are you hurting? Pray. Do you feel great? Sing. Are you sick? Call the church leaders together to pray and anoint you with oil in the name of the Master. Believing-prayer will heal you, and Jesus will put you on your feet. And if you've sinned, you'll be forgiven— healed inside and out. Make this your common practice: Confess your sins to each other and pray for each other so that you can live together whole and healed.

James 5:13-16 *(The Message)*

Lord, you are a God of Restoration. Thank you for revealing to me that in the presence of love, miracles happen. I invite your love in me by faith in Christ to search me and highlight my areas of brokenness. I acknowledge that the same power that raised Christ Jesus from the grave lives in me awaiting me to take hold by faith and release it to bring resurrection to my unresolved hurts. I choose to get down on my knees before you knowing you alone can raise me to my feet. Thank you for making it clear that whatever is within me that has not been brought out into the open still has a life of its own in the past and hiding it, denying it, or running from it does not heal it. Bring others into my life that you know will encourage me and not condemn me. Draw me to those of your choosing who have walked a similar path as mine. I repent of the pride I have been hiding behind and open myself to you gratefully open to your healing. Thank you for healing.

# OCTOBER 13

God sees
our past,
present
and
future
through
eternity.

Praise be to the God and Father of our Lord Jesus Christ, who has blessed us in the heavenly realms with every spiritual blessing in Christ. For he chose us in him before the creation of the world to be holy and blameless in his sight. In love he predestined us for adoption to sonship through Jesus Christ, in accordance with his pleasure and will— to the praise of his glorious grace, which he has freely given us in the One he loves. In him we have redemption through his blood, the forgiveness of sins, in accordance with the riches of God's grace that he lavished on us. With all wisdom and understanding, he made known to us the mystery of his will according to his good pleasure, which he purposed in Christ, to be put into effect when the times reach their fulfillment—to bring unity to all things in heaven and on earth under Christ.

Ephesians 1:3-10

Lord, you are Sovereign Creator. You chose me in Christ before the creation of the world to be holy and blameless in your sight. There is no past, present or future part of my life that you have not already seen. In Christ, I have redemption through his blood, the forgiveness of sins, in accordance with the riches of your Grace which you have already imparted to me by faith in Christ Jesus. A sin consciousness that satan uses to condemn me and draw me away from you is his attempt to steal back the authority in me Christ has given to me. Christ Jesus broke the power of sin, so in Christ I live free. As I live in the spirit, I do not fulfill the lusts of the flesh. I am a kingdom child chosen, blessed and highly favored. I live in my inheritance every day by faith. Fellowshipping with you and feasting on your Word stirs my faith which releases your abundance in my spirit into every area of my life. Your joy in my spirit overflows in my soul.

# OCTOBER 14

Forgiveness
is conditional
because it always
involves a
sacrificial exchange.

And when you stand praying, if you hold anything against anyone, forgive them, so that your Father in heaven may forgive you your sins.

Mark 11:25

Lord, you are Freedom. Thank you for rescuing me from the pit of death and releasing me from the debt of sin I could never repay. Thank you Jesus for rescuing me from the dominion of darkness and transferring me into your kingdom of light. I am overwhelmed that you loved me so much that Christ took my unholiness, my sin, my eternal death, and exchanged it for his holiness, his sinlessness and his eternal life. Your immeasurable gift draws me to my knees. I choose to quickly forgive others because you have powerfully demonstrated that forgiveness releases the debt that an offender can never repay. I forgive others through the strength of Christ, the Forgiver, who lives within me. Just as Jesus drew upon your strength while paying the price of my sins, I draw upon Christ who is my strength. Thank you for revealing your living and written Word which feeds my spirit and grounds my soul. I am free to live, free to give and free to be all you created me to be. My lips sing your praises. I live in the freedom of Christ Jesus.

# OCTOBER 15

When we examine our
anger, we begin to uncover
what we're trying to
protect, and that insight
will help us decide
if what we are trying
to protect
is worth the price
we're paying.

Don't have anything to do with foolish and stupid arguments, because you know they produce quarrels. And the Lord's servant must not be quarrelsome but must be kind to everyone, able to teach, not resentful.

2 Timothy 2:23-24

Lord, you are Truth. Thank you that in Christ I am free from the yoke of bondage and slavery to sin. Life by faith in you is no longer about me, but all about you. Thank you for establishing my worth and value in Christ Jesus. Your Word tells me to be angry and sin not. Anger is a warning sign that something needs attention. I open myself to your wisdom to shed light where light needs to be shed. I use my anger as a mirror of self-reflection humbling myself before you asking you to show me what needs to be yielded to you. I renew my mind to the truth of your Word and allow the Holy Spirit to teach, correct and guide me. Thank you that I can come before your throne of Grace and find help in my time of need. Thank you Jesus for inviting me to spend time with you, share the desires of my heart with you and cast my cares on you. I look to you to meet my needs for love, acceptance and worth and not others. I look at others as your masterpiece worthy of honor and respect. Your spirit of love alive within is the love I share with others.

## OCTOBER 16

Choices are gifts
we give to others
and ourselves.

This day I call the heavens and the earth as witnesses against you that I have set before you life and death, blessings and curses. Now choose life, so that you and your children may live and you may love the LORD your God, listen to his voice, and hold fast to him. For the LORD is your life, and he will give you many years in the land he swore to give to your fathers, Abraham, Isaac and Jacob.

Deuteronomy 30:19-20

Who, then, are those who fear the LORD? He will instruct them in the ways they should choose. They will spend their days in prosperity, and their descendants will inherit the land.

Psalm 25:12-13

Lord, you are Life. Christ is the Way, the Truth, and the Life. Thank you for leading me to the greatest choice in life and that is living by faith in Christ Jesus. I choose to praise you for you are worthy. I choose to yield to the spirit of Christ living in me by faith because he supplies all my needs according to his riches in glory. My joy overflows as I abide in Christ and rest in the fullness of his abundant supply of Grace. By choosing life in Christ, your blessings pour into me and come to me in unexpected times and in unexpected ways. In your loving goodness, you have blessed the works of my hands. You leave me with peace as I fix my mind on Christ. Your Word is life to me and health to my bones. Life in Christ has released me from bondage under the law. Christ has freed me with life in the spirit which is more wonderful than words can describe. My lips sing your praises. My soul magnifies your name. I shout, "Halleluiah praises."

# OCTOBER 17

The
secret to
lasting joy
is walking
in God's love.

Love comes from God. Everyone who loves is born of God and experiences a relationship with God. The person who refuses to love doesn't know the first thing about God, because God is love—so you can't know him if you don't love. This is how God showed his love for us: God sent his only Son into the world so we might live through him. This is the kind of love we are talking about—not that we once upon a time loved God, but that he loved us and sent his Son as a sacrifice to clear away our sins and the damage they've done to our relationship with God. My dear, dear friends, if God loved us like this, we certainly ought to love each other. No one has seen God, ever. But if we love one another, God dwells deeply within us, and his love becomes complete in us—perfect love! This is how we know we're living steadily and deeply in him, and he in us: He's given us life from his life, from his very own Spirit. Also, we've seen for ourselves and continue to state openly that the Father sent his Son as Savior of the world. Everyone who confesses that Jesus is God's Son participates continuously in an intimate relationship with God. We know it so well, we've embraced it heart and soul, this love that comes from God.

1John 4:7-16 *(The Message)*

Lord, you are Love and Joy. There is nothing in my flesh that has the ability to love apart from Christ in me. I love because you first loved me. I love you, myself and others because the source of love who is Christ Jesus lives in me. I abide in, rely on and trust in Jesus and he is perfecting his love in me. I live in abundant joy because Christ imparted his joy to me. Thank you Lord for making known to me the path of life in Christ Jesus where in his presence is fullness of joy. My spirit rejoices with joy that is inexpressible and filled with glory. My soul shouts for joy for your immeasurable love that is mine in Christ Jesus. My body joins in the celebration of being filled with the love and joy of Christ Jesus by opening my lips in praise, falling to my knees in adoration, and raising my hands in worship. Thank you for life abundant in Christ Jesus.

# OCTOBER 18

Gods Word
is the
GPS
that
never fails
to direct
us to our
destiny.

You will keep in perfect peace those whose minds are steadfast, because they trust in you. Trust in the LORD forever, for the LORD, the LORD himself, is the Rock eternal.

Isaiah 26:3-4

Just think—you don't need a thing, you've got it all! All God's gifts are right in front of you as you wait expectantly for our Master Jesus to arrive on the scene for the Finale. And not only that, but God himself is right alongside to keep you steady and on track until things are all wrapped up by Jesus. God, who got you started in this spiritual adventure, shares with us the life of his Son and our Master Jesus. He will never give up on you. Never forget that.

1 Corinthians 1:7-9 *(The Message)*

Lord, you are my Destiny. My hope is in you. All things come to me in Christ Jesus. Every blood bought blessing of Christ is mine by faith. My heart overflows in continuous praise for life in Christ Jesus. His completed work of the cross has brought his unending bounty of righteousness, peace and joy into my spirit. His abundant blessings spring forth from my spirit into my natural circumstances as I renew my mind to your Word and release my faith in your Covenant promises. Your Word is a lamp unto my feet and life to my very being. You have created me for the praise of your glory. Every part of my being praises you for making the way where I can rest in Christ and allow him to bring forth your anointed kingdom works. I bear abundant and lasting fruit in Christ. Thank you. Thank you. Thank you wonderful and magnificent God.

# OCTOBER 19

Jesus did more
than leave heaven
to save us from a devil's hell;
He came to get heaven into us.

That all may honor the Son just as they honor the Father. Whoever does not honor the Son does not honor the Father, who sent him. Very truly I tell you, "whoever hears my word and believes him who sent me has eternal life and will not be judged but has crossed over from death to life."

John 5:23-24

Jesus said, "Very truly I tell you, the one who believes has eternal life."

John 6:47

Lord, you are Life. My life is hidden in you in Christ Jesus. Jesus is the first and the last. He was nailed to the tree exchanging his life for the payment of my sin debt becoming the tree of life for me. In Christ, I am an oak of righteousness lofty, strong and magnificent by faith in Christ Jesus. My life joined to and yielded to Christ is the planting of the Lord that he may be glorified. In Christ, I am a tree planted beside the living waters where my roots are strong and my branches brim with fruit. Even when adverse circumstances come against me in Christ, I bear much fruit. Thank you God for reconciling heaven and earth under one head and that is Christ Jesus. Your plan of creation and redemption are far greater than my mind can comprehend. I live humbled by the depth of your love. I celebrate with gratitude and thanksgiving my security of spending eternity with you now and forevermore. Thank you for placing your kingdom within me. I joy in your magnificent plan to bring heaven to earth supplying all my needs every day in Christ Jesus.

# OCTOBER 20

In
God's Grace,
everyone
can be
saved.

Look at it this way. If someone has a hundred sheep and one of them wanders off, doesn't he leave the ninety-nine and go after the one? And if he finds it, doesn't he make far more over it than over the ninety-nine who stay put? Your Father in heaven feels the same way. He doesn't want to lose even one of these simple believers.

Matthew 18:12-14 *(The Message)*

He has saved us and called us to a holy life—not because of anything we have done but because of his own purpose and grace. This grace was given us in Christ Jesus before the beginning of time, but it has now been revealed through the appearing of our Savior, Christ Jesus, who has destroyed death and has brought life and immortality to light through the gospel.

2 Timothy 1:9-10

Lord, you are Salvation, Redemption, and Newness of Life. I live as a holy and blameless saint because of the blood of Christ Jesus. I am righteous in Christ. I am filled with all the fullness of God in Christ Jesus. As I abide in Christ, my life expresses righteousness, joy and peace. My arms are outstretched in praise, as your grace saved me and supplies me. I magnify you with shouts of praise. My heart rejoices overflowing with thanksgiving. I serve you with gladness. I am what I am by the Grace of Christ Jesus. You take pleasure in the prosperity of your servant. I receive with gladness. All the works of my hands to honor you and serve others are blessed by your Grace. Your divine favor unfolds all around me. I am your child and you are my God. Thank you Jesus for loving me, saving me, and supplying me. Halleluiah praises.

# OCTOBER 21

God's Word
is a gift
He has
laid before
us to save us
from self-destruction
and eternal separation.

There's nothing like the written Word of God for showing you the way to salvation through faith in Christ Jesus. Every part of Scripture is God-breathed and useful one way or another—showing us truth, exposing our rebellion, correcting our mistakes, training us to live God's way. Through the Word we are put together and shaped up for the tasks God has for us.

2 Timothy 3:16-17 *(The Message)*

Above all, you must understand that no prophecy of Scripture came about by the prophet's own interpretation of things.

2 Peter 1:20

My word that goes out from my mouth: It will not return to me empty, but will accomplish what I desire and achieve the purpose for which I sent it.

Isaiah 55:11

Lord, your Word is life. Christ Jesus is the Word. I live in exuberance as I spend time with Christ and feast on his living written Word. As Christ is my Shepherd, and I am a member of his flock. I delight in listening for and hearing his voice. As I listen, I joyfully receive the truth and fullness of his wisdom. With my spirit alive in Christ Jesus and full of his abundance, my will gratefully and humbly follows your will. Your Word always returns to me with favor and blessings. Your Word is life to me and health to my bones. I surrender myself to be molded by the Holy Spirit. As I trust in and speak your Word, it never returns void. Thank you that in Christ your promises are "yes and amen." My storehouses are full. My cup runs over. Goodness and mercy follows me all the days of my life. Thank you that all things were created by you and for you being made by your power according to your pleasure and for your praise and your glory. Thank you.

# OCTOBER 22

Our inheritance
in Christ,
exceeds our wildest
imaginations
and
surpasses our
greatest expectations.

You can be sure that God will take care of everything you need, his generosity exceeding even yours in the glory that pours from Jesus. Our God and Father abounds in glory that just pours out into eternity. Yes.

Philippians 4:19 *(The Message)*

I don't think the way you think. The way you work isn't the way I work. God's Decree. For as the sky soars high above earth, so the way I work surpasses the way you work, and the way I think is beyond the way you think. Just as rain and snow descend from the skies and don't go back until they've watered the earth, doing their work of making things grow and blossom, producing seed for farmers and food for the hungry, so will the words that come out of my mouth not come back empty-handed. They'll do the work I sent them to do, they'll complete the assignment I gave them.

Isaiah 55:8-11 *(The Message)*

Lord, you are Divine Supply. Thank you for supplying all my needs according to your riches in glory in Christ Jesus. Thank you for blessing me in my going out and my coming in. Thank you that in Christ I can do all things through him who gives me strength. My life and all you have called me to is hidden in Christ. My lips sing the praises of your glory. In Christ, you empower me to gather in my harvest in a remarkable way. Your Word is seed that brings abundant harvest in Christ as I plant in faith. Abiding in Christ, relying on Christ and trusting in Christ is the joy of my life. When I think on your goodness, your immeasurable love, your glory in Christ who lives in me, the gift of life Christ died to give me and all the blessings you pour out on me I am overcome with thanksgiving and praise. I am created for the praise of your glory. Thank you.

# OCTOBER 23

Oppression
has a destination
of
stealing
our destiny.

You're blessed when you stay on course, walking steadily on the road revealed by God. You're blessed when you follow his directions, doing your best to find him. That's right—you don't go off on your own; you walk straight along the road he set. You, God, prescribed the right way to live; now you expect us to live it. Oh, that my steps might be steady, keeping to the course you set; Then I'd never have any regrets in comparing my life with your counsel. I thank you for speaking straight from your heart; I learn the pattern of your righteous ways. I'm going to do what you tell me to do; don't ever walk off and leave me.

Psalm 119:1-8 *(The Message)*

Lord, you are Sovereign Order, and Divine Direction. I seek and treasure your counsel. Your divine instructions in your Word are unfailing. Thank you that your wisdom is first of all pure, then peace-loving, considerate, submissive, full of mercy and good fruit, impartial and sincere. Thank you for the gift of the Holy Spirit which lives within me teaching me, guiding me and correcting me. Because my mind is the mediator between my spirit and my soul, I renew my mind to your Word. Christ alive in me brings forth his truth through my spirit to my soul where he manifests in my thoughts, my words and my actions. I am yoked to Christ by faith. Christ is my supply and my victory. I find favor and good understanding in your sight and the sight of men because it is the favor of Christ that reflects through me. Thank you for placing everything for life and godliness inside of me by faith in Christ Jesus. As I abide, Christ supplies. Nothing or no one can steal the destiny you have set forth for me in Christ. I live in grateful praise.

# OCTOBER 24

God is
constantly
changing
and
rearranging us
as we yield our will
to His.

When you heard about Christ and were taught in him in accordance with the truth that is in Jesus. You were taught, with regard to your former way of life, to put off your old self, which is being corrupted by its deceitful desires; to be made new in the attitude of your minds; and to put on the new self, created to be like God in true righteousness and holiness.

Ephesians 4:21-24

Lord, you are Truth. Thank you for the honor and privilege of feasting on Your Word, yielding to Christ and waiting expectantly as he transforms his Word in me. My life is clay submitted to you by faith in Christ Jesus. My lips shout, "Press what needs pressing, mold what needs molding, and shape what needs shaping." I joy in knowing that you have placed within me your masterpiece and as you shape and mold me, you bring that masterpiece into manifestation. I am not the same today as I was yesterday. Every day my soul is aligning to the abundance of Christ in me and my life by the spirit. My beliefs, my perceptions, my thoughts, my attitudes, my feelings, my words and my actions are changing because you are faithful to perform your Word as I renew my mind to it. Things of this earth pale in comparison to knowing and loving you. I am a chosen race, a royal priesthood, set forth for wonderful deeds. I display the virtues and perfections of him who called me out of darkness into his marvelous light. Thank you for loving me, saving me and supplying me in Christ Jesus. I am your loved and accepted child.

# OCTOBER 25

God plants the
seeds of possibilities
in our spirit so
He can turn them into
His harvest in His time.

Jesus said, "The seed is the Word of God. The seeds on the road are those who hear the Word, but no sooner do they hear it than the Devil snatches it from them so they won't believe and be saved. The seeds in the gravel are those who hear with enthusiasm, but the enthusiasm doesn't go very deep. It's only another fad, and the moment there's trouble it's gone. And the seed that fell in the weeds—well, these are the ones who hear, but then the seed is crowded out and nothing comes of it as they go about their lives worrying about tomorrow, making money, and having fun. But the seed in the good earth—these are the good-hearts who seize the Word and hold on no matter what, sticking with it until there's a harvest."

Luke 8:11-15 *(The Message)*

Lord, you are Divine Seed. Thank you for the divine living seed which is your Word brought to living life by the Holy Spirit. I joy in spending time with you, feasting in your Word, learning of you and listening to your instruction. You have placed within the seed the potential to bring about a full and abundant harvest when it is planted in faith. I take your Word as seed and plant it in my heart. I water each seed in the fertile soil of your truth. I nurture the seed with faith and you bring about an abundant harvest. I tend the care of the garden of my life by abiding in, relying on and trusting in Christ Jesus. Christ fills my storehouses as I abide in him by faith. Seeds of love, mercy, compassion, truth, grace and hope are in me through Christ Jesus. As I water each seed in the fertile soil of your Truth, and nurture it with faith, my harvest overflows in abundance. Thank you for desiring to bless my life through the abundance of Christ Jesus. Glory Halleluiah.

# OCTOBER 26

We move forward
when we choose to
take our foot
off the brakes of pride.

Meanwhile, the moment we get tired in the waiting, God's Spirit is right alongside helping us along. If we don't know how or what to pray, it doesn't matter. He does our praying in and for us, making prayer out of our wordless sighs, our aching groans. He knows us far better than we know ourselves, knows our pregnant condition, and keeps us present before God. That's why we can be so sure that every detail in our lives of love for God is worked into something good. God knew what he was doing from the very beginning. He decided from the outset to shape the lives of those who love him along the same lines as the life of his Son. The Son stands first in the line of humanity he restored. We see the original and intended shape of our lives there in him. After God made that decision of what his children should be like, he followed it up by calling people by name. After he called them by name, he set them on a solid basis with himself. And then, after getting them established, he stayed with them to the end, gloriously completing what he had begun.

Romans 8: 26-30 *(The Message)*

Lord, you are my supply in all things. I have this treasure in jars of clay to show that this all-surpassing power is from you God and not from myself. I am hard pressed on every side, but not crushed; perplexed, but not in despair; persecuted, but not abandoned; struck down, but not destroyed. I always carry around in my body the death of Jesus, so that the life of Jesus may also be revealed in my body. I look to you and rest in Christ. You fill me to overflowing as I yield to Christ. I draw near to you and you draw near to me. I receive every Covenant blessing and every Blood Bought right that is mine in Christ Jesus. I live in the fullness of Christ Jesus. I joy in the fullness of Christ Jesus who lives within me. Thank you for creating and loving me.

# OCTOBER 27

The question is not
whether Jesus heals
but whether
we will believe
He wants to heal us.

The fundamental fact of existence is that this trust in God, this faith, is the firm foundation under everything that makes life worth living. It's our handle on what we can't see. The act of faith is what distinguished our ancestors, set them above the crowd. By faith, we see the world called into existence by God's word, what we see created by what we don't see. By an act of faith, Abel brought a better sacrifice to God than Cain. It was what he believed, not what he brought, that made the difference. That's what God noticed and approved as righteous. After all these centuries, that belief continues to catch our notice. By an act of faith, Enoch skipped death completely. "They looked all over and couldn't find him because God had taken him." We know on the basis of reliable testimony that before he was taken "he pleased God." It's impossible to please God apart from faith. And why? Because anyone who wants to approach God must believe both that he exists and that he cares enough to respond to those who seek him.

Hebrews 11:1-6 *(The Message)*

Lord, you are Healer. Miracles and wonders are mine in faith. I am nourished and sustained by your Spirit as Christ lives in me. Thank you for teaching me in your Word that healing is your will. At the cross, Christ took my pain and bore my sufferings. He was pierced for my transgressions and crushed for my iniquities. He took upon himself the punishment that brought me peace and by his wounds I am healed. My healing is complete in Christ. I access that provision placed in my spirit at the time of salvation by speaking your word in faith over my natural circumstances. Thank you that as I confess your word in faith, my mind takes hold of it bringing its harvest forth in my body. Thank you that as I abide in Christ by faith he brings forth his supply in my spirit to supply my needs. Thank you that in Christ I am assured all things work together for my good. I glorify and praise your faithfulness. I joy in worshipping you.

# OCTOBER 28

Praise and
thanksgiving
acknowledges
nothing happens
without His knowing
and everything
surrendered to
Him will be
used for
His glory
and our good.

With God rests my salvation and my glory; He is my Rock of unyielding strength and impenetrable hardness, and my refuge is in God!

Psalm 62:7 (AMP)

Lord, you are Abundant Supply. You have supplied me with life eternal and grace to meet my every need in Christ Jesus. I live clothed in the righteousness of Christ Jesus and dressed in his completed work of salvation. I am steadfast, immovable, always abounding in the work of the Lord, knowing that in the Lord my labor is not in vain. Your wisdom from above is first pure, then peaceable, gentle, willing to yield, full of mercy and good fruits, without partiality and without hypocrisy. All that is mine through the divine right of abiding in Christ is for your glory and my good. No one or nothing compares to your goodness, your grace, your love, your mercy and your provision. You comfort me in my pain. You bring victory over my enemies. You prosper me. Your protect and defend me. You heal my diseases. No encumbrance, no word of judgment spoken against me, no devil, and no demon can steal my identity or my supply in Christ Jesus. Inhale my worship. Exhale your glory. You are worthy to be praised. Thank you.

# OCTOBER 29

Jesus never
usurped
His
Father's
authority.

The Son is the image of the invisible God, the firstborn over all creation.

Colossians 1:15

The god of this age has blinded the minds of unbelievers, so that they cannot see the light of the gospel that displays the glory of Christ, who is the image of God.

2 Corinthians 4:4

Philip said, 'Master, show us the Father; then we'll be content.' You've been with me all this time, Philip, and you still don't understand? To see me is to see the Father. So how can you ask, 'Where is the Father?' Don't you believe that I am in the Father and the Father is in me? The words that I speak to you aren't mere words. I don't just make them up on my own. The Father who resides in me crafts each word into a divine act.

John 14:8-10

Lord, you are Sovereign Authority. All things were created by you through your spoken Word. Your Word is Light and Truth. You have created me in your image with value and purpose. Yielded to Christ who lives within me by faith, the divine purpose of my life unfolds. I am created for your glory. My life is a reflection of your life within me. When others see me, they see your life in me manifesting your fruits of the spirit. With Christ, I can do all things. Apart from Christ, I can do nothing. I yield the clay of my life for your molding. I humble myself before you and you lift me up. I joy in beholding your glory. I live to praise you. I live to share your goodness with those around me. I live as a vessel that overflows with your love. Thank you.

# OCTOBER 30

By grace through faith
we share everything that
belongs to God.

This resurrection life you received from God is not a timid, grave-tending life. It's adventurously expectant, greeting God with a childlike "What's next, Papa?" God's Spirit touches our spirits and confirms who we really are. We know who he is, and we know who we are: Father and children. And we know we are going to get what's coming to us—an unbelievable inheritance! We go through exactly what Christ goes through. If we go through the hard times with him, then we're certainly going to go through the good times with him!

Romans 8:15-17 *(The Message)*

Lord, you are Divine Father. You have accepted me into you family, wrapping your love around me in Christ Jesus who has supplied all my needs according to his riches in glory. I am one with you in spirit in Christ Jesus where I am accepted, I am secure, I am loved, I am a new creation, I am redeemed, I am justified, I am blessed, I am chosen, I am adopted, I am forgiven, I am alive, I have access to you, I am free, I am light, I am complete, I am victorious, I am your workmanship, I am a joint heir with Christ, I am delivered, and I am redeemed from the curse of the law. In addition to your overwhelming gift of identity, position, authority and access, I have your manifold grace that flows to me through Christ in me to bring forth the promises of your Word for me. Your wondrous Grace has only left me one labor which is the greatest joy of my life and that is resting in Christ. I praise you for you are worthy to be praised. I worship you for you are worthy to be honored and adored. Halleluiah praises now and forevermore. Thank you.

# OCTOBER 31

Every
relational
conflict
has a
self-righteous
issue in it.

Don't pick on people, jump on their failures, criticize their faults—unless, of course, you want the same treatment. Don't condemn those who are down; that hardness can boomerang. Be easy on people; you'll find life a lot easier. Give away your life; you'll find life given back, but not merely given back—given back with bonus and blessing. Giving, not getting, is the way. Generosity begets generosity.

Luke 6:37-38 *(The Message)*

Jesus said, "'Love the Lord your God with all your passion and prayer and intelligence. This is the most important, the first on any list. But there is a second to set alongside it: Love others as well as you love yourself. These two commands are pegs; everything in God's Law and the Prophets hangs from them.

Matthew 22:37-40 *(The Message)*

Lord, you are True Love. When I accepted Jesus as my Lord and Savior, I gave up my rights to myself. I yielded to you to receive Christ by faith. I yield my life abiding in Christ as I live by the spirit. I renew my mind to the truth of your Word and humble my will to your will. Search and reveal to me my mind sets that do not line up with your Word producing the fruits of selfishness, demand, self–centeredness and pride. I repent where I have failed and gratefully receive your loving correction. With love living within me, I look for ways to serve others. My relationships reflect the revelation of honor and understanding that everyone I meet is created in your image. My words are kind, encouraging, gentle and loving regardless of the actions of another towards me. I bear the fruit of love because I abide in Christ who is the vine. I love others with Christ in me. The love I give out is multiplied and returned to me in wondrous ways.

# NOVEMBER 1

God always
shows
up
when we
open
up.

So I say to you: Ask and it will be given to you; seek and you will find; knock and the door will be opened to you. For everyone who asks receives; the one who seeks finds; and to the one who knocks, the door will be opened.

Luke 11:9-10

Cast your cares on the Lord and he will sustain you; he will never let the righteous be shaken.

Psalms 55:22

Lord, you are my Portion. There is nothing that escapes your eyes or your knowledge. You know my thoughts before the words are formed on my tongue. You have created me with free will giving me the freedom of making choices. When I draw near to you, you draw near to me. As your loved, accepted and righteous child in Christ Jesus, thank you for inviting and allowing me to cast my cares on you. Thank you for hearing me when I call. Thank you for honoring my desire to grow in your Grace and pouring out revelation as I feast on your Word. I delight myself in Christ and He brings forth the desires of my heart which is to be a mirror that reflects him to all those I meet. I yield the pieces of my life to the altar of your Grace and wait excitedly and expectantly in faith as you knit them together. Your divine plan for my life unfolds minute by minute and day by day. I joy resting in the fullness of your Grace which is provision and supply. Every day, I write another chapter of Halleluiah praises as I fellowship with you in your Word.

# NOVEMBER 2

Sin
takes
a back
seat when
Jesus
is
steering.

So, since we're out from under the old tyranny, does that mean we can live any old way we want? Since we're free in the freedom of God, can we do anything that comes to mind? Hardly. You know well enough from your own experience that there are some acts of so-called freedom that destroy freedom. Offer yourselves to sin, for instance, and it's your last free act. But offer yourselves to the ways of God and the freedom never quits. All your lives you've let sin tell you what to do. But thank God you've started listening to a new master, one whose commands set you free to live openly in his freedom!

Romans 6:15-18 *(The Message)*

Lord, you are Freedom. Thank you Jesus for paying my sin debt in full. Sin or satan can no longer accuse me or condemn me. Where the spirit is, there is freedom. I am one in spirit with you in Christ Jesus. Thank you Jesus for breaking the power of sin. Thank you for shedding your life giving blood for my eternal death. You have restored my relationship to the Father that sin once separated. You took upon yourself my sin nature and exchanged it for a holy and blameless nature. Your gift of life is one I celebrate with every fiber of my being. My spirit desires to fellowship with you and feast on your Word. My soul delights in you as your life in the spirit pours over into my soul. By body joins the celebration by wanting to honor you. I submit my soul to the work of salvation which began on the day I accepted Jesus as my Lord and Savior. I walk uprightly as my mind is fixed on you. You are my God. I am your child. Thank you.

# NOVEMBER 3

What we
release to
God,
He
restores.

With the arrival of Jesus, the Messiah, that fateful dilemma is resolved. Those who enter into Christ's being-here-for-us no longer have to live under a continuous, low-lying black cloud. A new power is in operation. The Spirit of life in Christ, like a strong wind, has magnificently cleared the air, freeing you from a fated lifetime of brutal tyranny at the hands of sin and death. God went for the jugular when he sent his own Son. He didn't deal with the problem as something remote and unimportant. In his Son, Jesus, he personally took on the human condition, entered the disordered mess of struggling humanity in order to set it right once and for all. The law code, weakened as it always was by fractured human nature, could never have done that. The law always ended up being used as a Band-Aid on sin instead of a deep healing of it. And now what the law code asked for but we couldn't deliver is accomplished as we, instead of redoubling our own efforts, simply embrace what the Spirit is doing in us.

Romans 8:1-4 *(The Message)*

Lord, you are Divine Restoration. I am no longer condemned. I am a new creation in Christ. When you look at me, you see me holy and blameless in Christ Jesus. I am signed and sealed by the Holy Spirit. I yield myself to the work of the Holy Spirit to continue to be molded into Christ likeness. I feast on your Word with gladness knowing that your Word is living and filled with your power. I confess your Word over my circumstances and wait in faith as it holds the power to move mountains. I joyfully live free from the curse and loosed from the demands of the law. With Grace, the person of Christ Jesus and his power living in me, my spirit is drawn to your goodness. I breathe in the air around me as a reminder of my life in Christ. I praise the wonder of your Majesty as I see your divine hand in creation. I feel the wind against my face and live mindful you breathed life in me. I live to praise, glorify you and serve others. I joy in resting and abiding in Christ who is my supply for and in every thing. Thank you. Halleluiah praises.

# NOVEMBER 4

Where faith
goes,
something
supernatural
returns.

Jesus was matter-of-fact: "Embrace this God-life. Really embrace it, and nothing will be too much for you. This mountain, for instance: Just say, 'Go jump in the lake'—no shuffling or shilly-shallying— and it's as good as done. That's why I urge you to pray for absolutely everything, ranging from small to large. Include everything as you embrace this God-life, and you'll get God's everything. And when you assume the posture of prayer, remember that it's not all asking. If you have anything against someone, forgive—only then will your heavenly Father be inclined to also wipe your slate clean of sins.

Mark 11:22-25 *(The Message)*

Lord, you are the I AM. There is no other God like you. You formed me before the foundation of the world. By faith, I am high and lifted up with Christ seated in the heavens with every spiritual blessing. My lips shout your praises as I receive by faith every blood bought blessing of Christ Jesus. My cup runs over in your goodness and blessing. Christ has restored my relationship with you. I am your child and you are my God. I enter your gates with thanksgiving and your courts with praise for you are worthy. Your faithfulness is unmoving and your love is forever steadfast. In Christ, I live in the fullness of your unending blessings. You have given me the measure of your faith. You have given me Eternal life through Christ Jesus. You have redeemed me for your Glory. I receive the crown of life with thanksgiving and joyfully respond to your one request and that is to only believe. I seek you. I yield to you. I rest in you. Thank you. Glory Halleluiah.

# NOVEMBER 5

Our mouth hinders or enhances
God's
manifestations in our life.

Words kill, words give life; they're either poison or fruit—you choose.

Proverbs 18:21 *(The Message)*

Watch the way you talk. Let nothing foul or dirty come out of your mouth. Say only what helps, each word a gift.

Ephesians 4:29 *(The Message)*

For by your words you will be acquitted, and by your words you will be condemned.

Matthew 12:37

The soothing tongue is a tree of life, but a perverse tongue crushes the spirit.

Proverbs 15:4

But what does it say? "The word is near you; it is in your mouth and in your heart," that is, the message concerning faith that we proclaim: If you declare with your mouth, "Jesus is Lord," and believe in your heart that God raised him from the dead, you will be saved.

Romans 10:8-9

Lord, you are Life. I hide myself in Christ and come before your Throne of Grace yielded to hear you speak to me. Preserve my life and lead me in the way everlasting. I live that the words of my mouth and the meditations of my heart will be acceptable to you. I guard my mouth for it is the wellspring of life. I use my words to glorify you and build others up. I put away perversity and keep corrupt talk far from my lips. I feed my spirit with the Truth of your Word beholding you. What I behold, I become. My words are an overflow of your presence and goodness within me.

# NOVEMBER 6

Wisdom is
knowing what is
right and
doing
it.

God, teach me lessons for living so I can stay the course. Give me insight so I can do what you tell me— my whole life one long, obedient response. Guide me down the road of your commandments; I love traveling this freeway! Give me a bent for your words of wisdom, and not for piling up loot. Divert my eyes from toys and trinkets, invigorate me on the pilgrim way. Affirm your promises to me— promises made to all who fear you. Deflect the harsh words of my critics— but what you say is always so good. See how hungry I am for your counsel; preserve my life through your righteous ways!

Psalm 119:33-40 *(The Message)*

Lord, you are Wisdom. I am guided and nourished by your spirit. I joy in spending time with you. I am an open vessel to you. Teach me knowledge and good judgment as I abide in Christ. Wisdom is sweet to my soul. Wisdom makes one wise man more powerful than ten rulers in a city. I live to seek you. I live to praise you. I live to glorify you. I live to be all and do all you created me to be and do. Hidden mysteries unfold as I spend time in your Word. Thank you for the Holy Spirit who unfolds revelations. Your wisdom is first of all pure; then peace-loving, considerate, submissive, full of mercy, and good fruit, impartial, and sincere. I yield by faith to Christ living in me and desire a deeper understanding of you. I renew my mind to your Word and take my thoughts captive to the obedience of Christ because I know my thoughts form my words and actions. Thank you for watching over your Word to perform it. All your Covenant promises are mine in Christ Jesus. My lips sing your praises. My soul magnifies you. Thank you.

# NOVEMBER 7

Outer turmoil
comes from
inner unrest.

You're blessed when you can show people how to cooperate instead
of compete or fight. That's when you discover who you really are,
and your place in God's family.

Matthew 5:9 *(The Message)*

Evil scheming distorts the schemer; peace-planning brings joy to
the planner.

Proverbs 12:20 *(The Message)*

Lord, you are Peace. I have peace as a fruit of my spirit because Christ, the
Prince of Peace lives within me. Peace overflows into my soul as I worship
you in spirit and truth. Peace springs forth from your Word as I feast on it.
Thank you for peace that overflows from my spirit as I trust in, meditate on
and speak your Word. Man-made peace is getting your way. World-made
peace is the absence of disturbance. Your peace passes all understanding. I
yield, abide and trust you Jesus and you bring peace to my very being. The
peace of Christ rules my mind and guards my heart. I look to you Jesus
to satisfy my longing for love and approval and not to others. I am able to
hold my peace when adversity comes because you have taught me to trust
in your Grace provision. Thank you for working all things together for my
good. Thank you that as I walk in the spirit I reap your peace. I joyfully
declare, "Not my will, but yours be done." Halleluiah.

# NOVEMBER 8

Until
we rest
in the finality
of the
Cross,
we will never
experience
the reality of
resurrection.

What a God we have! And how fortunate we are to have him, this Father of our Master Jesus! Because Jesus was raised from the dead, we've been given a brand-new life and have everything to live for, including a future in heaven—and the future starts now! God is keeping careful watch over us and the future. The Day is coming when you'll have it all—life healed and whole.

1 Peter 1:3-5 *(The Message)*

Lord, you are Life. The same power that raised Christ from the dead is living in my spirit and bringing power to every area of my life. The moment I accepted Christ as Lord and Savior I was crucified, my sin nature died and I was resurrected in Christ. The life which I now live in the flesh I live by faith in Christ Jesus, who loved me, and gave himself for me. Neither death nor the powers of darkness have dominion over me in Christ. I receive that which is before me as a hidden treasure and an opportunity to see your love revealed. I live in your abundant Grace who is Jesus. Your immeasurable love has gifted me with every blood bought blessing of Christ Jesus. I live to sing your praises. Inhale my worship and exhale your glory. Strike up the band of praise. I live to the beat of a different drummer. My life holds the beat of harmonious rhythm because I know the one who writes every melody. Praises flow from within like a flowing stream.

# NOVEMBER 9

Praise is the ultimate
relinquishment
of our tight grip
of control.

Be cheerful no matter what; pray all the time; thank God no matter what happens. This is the way God wants you who belong to Christ Jesus to live.

1 Thessalonians 5:16-18 *(The Message)*

God made the heavens— Royal splendor radiates from him, A powerful beauty sets him apart. Bravo, God, Bravo! Everyone join in the great shout: Encore! In awe before the beauty, in awe before the might. Bring gifts and celebrate, Bow before the beauty of God, Then to your knees—everyone worship! Get out the message—God Rules! He put the world on a firm foundation; He treats everyone fair and square.

Psalm 96:5-10 *(The Message)*

Lord, you are Great and worthy of praise. I marvel at your wonder as I see your imprint of majesty upon creation. Your attention to every detail of creating the universe is only a glimpse of your power and might and yet you are so personal you know the number of hairs on my head. Your Word brings order and life. It calls things that are not into being. All of creation is subject to the authority of your Word. I delight in living in submission to Christ who is my life. Yielding my thoughts and my will opens the door of freedom for the Holy Spirit to bring forth all Christ planted in my spirit to a bountiful harvest in the natural. Like God, creator of all, designed the universe with the seed principle of sowing and reaping, I delight in sowing your Word in my spirit and reaping abundant blessings by placing my faith in Christ who brings your abundant harvest to me and through me. When I consider your immeasurable love, outbursts of heartfelt praise pours from the depths of my soul. There is no greater joy than loving you. Thank you.

## NOVEMBER 10

God knows
every act
of kindness
regardless
of its size.

So, chosen by God for this new life of love, dress in the wardrobe God picked out for you: compassion, kindness, humility, quiet strength, discipline. Be even-tempered, content with second place, quick to forgive an offense. Forgive as quickly and completely as the Master forgave you. And regardless of what else you put on, wear love. It's your basic, all-purpose garment. Never be without it.

Colossians 3:12-14 *(The Message)*

The LORD does not look at the things people look at. People look at the outward appearance, but the LORD looks at the heart.

1 Samuel 16: 7b

Lord, You are all seeing and all knowing. Nothing escapes you as you look upon my heart. By faith in Christ, my spirit is alive and one with you. Thank you for the transforming power of the Holy Spirit living within me that is transforming me into the image of Christ Jesus as I feast on your Word and yield my will to you. You have given me life in Christ Jesus and planted in my heart the desire to drink his living water and feast on his truth. Thank you for giving me the garment of your love by allowing me to put on Christ who is love. Thank you for molding and shaping me daily into the masterpiece that you have created me to be through the life of Christ who lives in me. You have a plan for my life and you are fulfilling your purpose in me as I yield to Christ. You think thoughts of peace towards me, and not of evil. You give me a future and a hope. You order my steps and delight in how I walk. The aliveness of my spirit and the joy of my soul writes a symphony of praise to you throughout the day. Halleluiah choruses to you.

# NOVEMBER 11

We are invited
to reason
and
privileged to trust.

Your kingdom is an everlasting kingdom, and your dominion endures through all generations. The LORD is trustworthy in all he promises and faithful in all he does. The LORD upholds all who fall and lifts up all who are bowed down. The eyes of all look to you, and you give them their food at the proper time. You open your hand and satisfy the desires of every living thing. The LORD is righteous in all his ways and faithful in all he does. The LORD is near to all who call on him, to all who call on him in truth. He fulfills the desires of those who fear him; he hears their cry and saves them. The LORD watches over all who love him, but all the wicked he will destroy.

Psalm 145:13-20 *(The Message)*

Lord, you are Trustworthy and Unfailing. You are my fortress, my shield, my refuge, my hope, my defender and my deliverer in all things. In Christ, all things work together for my good and for your glory. All that I am comes from you. You have created me in your image, created my spirit anew and alive, supplied my every need according to your riches in glory, given me access to every spiritual blessing in heavenly places, paid by sin debt in full, provided your measure of faith to come boldly before your throne of grace, healed my diseases, broken the power of sin, defeated the kingdom of darkness, shared your authority to reign, rule, and create through my spoken words, invited me to cast my cares on you and live free, all by relationship with and by faith in the name and blood of Jesus Christ. There is only one self-effort I can add to your full provision in Jesus and that is to fall to my knees in grateful humility, worship you, thank you, and shout continual praises forevermore. Receive my offering of thanksgiving. Thank you.

# NOVEMBER 12

Every time we claim
our identity as a child
of God,
we are resting
on His
promises
by faith.

Because you are his sons, God sent the Spirit of his Son into our hearts, the Spirit who calls out, *"Abba*, Father." So you are no longer a slave, but God's child; and since you are his child, God has made you also an heir.

Galatians 4:6-7

The Spirit himself testifies with our spirit that we are God's children. Now if we are children, then we are heirs—heirs of God and co-heirs with Christ, if indeed we share in his sufferings in order that we may also share in his glory.

Romans 8:16-17

Lord, you are my Father and I am your child. You have adopted me into your family by faith in Christ Jesus. I am signed, sealed and delivered in the Holy Spirit. I humbly and gratefully receive your incomparable riches of grace in Christ Jesus. I delight in spending time with Christ, yielding to his spirit living within, and seeing his divine grace mold and shape me into his likeness. I am united with Christ in one spirit. I am a member of Christ's body. I am an heir to your divine promises. I am free from condemnation. I am fully and completely loved. I am hidden in Christ. I am a minister of reconciliation. I am God's workmanship. I am chosen to bear much fruit. I am living in the abundance of Christ. I can do all things through Christ who gives me strength. I live by faith. I am empowered by Grace and under girded in your love. I am a child of the King divinely created, fully loved, and totally accepted. Thank you.

# NOVEMBER 13

Freedom
is rarely captured,
it's usually
surrendered.

So here's what I want you to do, God helping you: Take your everyday, ordinary life—your sleeping, eating, going-to-work, and walking-around life—and place it before God as an offering. Embracing what God does for you is the best thing you can do for him. Don't become so well-adjusted to your culture that you fit into it without even thinking. Instead, fix your attention on God. You'll be changed from the inside out. Readily recognize what he wants from you, and quickly respond to it. Unlike the culture around you, always dragging you down to its level of immaturity, God brings the best out of you, develops well-formed maturity in you.

Romans 12:1-2 *(The Message)*

Lord, you are Freedom. Thank you for releasing me from sin consciousness which held me in bondage of believing that my self-generated works would allow me to be acceptable to you. You have revealed the truth that true freedom is abiding in Christ by faith and he supplies. Jesus is my justification, my righteousness and my access to you. I delight in sharing my thoughts, my desires and my dreams with you. As I rest in you, the person and supply of Christ Jesus knows fully and perfectly how to reveal your will and join it in perfect union to the gifts you have already placed in me. Thank you for continually unfolding and enlarging your love in my spirit. Thank you for bringing the truth you have placed in my spirit to revelation where my mind can take hold and apply it by faith. I am chosen, fully loved and completely accepted in Christ Jesus. I speak your promises by faith over my life and I joy in knowing you are working all things out for my good. I abide and Christ supplies. What Freedom. What joy. What life. Thank you.

# NOVEMBER 14

Faith is the
road map
to our
destination.

And without faith it is impossible to please God, because anyone who comes to him must believe that he exists and that he rewards those who earnestly seek him.

Hebrews 11:6

Jesus said, "Everything is possible for one who believes."

Mark 9:23

So then, just as you received Christ Jesus as Lord, continue to live your lives in him, rooted and built up in him, strengthened in the faith as you were taught, and overflowing with thankfulness.

Colossians 2:6-7

Lord, you are Divine Destiny. You bridged the relationship between us that sin divided in Christ Jesus. The blood of Jesus has made the final and lasting exchange of his life for my death. His spirit, one with me by faith, has provided the opening where I can meet your abundant and immeasurable love face to face. Your love opened the Lamb's book of life and Christ Jesus wrote my name in it. My destiny by faith in Christ Jesus, is intimate fellowship with you, an unbreakable relational connection to you, a place of secure and constant rest where the Grace of Christ Jesus lives in me and brings your goodness through me to glorify you, serve others, and receive your lavish blessings. I joy in your truth that I can do all things through Christ who is my strength. I delight in knowing that Christ has broken the power of sin that once bound me. I live in the spirit where there is freedom and life. My joy, which is no labor, is to abide in Christ by faith and rest in his provision. Thank you for my divine destiny in Christ Jesus.

# NOVEMBER 15

Faith
without action
binds us to the
natural world
and hold us to its
limitations.

Dear friends, do you think you'll get anywhere in this if you learn all the right words but never do anything? Does merely talking about faith indicate that a person really has it? For instance, you come upon an old friend dressed in rags and half-starved and say, "Good morning, friend! Be clothed in Christ! Be filled with the Holy Spirit!" and walk off without providing so much as a coat or a cup of soup—where does that get you? Isn't it obvious that God-talk without God-acts is outrageous nonsense? I can already hear one of you agreeing by saying, "Sounds good. You take care of the faith department, I'll handle the works department." Not so fast. You can no more show me your works apart from your faith than I can show you my faith apart from my works. Faith and works, works and faith, fit together hand in glove. Do I hear you professing to believe in the one and only God, but then observe you complacently sitting back as if you had done something wonderful? That's just great. Demons do that, but what good does it do them? Use your heads! Do you suppose for a minute that you can cut faith and works in two and not end up with a corpse on your hands?

James 2: 14-20 *(The Message)*

Lord, you are Faithful. Your Word is a mirror that reflects your nature, your faithfulness and your Covenant promises which are mine by faith in Christ Jesus. Jesus is the Word and the fulfillment of the Word. I delight in renewing my mind to the truth of your Word, putting it in my mouth and placing a demand of faith on it to call forth that which is unseen into the seen. I am a vessel of your supply by faith in Christ Jesus. All that I am is already complete in Christ Jesus. I joy in responding to your immeasurable love by being obedient to where you lead me to glorify you and serve others. The works I do are divinely anointed, created by the spirit, blessed and released in the Grace of Christ Jesus. I live to glorify you and serve others out of the abundance of Christ living in me. Thank you. Inhale my worship. Exhale your glory. My lips sing your praises.

# NOVEMBER 16

The devil rarely
brings us into bondage
through an all out
frontal assault,
but systematically
restricts one freedom
after another until we find
ourselves stumbling in the darkness.

And no wonder, for Satan himself masquerades as an angel of light. It is not surprising, then, if his servants also masquerade as servants of righteousness. Their end will be what their actions deserve.

2 Corinthians 11:14-16

Lord, you are Light. In you is no darkness. As I live in Christ, I live in the light. I guard my mind with the truth of your word because my mind is the portal in which satan desires to enter to deceive me from my identity in Christ. Thank you Jesus that I have your authority to cast down vain imaginations, confess your Word as my weapon of victory over the powers of darkness, use the name of Jesus as the name above all names, and plead your blood over the attacks that come against me. No weapon formed against me can prosper. Every tongue that rises up against you in judgment, you will condemn. Thank you for rescuing me from every evil attack and bringing me safely into your heavenly kingdom. Thank you for triumphant victory in Christ Jesus. Every plant which my heavenly Father did not plant shall be uprooted up in the name of Jesus. Nothing or no one is more powerful than your Word or my confession of faith in it. I take up the whole armor of God and overcome by faith in Christ Jesus. Thank you for giving me victory in Jesus.

# NOVEMBER 17

Unhealed
hurts choke life
out of our relationships
when they become
the noose around our souls.

The Lord is close to the brokenhearted and saves those who are crushed in spirit. The righteous person may have many troubles, but the Lord delivers him from them all.

Psalms 34:18-19

Lord, you are Healer. Your hands fashioned and formed me before I knew you. You saw my beginning and my end before the foundation of the world. You knew every trial and every suffering I would face before I was even formed in my Mother's womb. I cannot read the minds of others. Only you can read the minds and heart of others. You have invited me to partake of your healing of my hurts by honestly acknowledging them before you and those you have brought into my life. I ask you to search me and bring the remembrances of those emotions that rooted deep within me when my wound occurred. I release my pain to Christ by inviting him into it and asking him to go through it transforming it into his peace. Thank you for drawing me to your love and healing. Thank you for desiring me to be free of unresolved emotions so that the place it has been occupying in my soul will no longer bring a hindrance for me to receive the fullness of your love in my spirit. In the glory of your presence, I find rest. In the depths of your love, I find peace. In the grace of your healing, I am free to be all that you created me to be by faith in Christ Jesus. Thank you for loving me and caring about every detail of my life.

# NOVEMBER 18

Loss of joy
usually indicates
the withdrawal
of an area
of our lives
away from the
Lordship of Christ.

May the God of your hope so fill you with all joy and peace in believing [through the experience of your faith] that by the power of the Holy Spirit you may abound *and* be overflowing (bubbling over) with hope.

Romans 15:13 (AMP)

Lord, you are Joy. I sing your praises every morning for your new mercies. I sing your praises at noon day because your eyes are forever watching over me and your steadfast love is forever covering me. I sing your praises as I lay my head on the pillow to sleep because your steadfast love and abounding Grace by faith in Christ Jesus has supplied my every need. Nothing or no one can steal my joy because my joy comes to me in the abundance of Christ living in me. In Christ, your steadfast love and mercy covers me, you enlarge my territory, you are my refuge and fortress, you bless me with a shield, and you pour out your blessings upon me. I live in complete triumphant joy in Christ regardless of my circumstances. In Christ, my life flows in divine provision and my soul rejoices. Joy spills over from my spirit into my soul as I spend time with you and feast on your Word. I live in the fullness of your love poured out for me in Christ Jesus. Every day I write another chapter of Halleluiah praises to you. My spirit is filled with you.

# NOVEMBER 19

The
Kingdom of God
is not mere
talk it's
supernatural power.

I know there are some among you who are so full of themselves they never listen to anyone, let alone me. They don't think I'll ever show up in person. But I'll be there sooner than you think, God willing, and then we'll see if they're full of anything but hot air. God's Way is not a matter of mere talk; it's an empowered life.

1 Corinthians 4:18-20 *(The Message)*

Lord, You are Majestic and Glorious. Your Word is a rich faithful and full supply of never ending living power. You created me and called me forth in Christ. Your Word is life and spirit. I am joined as one spirit with you by faith in Christ Jesus. You have given me the authority in Christ Jesus to release your Word from my lips and plant it over my circumstances. My mouth is the instrument of my spirit releasing the blessings that are mine in Christ I fill my mouth with the sword of the Spirit and you are faithfully watching over it to perform it. Thank you for teaching me that faith-filled words move mountains and not my begging, pity, repetitive or self-centered requests. As I speak your Word which is your will, I release your creating power in the spirit to manifest in my natural circumstances. Thank you that as your Word goes forth out of my mouth, it does not return void, but it accomplishes and prospers that which it was sent forth. Thank you for empowering and supplying me with your Word. Your Word is life and power.

# NOVEMBER 20

All of God's
promises
are
'Yes and Amen'
in
Christ.

How blessed is God! And what a blessing he is! He's the Father of our Master, Jesus Christ, and takes us to the high places of blessing in him. Long before he laid down earth's foundations, he had us in mind, had settled on us as the focus of his love, to be made whole and holy by his love. Long, long ago he decided to adopt us into his family through Jesus Christ. (What pleasure he took in planning this!) He wanted us to enter into the celebration of his lavish gift-giving by the hand of his beloved Son."

Ephesians 1:3-6 *(The Message)*

Lord, you are Unending Faithfulness. You take me to the high places of blessing in Christ Jesus. Your love for me through Christ has redeemed me, resurrected my dead spirit to life and pours out your full provision of supply. I am one with you never to be orphaned or abandoned. Your Grace is sufficient. Your Word is seed life that I plant in my spirit to bring forth your purposed harvest. I delightfully renew my mind to your Word which is life to me and for me. I confess your Word out my mouth and it has the power of a two edged sword penetrating to that which it is purposed bringing forth your will. Your Word is my well spring of life making a way to bring every promise you have faithfully declared into manifestation. As I hear your Word, it stirs and nourishes my faith. It takes root in my spirit where it is watered by faith in Christ who lives in me. I joy in abiding in Christ Jesus, spending time with him and listening to his voice. Thank you for lavishing your love on me and allowing me to praise you and serve others.

# NOVEMBER 21

Our human
weaknesses
provide the ideal
opportunity
for the
display
of
Divine Power.

My grace is enough; it's all you need. My strength comes into its own in your weakness.

2 Corinthians 12:9 *(The Message)*

Lord, you are Grace which is the person of Christ Jesus and his supply. You deal bountifully with me. You preserve, guard and pour all goodness into me. You are my unfailing and immediate supply of all good. I am a watered tree bearing fruit. Thank you for the Holy Spirit who comes to my aid and bears me up in my weaknesses interceding on my behalf according to the will of God. Thank you for Jesus who is my life and my strength. Thank you for teaching me I have the full measure of the God-head living in me. With the creating power of the Father, the mind of Christ, and the help of the Holy Spirit, I live in the gift of freedom, joy, and hope they bring. Jesus is the High Priest of my confessions as I speak the Word over my life. I stand in the gift of faith by the measure you placed in me. I hold unswervingly to your steadfast love. I glory in your presence. I praise your goodness. I celebrate your mercies which are new every day. No matter what comes I know I am more than a conqueror in Christ. Thank you Jesus for being my supply.

# NOVEMBER 22

Only the light
of truth,
can abolish
the darkness
of deception.

You, LORD, are my lamp; the LORD turns my darkness into light.

2 Samuel 22:29

Send me your light and your truth, let them lead me; let them bring me to your holy mountain, to the place where you dwell.

Psalm 43:3

Lord, you are Truth and Light. Your wisdom reveals my way and your Grace lights it. My life is hidden in Christ by faith, where I forever live in the light. Shame, guilt, condemnation, the power of sin and all fruits of darkness have been broken by the blood of Christ Jesus. By faith, I exercise the authority that Jesus gave to me to use his name to bind and loose. What I bind on earth is bound in Heaven. What I loose on earth is loosed in Heaven. In Jesus name, I bind the principalities, the powers, and the rules of the darkness of this world. I bind and cast down spiritual wickedness in high places and render them harmless and ineffective against me in the name of Jesus. I loose the blessings of Heaven over my life as a child of the light. The light of Christ in me shines from me like a city on a hill. As I stand steadfast and immovable in faith, I bring others to your light. Thank you Jesus. You are Truth and Light. I sing your praises.

# NOVEMBER 23

God
equips and
lends His armor
to us;
we have
to put it on.

Be prepared. You're up against far more than you can handle on your own. Take all the help you can get, every weapon God has issued, so that when it's all over but the shouting you'll still be on your feet. Truth, righteousness, peace, faith, and salvation are more than words. Learn how to apply them. You'll need them throughout your life. God's Word is an indispensable weapon. In the same way, prayer is essential in this ongoing warfare. Pray hard and long. Pray for your brothers and sisters. Keep your eyes open. Keep each other's spirits up so that no one falls behind or drops out.

Ephesians 6:13-19 *(The Message)*

Lord, you are my Divine Protection. You have supplied me for victory. I stand by faith on your written Word as I confess it over my life. I abide in the strength of Christ by faith who is the living Word. As your child in Christ, you have given me authority to use his name and plead his blood. The weapons of my warfare are no carnal but mighty for pulling down every stronghold and defeating the powers of darkness. No weapon formed against me shall prosper. You keep me safe from the hands of the wicked and dissipate the plans of evil against me. Your angels of assignment watch over me and protect me. I have peace of mind because I keep my mind on Christ. I embrace each day with your living power as I suit up in my divine armor by faith. I place your salvation on my head as a helmet. Your breastplate of Righteousness covers me. I wear your belt of truth. I carry your peace as sandals on my feet. I grasp the sword of your spirit as my armored weapon. I wear the shield of faith to quench any fiery darts of darkness. Greater is he that is in me that he that is in the world. Christ is my victory. Thank you.

# NOVEMBER 24

A circumstance
does not have the
power to bring
us down,
but how
we view
it does.

So do not fear, for I am with you; do not be dismayed, for I am your God. I will strengthen you and help you; I will uphold you with my righteous right hand.

Isaiah 41:10

But the Lord is faithful, and he will strengthen you and protect you from the evil one.

2 Thessalonians 3:3

Lord, you are Life. I look to you as my Divine Security. I have the eyes to see, the ears to hear and the heart to connect with all the fullness of your spirit because Christ lives in me by faith. I live in this world, but I am not of this world. I rest and abide in Christ trusting in his provision which he graciously lavishes on the righteous. Christ has imparted his righteousness to me. Your Word reveals your loving nature and your divine provision. You are the God who parted the Red Sea. You are the God who called forth dry bones unto life. You are the God who spoke to the waves and they obeyed you with calmness. You are the God who died to pay my sin debt in full and exchange your life for my death. Nothing or no one compares to you. No circumstance can agitate, stir or move me from my place of rest and trust in Christ Jesus who brings forth your divine supply to me and through me. You are an awesome God. Thank you.

# NOVEMBER 25

A set
back
is not
a
sit back
when
we live
by faith.

What marvelous love the Father has extended to us! Just look at it—we're called children of God! That's who we really are. But that's also why the world doesn't recognize us or take us seriously, because it has no idea who he is or what he's up to. But friends, that's exactly who we are: children of God. And that's only the beginning. Who knows how we'll end up! What we know is that when Christ is openly revealed, we'll see him—and in seeing him, become like him. All of us who look forward to his Coming stay ready, with the glistening purity of Jesus' life as a model for our own.

1John 3:1-3 *(The Message)*

Lord, you are Supernatural Provision. You make a way where there doesn't appear to be one. By faith in Christ, I am the righteousness of God, chosen to bear fruit. I am seated in the Heavenly realm with Christ and have unbroken access to the Father. I am a child of the King and a royal priesthood. In Christ, all things are possible. I call forth my ministry of reconciliation and every day door after door opens in faith. You have anointed my hands to bear fruit for the Kingdom, to bring forth an abundant harvest, to glorify you and to serve others. Thank you for your Covenant Promises which are mine by faith in Christ Jesus. I delight in spending time with you, worshipping you, sharing the desires of my heart with you and placing a demand by faith on your Word. Christ is provision and breakthrough. I can advance in victory against any adverse troop. I can scale a wall in his strength. I live in Christ believing your divine way unfolds before me. I live in joyful thanksgiving in Christ. Praise God from whom all blessings flow. Thank you.

# NOVEMBER 26

When God
does the
leading,
we always
get
where we're
going.

You are my hiding place; you will protect me from trouble and surround me with songs of deliverance. I will instruct you and teach you in the way you should go; I will counsel you with my loving eye on you.

Psalm 32:7-8

Lord, you are Divine Guidance. My promised land is before me and you are leading me one step at a time. My destiny is to fulfill the purpose you created me for which is to glorify you and serve others through the gift of your love living in me in Christ Jesus. I still my soul and quiet the noise of the world as I spend time with you. I listen for your voice that directs, guides and teaches me. I offer the gifts you have placed in me as yielded sweet offerings desiring they be pleasing in your sight and surrendered for your will and not mine. I have the mind of Christ. Thank you for the Holy Spirit that guides, teaches and corrects me. I rest and abide in Christ to unfold and bring forth all his fullness to the works of my hands. I gratefully receive the spirit of wisdom and revelation in the knowledge of Christ who enlightens the eyes of my understanding. I feast on your Word which nourishes my spirit and stirs my faith. Thank you for your Grace which supplies all my needs in Christ Jesus. I seek you. I yield to you. I abide in you.

## NOVEMBER 27

God is the
giver of all
things;
His
supply never
runs dry.

You can be sure that God will take care of everything you need, his generosity exceeding even yours in the glory that pours from Jesus. Our God and Father abounds in glory that just pours out into eternity. Yes.

Philippians 4:19 *(The Message)*

Lord, you are Supply and Abundance. You are my shelter, my fortress, my shield, my refuge, my rock, my stronghold, my deliverer, my dwelling place, my safe haven, my supply and my provision. Your love for me has delivered your supply of abundance in Christ Jesus. By faith in Christ, I have every spiritual blessing of Heaven. No weapon can destroy what you have built up in me. No word of discouragement heard in my ears can linger in my heart. All that you are and all that you do has no limits and no boundaries of containment. You are living water to my thirst and Heaven's provision of Grace to my hungry soul. You can part any Red Sea in my life so I can pass through on dry land and be separated from my enemies. You have established me as your child in Christ Jesus. My life is hidden in the life of the King of Kings and the Lord of Lords. No other is higher than you. I plant seeds of faith in your Word and harvest according to your established provision. My well never runs dry. Thank you for the wondrous joy of life in Christ.

# NOVEMBER 28

Who and
what we
associate
with
becomes
a part
of us.

Do not be misled: Bad company corrupts good character. Come
back to your senses as you ought, and stop sinning; for there are
some who are ignorant of God—I say this to your shame.

1 Corinthians 15:33-34

Lord, you are Divine Supply, full of all Truth, and all Wisdom. You lavish
your love of unending supply on me by faith in Christ Jesus. The full
provision of your Truth and your Wisdom lives in my spirit as Christ
quickened my spirit alive unto him at my salvation. Christ has already
imparted everything that pertains to life and godliness in my spirit. I
gratefully receive every portion of favor you lavish on me. I renew my mind
to the truth of your Word and Christ brings your Word alive in me. I take
my thoughts captive to the obedience of Christ. I meditate on your Word
and ask you to search me with the truth of it. Make clear as you bring to
mind those areas of my life that need washing with your truth. I guard my
heart, for out of it comes the issues of life. As I meditate on your Word and
behold Christ, I partake of his divine nature. His life in me is transforming
me into his likeness. Thank you for sifting me in your loving Grace and
pouring me out for your glory and service of others. Thank you for taking
me from glory to glory.

# NOVEMBER 29

Envy focuses
our attention
outside our
boundaries
onto others
and is a signal
something
is lacking
in our
own hearts.

Each one should test their own actions. Then they can take pride in themselves alone, without comparing themselves to someone else, for each one should carry their own load.

Galatians 6:4-5

Lord, you are Life by the Spirit. With Christ living in me by faith, I live in the world but I am no longer conformed to the world. I no longer live in the kingdom of darkness where pride rules and envy reigns. I am a new creation alive by faith in Christ Jesus. The old man with all its ways of unforgiveness, impatience, irritation, selfishness and passing of judgments does not align with life in the spirit. As I live in the spirit, I no longer fulfill the desires of the flesh. Christ has freed me from the bonds of sin and its power has been crushed under the feet of my Savior. As I abide in Christ, he releases his power in me which is constantly at work in me transforming me into his image. I lay aside every weight which so easily besets me yielding my life to Christ so he can bring forth his nature through me. I yield my spirit to your Word. As I feed on, meditate in, and mix my faith with your Word, my soul nature joys in lining up with the truth of it. I walk in love as Christ is love. I joy in Christ Jesus who is my life. I live for the praise of your glory.

# NOVEMBER 30

When
anger
becomes our
fruit,
bitterness
has likely taken
root.

Get rid of all bitterness, rage and anger, brawling and slander,
along with every form of malice. Be kind and compassionate to one
another, forgiving each other, just as in Christ God forgave you.

Ephesians 4:31-32

Lord, you are Complete Freedom. Through your Grace, I yield to your love
in Christ Jesus that examines me and chides me to acknowledge those
areas of my life that do not line up with the truth of who I am as a new
creation in Christ. In Christ, my spirit contains all the fullness of God.
My spirit renewed in Christ now reigns and rules in submission to him.
Old patterns of fleshly mindsets that once ruled and reigned in my flesh
are being transformed by the Grace of Christ Jesus as I renew my mind
to your Word. Desiring to not have anything hinder your flow of grace in
my life, I confess what needs confessing, grieve what needs grieving and
forgive what needs forgiving. I look in the mirror of my past hurts so your
light can reveal the shadows and smudges of buried pain. I courageously
acknowledge any offense that is living in my heart. I cast my burdens on
Christ and open myself to those you are bringing into my life to serve as
vessels of your compassion, your love and your healing. I welcome and
embrace my hurts and see them as stepping stones to my future of freedom.
I can forgive others through Christ the Forgiver who lives in me. I pray for
my enemies and use my words to speak blessings over them. Thank you.

# DECEMBER 1

Every offense
provides the
opportunity
to plant a seed
of forgiveness,
and reap a harvest
of peace in
our souls.

Therefore, if you are offering your gift at the altar and there remember that your brother has something against you, leave your gift there in front of the altar. First go and be reconciled to your brother; then come and offer your gift.

Matthew 5:23-24

Lord, you are Peace. In Christ, I overflow with forgiveness towards others. I am one with his spirit where love and forgiveness reside. When the choice of offense arises within me, I seek quiet time with you and the Word. I cast my burdens on you knowing that you are my defender and my avenger. I seek the Word as a mirror to look in. Knowing that anger, irritation and self-centeredness can create distance in my relationships, I quickly choose my response of truth and love. I yield my fleshly mindsets to Christ the Forgiver. I invite Christ to go to and through my emotions that need His touch. I communicate my needs to others openly and without demand. I allow others to be who you created them to be. I live in your Spirit of reconciliation. I am open to hear and consider others opinions. I value others as created in your image. I live for God approval and not people approval. I speak unity over all things and all those I meet. In Christ, I take authority over the devil or any power of darkness who brings confusion, fear, or any evil work in my life. I am a kingdom child pursuing peace. I reap peace because I sow peace.

# DECEMBER 2

When we
reject
the
Holy life,
we reject
the work of the Cross.

It is impossible for those who have once been enlightened, who have tasted the heavenly gift, who have shared in the Holy Spirit, who have tasted the goodness of the word of God and the powers of the coming age and who have fallen away, to be brought back to repentance. To their loss they are crucifying the Son of God all over again and subjecting him to public disgrace.

Hebrews 6:4-6

Whoever is not with me is against me, and whoever does not gather with me scatters. And so I tell you, every kind of sin and slander can be forgiven, but blasphemy against the Spirit will not be forgiven. Anyone who speaks a word against the Son of Man will be forgiven, but anyone who speaks against the Holy Spirit will not be forgiven, either in this age or in the age to come.

Matthew 12:30-32

Lord, you are Grace and Truth. Thank you for the gift of life in Christ. All I am and all I have is because of your extravagant love for me which drew me to accept Christ as my Lord and Savior. Christ Jesus has completed for me what I had no power or authority to do and that is cancel my sin debt, defeat the power of sin, restore my relationship with you now and to eternity and transfer me into the Kingdom of Light. My life following salvation is one of resting in Christ's finished work, yielding to his voice, renewing my mind to your truth, and releasing your provision of Grace by faith. I live humbled and overwhelmed with your abounding love that has accomplished my every need in Christ Jesus. I glory in every blood bought blessing that is mine in Christ Jesus. I joyfully submit daily and throughout the day to the Holy Spirit who teaches, guides and corrects me. Everyday my soul is aligning to your presence in my spirit. Thank you.

## DECEMBER 3

Every drop
of
blood
Jesus
shed
had your
name on it.

In him we have redemption through his blood, the forgiveness of sins, in accordance with the riches of God's grace.

Ephesians 1:7

Without the shedding of blood, there is no remission of sins.

Hebrews 9:22

They triumphed over him by the blood of the Lamb and by the word of their testimony;

Revelations 12:11a.

Lord, you are Restoration. Every part of my life is about you. You are my creator, my provider, my defender, my strength and my supply. You have opened the door of relationship that sin once closed through the holy blood of Christ Jesus. His blood is my salvation, my freedom, my authority, my identity, my righteousness, my forgiveness, my redemption, my restoration, my acceptance and my adoption as your holy, accepted and beloved child. You have moved Heaven and earth for me to bring me in perfect harmony with your Love wrapped in Grace and Truth. Jesus is Grace and Truth. No power of darkness or word of destruction has authority to rob me of my position in Christ. I engage the enemy with the blood of Christ and no sea of trouble can overtake me. Your blood gives me Kingdom identity, Kingdom authority, Kingdom power and Kingdom access. I live in Christ. Thank you for abundant life in Christ Jesus. Halleluiah.

# DECEMBER 4

When we
meet
God
face to face,
an inner
metamorphoses
begins.

So from now on we regard no one from a worldly point of view. Though we once regarded Christ in this way, we do so no longer. Therefore, if anyone is in Christ, the new creation has come: The old has gone, the new is here! All this is from God, who reconciled us to himself through Christ and gave us the ministry of reconciliation: that God was reconciling the world to himself in Christ, not counting people's sins against them. And he has committed to us the message of reconciliation. We are therefore Christ's ambassadors, as though God were making his appeal through us. We implore you on Christ's behalf: Be reconciled to God. God made him who had no sin to be sin for us, so that in him we might become the righteousness of God.

2 Corinthians 5:16-22

Lord, you are Creative Power. Thank you for the finished work of the cross where the sacrifice Jesus made of his life for my death has brought to me resurrection life in him by faith. I live alive in spirit with Christ where there is freedom from the sin consciousness and the power of sin. I joy in feeding my spirit with the truth. As I renew my mind and trust in the Word, my soul is drawn to the truth. As my spirit is nurtured with truth, my mind aligns with what it takes hold of in the spiritual mirror of the Word and the living power of Christ who is the Word begins transforming me from the inside out. Thank you that your Grace pulls me and your love holds me to your spirit as I abide in, rely on and trust in Christ by faith. I live every moment in the pure joy, pure light and pure love of Christ Jesus. I hold fast to my faith which grounds me in truth and floods my soul with peace. No one or nothing compares to you. I burst forth in resounding praises. My soul magnifies you. Life in Christ is overflowing joy. Thank you.

# DECEMBER 5

With
open eyes
we see,
with
open ears
we hear,
with
open hearts we love.

The eye is the lamp of the body. If your eyes are healthy, your whole body will be full of light. But if your eyes are unhealthy, your whole body will be full of darkness. If then the light within you is darkness, how great is that darkness!

Matthew 6:22-23

"Consider carefully what you hear," he continued. "With the measure you use, it will be measured to you—and even more.

Mark 4:24

This is how we know what love is: Jesus Christ laid down his life for us. And we ought to lay down our lives for our brothers and sisters.

1John 3:16

Lord, you are Life. I am one in spirit with you by faith in Christ Jesus. In the glory of your presence, I find pure joy. In the depths of your love, I find fullness. In the width of your Grace, I find life and truth. You shared your authority and imparted life to me through Jesus. You have given me the Holy Spirit to open my spiritual eyes to the deep things that are hidden from the world. Thank you for the Holy Spirit which imparts and reveals your truth to me by the spirit of Christ Jesus who lives in me. You have given me spiritual ears to hear your voice like a sheep hears their shepherd. Jesus is my shepherd who leads, guides, feeds and protects me. I abide in Christ Jesus by faith. I go where you send me. I serve others out of the abundance of Christ Jesus who lives in me. Thank you for life in Christ Jesus. My life is a continuous song of praise to you.

# DECEMBER 6

God's love
takes hold
of us
when
we yield
to Jesus.

I have been crucified with Christ and I no longer live, but Christ lives in me. The life I now live in the body, I live by faith in the Son of God, who loved me and gave himself for me.

Galatians 2:20

For we are God's handiwork, created in Christ Jesus to do good works, which God prepared in advance for us to do.

Ephesians 2:10

Lord, you are Salvation, Restoration, Redemption, and Provision. I lay myself aside to abide in the richness of your Grace. Your Grace is alive in the person of Jesus Christ. I sing of your mercies every morning. I sing of your beauty at noon. I sing of your greatness each night. An unending song of thanksgiving and praise lives in my heart. Symphonies pour out of me to celebrate your goodness. I bind your faithfulness around my neck and write your love on the tablet of my heart. In Christ, I am alive writing endless praise music. The fullness of harmony flowing in me is my never ending song of praise written to honor and glorify you. Your gift of love and life in Christ Jesus is comparable to no other. Breathing in your goodness and living life in Christ is joy unspeakable. I offer my life of glorifying you and serving others as a thank offering. Inhale my worship and exhale your glory. You are worthy to be praised. Thank you.

# DECEMBER 7

Our tithe
is much
more than
money;
it testifies
that God
is alive in our
hearts.

Remember this: Whoever sows sparingly will also reap sparingly, and whoever sows generously will also reap generously. Each of you should give what you have decided in your heart to give, not reluctantly or under compulsion, for God loves a cheerful giver.

2 Corinthians 9:6-7

Lord, you are God, Master and Creator of all things. All that you provide comes from the abundance of your love and has been delivered to me by the blood of Christ Jesus. I give to you and serve others out of the overflowing gratitude and love for you. Honoring you with my gifts, tithe, service and talents is a joy that pales in comparison of your great offering of love for me. Christ is my everlasting provision and unending supply. Nothing hinders the enlarging of my territory in Christ. No power, no walls, no division, no darkness, no evil and no stumbling blocks come against your divine blessings in Christ. I am free to love, free to sing, free to dance and free to be all you created me to be. I live by faith in the marvelous Grace of Jesus who is my life. I yield to Christ and wonders manifest in him which he lavishes on me. Your living love in me is what I lavish on everyone I meet. In Christ, I am high and lifted up. You are my God and I am your child. I sow generously, faithfully and lovingly. Christ in me brings abundant harvest to me and through me for His glory and the service of others. Thank you. Thank you. Thank you.

# DECEMBER 8

Our smile is
authentic
on the
outside,
when our
heart is
authentic
on the inside.

Just as water mirrors your face, so your face mirrors your heart.

Proverbs 27:19 *(The Message)*

Lord, you are my portion. I am blessed, highly favored and deeply loved in Christ. I live free from condemnation. I am redeemed and complete in Christ. I am established, anointed and sealed by the Holy Spirit. Your Spirit of Truth and Life lives on the inside of me testifying I belong to you. I am complete in your wholeness and called to Kingdom boldness by your Grace and in the power of Christ Jesus. Lord GOD you help me. I am not confounded. I set my face like a flint. I come boldly to the throne of God and receive your mercy. I find grace to help me when I need it most. Christ lives in me. He will neither fail nor abandon me. Thank you for your Word which is living life to my spirit. You are faithful to your Word and always watching over it to perform it. All that I lay my hands to by faith in Christ Jesus bears Kingdom fruit. By faith, I receive all the Covenant Promises of Abraham as my own. I am open, expectant and ready to receive my greatest expectations manifesting in miraculous ways in Christ. I reflect Christ as the Lord of my life. My lips sing your praises forevermore. My soul magnifies you. Thank you.

# DECEMBER 9

God is our
beginning and our end
and He knows how
to navigate
us through
all the
in-between.

You know when I sit and when I rise; you perceive my thoughts from afar. You discern my going out and my lying down; you are familiar with all my ways. Before a word is on my tongue you, LORD, know it completely. You hem me in behind and before, and you lay your hand upon me. Such knowledge is too wonderful for me, too lofty for me to attain.

Psalm 139:2-6

He who was seated on the throne said, "I am making everything new!" Then he said, "Write this down, for these words are trustworthy and true." He said to me: "It is done. I am the Alpha and the Omega, the Beginning and the End. To the thirsty I will give water without cost from the spring of the water of life. Those who are victorious will inherit all this, and I will be their God and they will be my children.

Revelation 21:5-7

Lord, you are Alpha and Omega—the beginning and the end. I am your workmanship created in Christ for good works. I am a citizen of Heaven and a joint heir with Christ. Christ has redeemed by life from the pit and imparted his life in my spirit. His holiness, his kingdom inheritance and his resurrection power to overcome every adversity is mine by faith. By faith, I reap his abundant harvest every day in every way. Christ is my spring of living water. Christ is the bread of life that nourishes my spirit. In Christ, I'm complete and victorious. The only labor that is required of me, which is not labor, but pure joy is to abide in you, to worship you and to praise you. Thank you that in Christ my spirit is the Holy of Holies, my soul is the Holy place, and my body is the outer court. I marvel continuously that you dwell in my spirit. Your wonder is above description.

# DECEMBER 10

When God
is our
steering wheel,
we won't
need an
emergency brake.

Those who know your name trust in you, for you, LORD, have never forsaken those who seek you.

Psalms 9:10

For no matter how many promises God has made, they are "Yes" in Christ. And so through him the "Amen" is spoken by us to the glory of God.

2 Corinthians 1:20 *(The Message)*

Jesus Christ is the same yesterday and today and forever.

Hebrews 13:8

Lord, you are Reliable, Steadfast and Faithful. You have bathed me in your abundant love through the gift of life by faith in Christ Jesus. Your revealed and living Word of Christ alive in me nourishes my spirit with love and life. Abiding in Christ, I celebrate empowered life now and forevermore. Christ Jesus is unfolding every detail of your divine plan for my life. His wisdom maps out your will in my spirit. I joyfully yield my will to your will so that your divine desires of Heaven are manifest on earth in me and through me. I rejoice in sharing the call with all your children of being a minister of reconciliation. I surrender my life to you as a vessel to glorify you and serve others in the full and abundant love of Christ that lives within. I plant seeds of love with my words. I plant seeds of truth as I reflect the life of Christ in me to those around me. I feed my faith with your Word which is life and power in my spirit. I joy in spending time with you, worshipping you, praising you and praying to you. My soul magnifies you. Thank you.

# DECEMBER 11

We often see
what
is;
God always
sees
what can be.

God judges persons differently than humans do. Men and women look at the face; God looks into the heart.

1 Samuel 16:7 *(The Message)*

Lord, you are an Eternal Mirror. You see my beginning, my end and everything in-between. In Christ, I find purpose and meaning. As I continuously ponder your wonder, I know apart from Christ, I am powerless. Every word I speak in love, is an endless echo from your mountain of Grace in Christ Jesus. Every seed I plant in love, is a bountiful harvest in the fertile soil of Christ Jesus. Christ has created a pure heart in me and renewed my spirit. Yielding my mind and my will to you opens my soul to receive the fullness of your spirit living in me. Every loving act I share is a reflection of Christ in me. My spirit alive and one with Christ holds all the fullness of you. Christ sees the full measure of the masterpiece you have created inside of me. He is bringing that masterpiece to the manifestation of your will as I abide in him by faith. His miracle of life in me draws me to the joy of gladness and praise. Thank you for your love which pulls all the fullness of your goodness to me and through me in Christ. Every day I write another chapter of Halleluiah praises to you for you are worthy to be praised. Inhale my worship as thanksgiving.

# DECEMBER 12

The time to prepare
for a battle
is not in the
midst of it, but before
it ever takes place.

And that about wraps it up. God is strong, and he wants you strong. So take everything the Master has set out for you, well-made weapons of the best materials. And put them to use so you will be able to stand up to everything the Devil throws your way. This is no afternoon athletic contest that we'll walk away from and forget about in a couple of hours. This is for keeps, a life-or-death fight to the finish against the Devil and all his angels. Be prepared. You're up against far more than you can handle on your own. Take all the help you can get, every weapon God has issued, so that when it's all over but the shouting you'll still be on your feet. Truth, righteousness, peace, faith, and salvation are more than words. Learn how to apply them. You'll need them throughout your life. God's Word is an indispensable weapon. In the same way, prayer is essential in this ongoing warfare. Pray hard and long. Pray for your brothers and sisters. Keep your eyes open. Keep each other's spirits up so that no one falls behind or drops out.

Ephesians 6:10-18 *(The Message)*

Lord, you are Divine Provision. With the Blood of the Lamb and the Word of my testimony, I am more than a conqueror in Christ Jesus. In Christ, no weapon formed against me shall prosper. You condemn every tongue that rises up against me in judgment. By faith in Christ, I am victorious. In Christ, I prepare for the battle. I buckle the belt of truth around my waist. I wear the breastplate of righteousness. My feet are fitted with the readiness of the gospel of peace. I take up the shield of faith and extinguish all the flaming arrows of the evil one. I wear the helmet of salvation as I declare your Word in faith. I hold fast to the sword of the spirit which is the Word of God. Having done all, I stand. My eyes are open to the truth of your Word. Satan is a defeated foe who has no authority over me except that which I give him. I take my thoughts captive to the obedience of Christ and confess the Word in faith over those thoughts that satan stirs up for the purpose of killing, stealing and destroying my identity in Jesus. I live victoriously.

# DECEMBER 13

When our faith is tested,
we get a glimpse of what's
really on the inside of ourselves.

Whoever dwells in the shelter of the Most High will rest in the shadow of the Almighty. I will say of the LORD, "He is my refuge and my fortress, my God, in whom I trust. Surely he will save you from the fowler's snare and from the deadly pestilence. He will cover you with his feathers, and under his wings you will find refuge; his faithfulness will be your shield and rampart. You will not fear the terror of night, nor the arrow that flies by day, nor the pestilence that stalks in the darkness, nor the plague that destroys at midday. A thousand may fall at your side, ten thousand at your right hand, but it will not come near you. You will only observe with your eyes and see the punishment of the wicked. If you say, "The LORD is my refuge," and you make the Most High your dwelling, no harm will overtake you, no disaster will come near your tent. For he will command his angels concerning you to guard you in all your ways; they will lift you up in their hands, so that you will not strike your foot against a stone. You will tread on the lion and the cobra; you will trample the great lion and the serpent. "Because he loves me," says the LORD, "I will rescue him; I will protect him, for he acknowledges my name. He will call on me, and I will answer him; I will be with him in trouble, I will deliver him and honor him. With long life I will satisfy him and show him my salvation."

Psalms 91

Lord, you are Divine Provision. There is no one like you. You have given me life and redeemed my life by the blood of Jesus. Jesus supplies my every need by faith in his completed work of the cross. Thank you for protecting, defending and providing for the righteous. Righteousness has been accounted to me through my faith in Jesus. I have been crucified with Christ; and it is no longer I who live, but Christ lives in me and the life which I now live in the flesh I live by faith in the Son of God, who loved me and gave himself up for me. Christ dwells in my heart through faith. My faith is continually nourished and built up, as I feast on your

Word. I confess your Word by faith and you release its power in the name of Jesus. Thank you for unleashing the power of heaven to perform your Word. Thank you for angels that carry out your assignments on my behalf. I abide in Christ by faith. He supplies. I marvel at your unending provision in Jesus.

# DECEMBER 14

Our obedience in faith,
and God's provision
leads
us to our
Promised Land.

The LORD will send a blessing on your barns and on everything you put your hand to. The LORD your God will bless you in the land he is giving you. The LORD will establish you as his holy people, as he promised you on oath, if you keep the commands of the LORD your God and walk in obedience to him. Then all the peoples on earth will see that you are called by the name of the LORD, and they will fear you.

Deuteronomy 28:8-10

Lord, you are Creator and Author of all. You have created me in your image. You have given me the power to create with my words, a free will to choose life or death, a spirit alive unto you in Christ Jesus, overcoming power by confessing your Word in faith, freedom from the power of sin, identity in the name of Jesus, eternal life by the blood of Christ Jesus and the Grace of Jesus which supplies my every need. I have already arrived in my Promised Land which is relationship with you by faith in Christ Jesus. I gratefully receive every blood bought promise of Christ Jesus. In Christ, I abide by faith and bear endless kingdom fruits. Blessings come to me in unexpected times in unexpected ways. I am a seed planter of your Word casting it by faith into my future and waiting expectantly as it returns to me in the fullness of your purposed blessings. I am born again by faith in Christ Jesus of the incorruptible seed of your Word. I stand in faith shouting praises over every circumstance of my life knowing that you are the High Way. Inhale my worship and exhale your Glory. I live established in the abundance of Christ Jesus. Glory Halleluiah.

## DECEMBER 15

God
uses every
act of submission
on our part
to unleash change
on His part.

It's news I'm most proud to proclaim, this extraordinary Message
of God's powerful plan to rescue everyone who trusts him, starting
with Jews and then right on to everyone else! God's way of putting
people right shows up in the acts of faith, confirming what Scripture
has said all along: "The person in right standing before God by
trusting him really lives."

Romans 1:16-17 *(The Message)*

Lord, you are Sovereign Destiny. You are my rock, my defense, my
salvation and my fortress. Thank you for giving me access to you by faith in
Christ Jesus. In Christ, I am rooted, established, strong, bold, immovable,
determined and victorious. I confess your Word and you are faithful to
perform it. Your Word is a lamp to my feet and a light to my way. I joyfully
yield to Christ who is the hope of glory living in me. I delight in spending
time with you and learning of your ways. I openly and joyfully embrace the
revelation, teaching and correction of the Holy Spirit. I rest in your Love,
live in your Grace, work in your Anointing and praise your wondrous
and marvelous being. Everything I am and every good thing comes to
me through the abundance of Christ within. Thank you for revealing that
abiding and resting by faith in Christ unleashes your Grace over every
area of my life. I live in the righteousness, joy and peace of Christ. My lips
sing your praises. My soul magnifies you. My spirit is alive in Christ Jesus.
Thank you.

# DECEMBER 16

Our flesh
contributes
to our
impaired
vision.

Don't love the world's ways. Don't love the world's goods. Love of the world squeezes out love for the Father. Practically everything that goes on in the world—wanting your own way, wanting everything for yourself, wanting to appear important—has nothing to do with the Father. It just isolates you from him. The world and all its wanting, wanting, wanting is on the way out—but whoever does what God wants is set for eternity.

1 John 2:15-17 *(The Message)*

Lord, you are Divine Wisdom. Nothing escapes your divine vision. I joyfully live as a child of obedience hungering for your Word and thirsting after righteousness. I am engraved on the palm of your hand. Jesus has written my name in the Lamb's Book. In Christ, you call me by name. When you look at me, you see me as perfected in Christ. I live as a child in your Kingdom which cannot be shaken. I am loved with an everlasting love. I am your child holy, righteous, blameless, free from condemnation, eternally bound, blessed and favored, sealed by the Holy Spirit, called according to your purpose, created for good works, a citizen of Heaven, redeemed, saved and perfected by faith in Christ Jesus. I abide by faith in Christ and he opens my spiritual eyes to see beyond my natural circumstances. I walk by faith and not by sight. I fix my eyes on Christ and the truth of his Word which feeds my spirit and nourishes my soul. Thank you.

# DECEMBER 17

Our first
step toward
greatness in
God's economy
is to realize
that apart
from Him
we can do
nothing.

I am the Vine, you are the branches. When you're joined with me and I with you, the relation intimate and organic, the harvest is sure to be abundant. Separated, you can't produce a thing. Anyone who separates from me is deadwood, gathered up and thrown on the bonfire. But if you make yourselves at home with me and my words are at home in you, you can be sure that whatever you ask will be listened to and acted upon. This is how my Father shows who he is—when you produce grapes, when you mature as my disciples. I've loved you the way my Father has loved me. Make yourselves at home in my love. If you keep my commands, you'll remain intimately at home in my love. That's what I've done—kept my Father's commands and made myself at home in his love.

John 15:5-10 *(The Message)*

Lord, you are Divine Supply. By faith in Christ, I am united to you in one spirit. His presence, his life, his wisdom and his Grace streams through my spirit and quickens my soul. You have established your kingdom as one of sowing and reaping. You are the Sovereign and Master Gardener of all creation. Christ is the vine on which all fruit resides. As your chosen, loved and accepted child in Christ, I bear forth the fruit of Christ as I abide in him by faith. I sow seeds as I confess your Word, take my thoughts captive to the obedience of Christ Jesus, fix my mind on you and speak words of truth and love. I desire to sow seeds of your love for you have revealed to me that as I give it will be given to me, good measure, pressed down, shaken together, and running over. The measure that I give will be the measure that returns to me. Thank you for the joy and peace that fills me as I abide in Christ and he supplies. Your well never runs dry.

## DECEMBER 18

God's call
on our lives
requires
His
provision.

The Lord will send a blessing on your barns and on everything you put your hand to. The Lord your God will bless you in the land he is giving you. The Lord will establish you as his holy people, as he promised you on oath, if you keep the commands of the Lord your God and walk in obedience to him. Then all the peoples on earth will see that you are called by the name of the Lord, and they will fear you. The Lord will grant you abundant prosperity—in the fruit of your womb, the young of your livestock and the crops of your ground—in the land he swore to your ancestors to give you. The Lord will open the heavens, the storehouse of his bounty, to send rain on your land in season and to bless all the work of your hands. You will lend to many nations but will borrow from none. The Lord will make you the head, not the tail. If you pay attention to the commands of the Lord your God that I give you this day and carefully follow them, you will always be at the top, never at the bottom. Do not turn aside from any of the commands I give you today, to the right or to the left, following other gods and serving them.

Deuteronomy 28:8-14

Lord, you are Limitless Provision. Your overflowing Grace in Christ pours blessings into me beyond measure. You meet all my needs in Christ according to your riches in glory. You are the essence that gently touches and the hand that lovingly holds my being in all your Perfection. You live in me with delight, kindness and unlimited favor. You have anointed my thoughts with the mind of Christ. You have blessed me with every spiritual blessing in heaven. You can do exceedingly more than I can think, dream, or image according to the power that is at work in me. You have blessed my hands with strength to do the works you have created me to do. You have filled my spirit and enriched my soul with your love so I can be your voice of love to those around me. You have gifted me with every blessing by faith in Christ Jesus who brings all your goodness to manifestation in my life. Your work in Christ Jesus is complete and you simply invite be to abide in him by faith. Praise you from whom all blessings flow. Glory Halleluiah.

# DECEMBER 19

Every gift
God places
within us,
becomes a blessing
when we
open them
in the
presence of His grace.

For the Lord God is a sun and shield: the Lord will give grace and
glory: no good thing will
   He withhold from, them that walk uprightly.

Psalm 84:11

Lord, you are Grace. I am forever joined to you by faith through your saving Grace of Christ Jesus. Thank you for justifying me by faith in Jesus. I have peace with you through Christ Jesus. Through him I have obtained access by faith into your full assurance of grace and rejoice in the hope of glory which is Christ Jesus. Christ has made available to all who will take hold by faith in him your provision of saving Grace. Your Grace has come forward for the deliverance from sin and the eternal salvation for all mankind. Christ Jesus sacrificed his life to pay my sin debt in full, redeem me from a devil's hell and once and for all set me right with you. He has completed what no acts of my self-efforts or will-power could ever accomplish. By Grace, I have been set free from the curse of the law. As I abide in Christ, he brings forth the supply of his grace at the time of my need turning my weaknesses into his strengths. I rejoice continually for your amazing Grace. You are my God. I am your child. I rejoice in the joy of living in Christ. Thank you.

# DECEMBER 20

Living daily
in purposed
surrender and
exercised faith,
sends ripples
of love and grace
through us, touching
the lives of those around us.

And without faith it is impossible to please God, because anyone who comes to him must believe that he exists and that he rewards those who earnestly seek him.

Hebrews 11:6

Therefore, as God's chosen people, holy and dearly loved, clothe yourselves with compassion, kindness, humility, gentleness and patience. Bear with each other and forgive one another if any of you has a grievance against someone. Forgive as the Lord forgave you. And over all these virtues put on love, which binds them all together in perfect unity. Let the peace of Christ rule in your hearts, since as members of one body you were called to peace. And be thankful.

Colossians 3:12-15

Lord, you are Forgiveness Provision. Your gift of love in Christ permeates me with love, grace and peace. Your love that fills and grows in me is a springboard of endless love and grace that flows from me to others. Abiding and resting in Christ, brings an abundant harmony unmatched as I live, breathe and move in Christ. As I feast on your Word, I eat from your table of Grace and my spirit is satisfied. As I drink in your Living Water, my thirst is quenched. My cup overflows with joy. The peace of Christ rules in my heart and spills over onto those I meet. I have peace because Christ Jesus the peacemaker lives in me. I see others as your divine masterpiece worthy to be loved, valued and treasured in the same measure you love, value and treasure me. I love others through the love of Christ living inside of me. Your kingdom is righteousness, love and peace. Christ has brought the kingdom of God from heaven to earth to live in me by abiding in him by faith. Thank you for the gift of life in Christ Jesus within my spirit. Forever praises.

## DECEMBER 21

When we reflect
on all God has brought
us through, it proves
He
can stand
the test of time.

I'm proud to praise God, proud to praise GOD. Fearless now, I trust in God; what can mere mortals do to me? God, you did everything you promised, and I'm thanking you with all my heart. You pulled me from the brink of death, my feet from the cliff-edge of doom. Now I stroll at leisure with God in the sunlit fields of life.

Psalm 56:10-13 (The Message)

Lord, you are Life. You saw me before the foundation of the world, called me according to your purpose and saved be by your Grace through faith in Christ Jesus. Your Righteous Right Hand protects me. You have rescued me from every evil attack and brought me safely into your Heavenly Kingdom. I am established in the righteousness of Christ. I am far from oppression. Terror cannot come near me. Whatever things I ask when I pray, I believe that I receive them, and I will have them. I abide in the strength of Christ Jesus who is my victory and provision. No weapon formed against me can prosper. No power of darkness can defeat me in Christ. Greater is he that is in me than he that is in the world. Goliaths that purpose to mock you and claim victory in their own strength hold no power over me. I live in the fullness of the God-head where there is no lack. You are for me so who can be against me? I am strengthened with all might, according to the Lord's glorious power, for all patient endurance and longsuffering with joy. Nothing that is mine by divine right in Christ Jesus can be taken from me. Thank you for provision in Jesus.

# DECEMBER 22

God
specializes
daily
in the
miracle
working
business.

For since the message spoken through angels was binding, and every violation and disobedience received its just punishment, how shall we escape if we ignore so great a salvation? This salvation, which was first announced by the Lord, was confirmed to us by those who heard him. God also testified to it by signs, wonders and various miracles, and by gifts of the Holy Spirit distributed according to his will.

Hebrews 2:2-4

Lord, you are a God of miracles. Nothing is outside your reach, your power or your creativity. Through faith in Christ living in me, I have resurrection power to pull down strongholds, minister in love, bind and loose on earth, bind and loose in Heaven, resist the devil, move mountains, prosper beyond natural means, speak healing to the sick and call things forth from the spirit into the natural. The Holy Spirit is manifesting and demonstrating might and wondrous works as I live in Christ. Your Word is your will and as your child alive to you by faith in Christ Jesus you have given me access to every provision of your Covenant promises. As I stand on your Word by faith confessing it from my mouth, you are watching over it to perform it. I plant your Word as seed and trust expectantly as you bring it to manifestation in my natural circumstances. I joy in abiding in Christ and standing on your Word because I know your ways are higher than my ways. Your are a God of miracles. Thank you for your abounding goodness.

# DECEMBER 23

Even when
life doesn't
make sense
to us,
God
is never confused.

For God is not a God of disorder but of peace—as in all the congregations of the Lord's people.

1 Corinthians 14:33

In the beginning was the Word, and the Word was with God, and the Word was God. He was with God in the beginning. Through him all things were made; without him nothing was made that has been made. In him was life, and that life was the light of all mankind. The light shines in the darkness, and the darkness has not overcome it.

John 1:1-5

Lord, you are Sovereign Order. I trust in, rely on and faithfully lean on Christ as my Source and help in all things. Your Word is a lamp to my feet and a light to my path. I dwell in the love of Christ living in me. You have poured your divine Love into me through the work of the cross. Christ Jesus who is my life by faith has filled me with Heaven's divine order and rule. I reign and rule over my circumstances in submission to Christ Jesus by faith. As I abide in Christ by faith, and make your Word my confessions, your divine order manifests in my circumstances. Faith in your Word is my provision for every good thing you have purposed for my life. I rest in Christ as he is the living and revealed Word that defends and rescues me from every evil attack. Christ is victory. In Christ, I abound with overflowing hope, lasting joy and wondrous peace. Disorder, unrest, fear, guilt, condemnation, shame and confusion are fruits of the kingdom of darkness which in Christ by faith, I am a child of the light. I have been born again, not of corruptible seed but incorruptible, through the Word of God which lives and abides forever. Thank you.

# DECEMBER 24

We
move
towards
tomorrow
with the
steps
we take
today.

For we are God's handiwork, created in Christ Jesus to do good works, which God prepared in advance for us to do.

Ephesians 2:10

Lord, you are Sovereign Destiny. You have established my destiny and provision in Christ Jesus. In Christ, you brought forth creation. In Christ, you saved me. In Christ my needs are met. In Christ, I have freedom in the Spirit. In Christ, I am high and lifted up. In Christ, I am chosen, blessed and highly favored. In Christ, you delivered your immeasurable love for me. In Christ, you have provided the Light, the Truth, and the Way. In Christ, you have delivered the completion of your living and revealed Word which describes your nature and gives me access to your blessings. I glory in Christ who is the hope of glory. Nothing of this world can measure or compare to your goodness. You have provided everything I need for life in its fullness. I take hold of today and the future you have prepared for me as I abide by faith in Christ Jesus. You open doors and light the pathway for me to follow. You bring people into my life and knit together relationships of divine appointment. I joy in praising you. I delight in living in you.

# DECEMBER 25

Only the one true Living God
could orchestrate an ordinary night,
with ordinary animals,
in an ordinary stable,
in an ordinary town,
and unfold His
extraordinary birth,
so that every heart that opens
itself to His entrance
becomes a manger of Jesus.

For to us a child is born, to us a son is given, and the government
will be on his shoulders. And he will be called Wonderful Counselor,
Mighty God, Everlasting Father, Prince of Peace.

Isaiah 9:6

Lord, you are more wonderful than words can describe. Your ocean of
grace and your immeasurable depth of love wrapped flesh around the
Word who has redeemed, justified, sanctified and saved me. Jesus left
the glory of Heaven, walked among men and emptied himself for me.
By faith, I live in the living person of Jesus Christ now and forever. Lord,
you are the Extraordinary. You are Exquisite. You are Majesty. You are
Love. No one compares to You. My heart dances with you to the music of
perfect love and freedom – an everlasting song of continuous joyous praise.
The unspeakable joy of living in Christ Jesus by faith is an everlasting
symphony that permeates every fiber of my being. Glory and shouts of
Halleluiahs ring from the depths of my soul. I stand before you on bended
knees in awe of your wondrous display of love for all the world to see. My
mouth can't contain itself as a lungful of praise springs forth from the
depths of my spirit. Unending shouts of praise and halleluiah's! You are
beyond amazing.

# DECEMBER 26

Like a mirror reflects
our outer state,
our hearts reflect
our inner state,
revealing whether
we harbor a grudge or release grace,
seek self pity or seek Christ,
taste human misery, or drink in God's Grace.

Flee the evil desires of youth and pursue righteousness, faith, love and peace, along with those who call on the Lord out of a pure heart.

2 Timothy 2:22

Above all else, guard your heart, for everything you do flows from it.

Proverbs 4:23

For as a man thinks in his heart, so is He.

Proverbs 23:7

Lord, you are Spirit. As you have offered your full provision of love to me in celebrating the birth of Christ Jesus, I reflect on my heart in light of your gift of life. I desire to live my life surrendered to Christ Jesus trusting in him and living in his freedom and provision. As he is the manifestation of the true mirror of your nature, I yield all that I am by faith to take hold of all that he is. I drink in His overflowing grace and live in the Light of His love. Ancient doors open in the presence of your merciful Grace. Walls come down in your Love. Chains of offense are loosed. I hunger and thirst for righteousness and I am filled. I confess what needs confessing, grieve what needs grieving and forgive what needs forgiving. I joyfully fix my eyes on Christ who is my salvation and my hope. I joyfully drink from the well of His unending Grace.

# DECEMBER 27

Sometimes
we have
to block the noise
from our outer ears
to hear the wisdom
from our inner ones.

"Consider carefully what you hear," he continued. "With the measure you use, it will be measured to you—and even more."

Mark 4:24

Pay attention and turn your ear to the sayings of the wise; apply your heart to what I teach, for it is pleasing when you keep them in your heart and have all of them ready on your lips. So that your trust may be in the LORD, I teach you today, even you.

Proverbs 22:17-19

Lord, you are Life. I am created in your image joined to your spirit by the blood of Christ Jesus. You anoint my eyes to see beyond the natural and live in faith. I look to you with bold confidence which is faith. I wait with expectancy and hope in you. You are my creator and the God of my salvation. You hear the cries of the righteous and in Christ I am righteous. I quiet my soul to be still before you. As I yield by faith in Christ, and listen for his voice within, I am divinely inspired in my thoughts, my words and my actions. Receiving your divine wisdom, and clarity fills and frees me to be all you have created me to be. I feast on your Word which is your will wrapped in your Truth. I store your truth in my soul by meditating on it. I testify to your goodness to those I meet. I pour your love onto others because Jesus has poured his love into me. As I abide in Christ, you make all grace abound towards me that I have all sufficiency in all things and abundance for every good work in Christ Jesus. Thank you. Halleluiah praises.

# DECEMBER 28

Grace
spells
God's
Richs
At
Christ's
Expense.

For it is by grace you have been saved, through faith—and this is not from yourselves, it is the gift of God—not by works, so that no one can boast.

Ephesians 2:8-9

Salvation is found in no one else, for there is no other name under heaven given to mankind by which we must be saved.

Acts 4:12

Lord, you are Grace. You wrapped your gift of love in Christ and delivered it by your Grace. Your Grace is your supply which you lavished upon me through the person of Christ who lives in me and his works of the cross which have united my spirit with you. I am restored to you and live in right standing in and through your loving Grace in Christ Jesus. There was no work in my flesh that could redeem my spirit from a devil's hell. My sin nature and the mastery of sin over me was broken once and for all as Jesus crushed the powers of darkness. My boast is my shout of praise for the King of Kings and Lord of Lords who has paid my sin debt in full once and for all. Ransomed by the blood of Christ I boast of his love to all those I meet. My boasts of joy and thanksgiving will forever shine the spotlight on the one who is center stage and deserves the reward of praises for all of eternity. Your love has purchased my life from the jaws of death and condemnation. I am free to wrap my celebrations of praise around songs that flows continuously from my lips. Every fiber of my being joins in singing halleluiah praises to you. Thank you.

# DECEMBER 29

God's love
has a
boomerang effect;
as we give it out
it returns to us.

For the Lord God is a sun and shield; the Lord bestows favor and honor; no good thing does he withhold from those whose walk is blameless."

Psalm 84:11

By entering through faith into what God has always wanted to do for us—set us right with him, make us fit for him—we have it all together with God because of our Master Jesus. And that's not all: We throw open our doors to God and discover at the same moment that he has already thrown open his door to us. We find ourselves standing where we always hoped we might stand—out in the wide open spaces of God's grace and glory, standing tall and shouting our praise.

Romans 5:1-2 *(The Message)*

Lord, you are Divine Everlasting Love. No greater demonstration of love has or will ever be displayed than the love you poured out for the world when you gave your only Son, Christ Jesus, that everyone who believed in him would not perish but have eternal life. You threw open the doors of heaven and invited all to enter by faith in Christ Jesus graciously extending the righteousness of Christ to all who will believe. Your love is giving and not taking. Your love is unconditional and not conditional. Your love is forgiving and not condemning. Your love invites freedom and is not manipulative. United to Christ by faith, your love is the essence that fills my spirit and overflows into my soul moving me to share it with everyone I meet. I am sure that neither death nor life, nor angels nor rulers, nor things present or things to come, nor powers, nor height nor depth, nor anything else can separate me from your love in Christ Jesus. I live every moment of the day in awe of your love. Inhale my worship. Exhale you glory. Thank you.

# DECEMBER 30

The same
hands that
once bore the
Roman spikes
will hold
our hearts
for eternity.

Could it be any clearer? Our old way of life was nailed to the cross with Christ, a decisive end to that sin-miserable life—no longer at sin's every beck and call! What we believe is this: If we get included in Christ's sin-conquering death, we also get included in his life-saving resurrection. We know that when Jesus was raised from the dead it was a signal of the end of death-as-the-end. Never again will death have the last word. When Jesus died, he took sin down with him, but alive he brings God down to us. From now on, think of it this way: Sin speaks a dead language that means nothing to you; God speaks your mother tongue, and you hang on every word. You are dead to sin and alive to God. That's what Jesus did.

Romans 6:6-11 *(The Message)*

Lord, you are Life. You have given me the gift of life through the blood of Christ Jesus. Blood is the source of life. Thank you Jesus for fulfilling the requirement of your Father, a Holy God, by sprinkling your blood on Heaven's mercy seat to pay the price for my sins and give me access to eternal life. Thank you for sanctifying me and purging my sin-filled conscious. Your blood has given me redemption the forgiveness of my sins according to the riches of your Grace. Thank you for your blood which has restored my relationship in spirit back to my Father. Thank you Jesus for delivering me from the powers of darkness and translating me into the kingdom of light. Thank you for the power of your blood which has broken the death jaws of sin from me. Your blood has given me access to the Father and power to live life this side of heaven. Thank you Jesus that your blood has won the victory over all the power of the enemy. Thank you Jesus that by the Word of my testimony and the power of your blood I have your authority to overcome. Nothing compares to life by faith in you. Receive my resounding thank you.

# DECEMBER 31

Every breath we take
is a personal assurance
that a loving and all
powerful God
is in control;
for to wait
on Him
to move,
is to know
He will.

For it is with your heart that you believe and are justified, and it is with your mouth that you profess your faith and are saved. As Scripture says, "Anyone who believes in him will never be put to shame." For there is no difference between Jew and Gentile—the same Lord is Lord of all and richly blesses all who call on him, for, Everyone who calls on the name of the Lord will be saved.

Romans 10:10-13

Lord, you are the HIGH WAY. You have created me, redeemed me and daily you supply all my needs according to your riches in glory in Christ Jesus. To know you is to seek you more. Your faithfulness is like no other. Your limitless and immeasurable love is like no other reaching to the heavens. You are compassionate and gracious, slow to anger, and abounding in love and faithfulness. Your mercies are new every morning. Creation holds the magnificent brushstrokes of your splendor. All of your Covenant promises are "yes and amen" to me by faith in Christ Jesus. I praise you with every fiber of my being. I joyfully seek to know you more. I live for the praise of your glory to shout the goodness of your name to everyone I meet. I will sing of your great love forever. With my mouth, I will make your faithfulness known through all generations. Praise you God from whom all blessings flow. You have created me for the praise of your glory.

# ABOUT CAROLYN

"I have always believed that ministry begins with **whose we are** and not **what we do**," says Carolyn Lynn Schwartz. The statement telegraphs an important balance Carolyn has learned about public ministry but downplays her wealth of talents. A gifted published songwriter, vocalist, keyboardist, producer, radio show host, author, speaker, and Christian Counselor she finds many ways to 'do' ministry. Her experience includes more than 20 years of professional training. Carolyn's gifts have opened doors for her to perform at church services across many denominations, civic organizations, banquets, retreats, concerts and conferences. An author of three books and the songwriter and vocalist behind multiple recorded music albums, Carolyn has been active in publicly expressing her faith since 1988. She has a bachelor's degree in nursing, is a Certified Temperament Counselor, Licensed Pastoral Counselor and has a PhD in Christian Counseling. She is a member of the National Christian Counselor's Association. She is currently an active member of Duane Sheriff ministries at Victory Life church and plays the keyboard or piano with their live praise band. Carolyn has a heart for God and a passion for loving people. Whether through music, public speaking, or Christian counseling, she draws upon her own background of pain and triumph to compassionately connect with other's who are experiencing inner brokenness and seeking freedom from captivity.

Carolyn's obvious passion for life, music, and helping others
embraces the desire and focus
of being a surrendered vessel to
Jesus Christ in such a way
that the transparency of her
heart open for others
to see, serves as a mirror for
others to experience the Incredible Grace and Power
of Jesus Christ who is the ultimate healer.
Jesus Christ says, "You shall know the truth,
and the truth will set you free!"

Carolyn is quick to share that although everyone experiences emotional bruises this side of Heaven it doesn't mean those inner bruises have to rob our joy, steal our peace, or kill our destiny. Our scars can serve as a reminder of where we've been, but they don't have to determine where we can go, nor do they have to limit who God created us to be. She recognizes the courage it takes to ask for help and the freedom that comes through Christ as we yield our unresolved hurts to His healing love.

The purpose of Carolyn's ministry is to reflect the empowering truth that living with unresolved hurts and losses from our past will keep us stuck emotionally and spiritually in our present, until we choose to offer our hurts to Christ through confessing, grieving, and forgiving allowing Him to bring about healing, freedom, and transformation from the inside out.

Unresolved pain affects our beliefs, our thoughts, our perceptions, our attitudes, our emotions, our actions, and our words. Whatever in us that has not been brought out into the open still has a life of its own in the past and its presence will affect our relationship to God, others, and ourselves. Wouldn't you agree it's time to live in all the fullness God created you to live in where there is genuine and lasting joy, freedom, and peace? Life is a gift…….. open yours!

I trust the Daily Cup has watered your thirsty soul as you have confessed the Word over your life. Where in your life do you see changes from when you started? Do you notice less anger? Are you quicker to forgive? Have you grown in expressing your faith? Is your life the mirror that reflects the Lord of Your Life?

> "God's Word is alive and active. Sharper than any double-edged sword, it penetrates even to dividing soul and spirit, joints and marrow; it judges the thoughts and attitudes of the heart."

> (Hebrews 4:12)

Carolyn is available for Women's Conferences or retreats at your church.

Visit her website for contact information.
*www.carolynschwartzministries.com*